KARGIL WAR:

THE TURNING POINT

COLONEL M B RAVINDRANATH, VrC

INDIA · SINGAPORE · MALAYSIA

ISBN 979-8-89322-935-6

Dedicated to all the valiant warriors of 2 RAJ RIF who played an integral part in evicting the Pakistani soldiers from Tololing and Three Pimples complex - Drass Sector, during the summer of 1999.
This book salutes their courage, grit and determination in extremely difficult and challenging conditions.

EVER VICTORIOUS

Veer Bhogya Vasundhara

Col M B Ravindranath
(Ever Victorious)

CONTENTS

ACKNOWLEDGEMENT

Our Dad had a dream to pen his thoughts, as seen through his eyes, about the sweat, tears, strategy, dedication and determination of the fearless warriors who fought the Battles of Tololing and Three Pimples in the summer of 1999.

At the cusp of realising his dreams, destiny had its say, and a valorous tale was left incomplete. But as always, the extended family of a soldier stepped in and fulfilled his unfinished dream. This book would not have been possible if not for the role many people played, who took upon themselves the challenge of completing the manuscript our dad had left behind.

With nothing but gratitude in our hearts, we extend heartfelt thanks to his course mates of the 56th NDA Course, especially Colonel David Devasahayam (Retired) who took it upon himself to have this book released. Lieutenant General JS Sandhu (Retired) and Major General Ajay Sah (Retired) for compiling the book, the numerous rounds of editing and all the co-ordination with the publishers. We also thank Brigadier Mohit Saxena, VrC for finishing some of the pending chapters and providing a first-hand account of the events. And Lieutenant General Mohinder Puri for the Foreword.

We are also eternally grateful to our extended family who have stood by us through it all and supported us in every which way they can.

To all the soldiers of the **2RAJ RIF** family who were part of the war, we have always been in awe and are huge admirers of your bravery and strength.

This book would not have been possible without each and every one of you. Thank you.

Prerna & Prarthana

ACKNOWLEDGEMENT

FOREWORD

I had the honour and privilege to command 8 Mountain Division during the Kargil War in the summer of 1999. The Division was deployed in a counter insurgency role in North Kashmir and at the outbreak of hostilities with Pakistan, it was tasked to take over the Drass - Mushko Sector in Western Ladakh on 01 June. 2 Rajputana Rifles (RAJ RIF), a battalion on the orbat of the Division, deployed in Kandi-Kigam area in North Kashmir, and under the able command of Colonel Ravindranath (Ravi) was the first battalion to be inducted into Drass in the first week of June 99.

Tololing, a dominating feature in the Drass sector, occupied by Pakistani troops, was effectively interdicting the NH1D and restricting movement of men and material to Kargil and Leh. Appreciating the importance of this feature, which since the third week of May had defied capture, I gave the task to Ravi to capture it earliest. Ravi, in his inimitable way went about the task by meticulously mustering his resources, bidding for additional resources, carrying out detailed reconnaissance (recce) of the objectives with his subordinates, putting the battalion through advance stages of acclimatisation and fine tuning battle drills and procedures, rusted during long years of counter insurgency operations. It was indeed remarkable to see how he transformed the battalion from the counter insurgency mind-set to conventional operations within a couple of days. I fixed 12 June as the day of the attack and on my visit to the battalion, was extremely satisfied to see their level of preparation and enthusiasm to take on the first operation of the Division.

Tololing feature comprises Point 4590, Tololing Top, South East (SE) Spur, South West (SW) Spur, South Spur and Hump to its North. Ravi's plan after discussion with me and the Brigade Commander, Brigadier Amar Aul, was to employ his D Company (Coy) with A Coy as reserve along the SW Spur, and this force was placed under his Second-in-Command (2iC). On the SE Spur he earmarked C Coy with B Coy as reserve and placed himself in command of this task force. With preponderance of artillery support, the attack was launched at 2030 hours on Night 12/13 June. By 0600 hours 13 June, 2 RAJ RIF had a fairly large chunk of the objective in their control. However, the dominating height of Point 4590 was still with the enemy and he was offering stiff resistance. Ravi sensed the problem on Top, and moved A Coy, the reserve, on the SW approach and at 0615 hours they rushed in and captured the feature. This timely action by Ravi was a typical example of exploiting fleeting opportunities to your advantage by anticipating problem areas and correctly responding to various contingencies at the unit level.

Ravi was a highly motivated soldier who had moulded his battalion into a fine and competent unit. With our victory at Tololing, the tide turned in our favour and changed the course of the war in Kargil. Though the battalion lost Major Vivek Gupta, two JCO's and some Other Ranks (OR), the morale of the unit was high and they were well set for the next operation.

Consequent to the capture of Tololing, 2 RAJ RIF was pulled back for rest and reorganising for the next task which was the capture of Knoll, Black Rocks / Three Pimples Complex and Lone Hill. I was keen that the attack should be launched on 26/27 June but Ravi was insistent that he needed time and would not be in a position to attack till 28/29 June. Despite my pressing him to attack on the earlier date, Ravi stood his ground and displayed a high degree of moral courage and confidence in his convictions. I relented and the attack was launched on 28/29 June with full preparations. This was perhaps one of the hardest fought battles of the war wherein the enemy offered stiff resistance resulting in heavy casualties to the battalion, losing Major Acharya, Captain Vijayant Thapar, Lieutenant Kenguruse, and 10 ORs while 32 including three JCO's were wounded. The performance in battle speaks volumes of Ravi's intrepid leadership under most trying conditions which rightly earned the battalion the **Chief's Unit Citation** and the award "Bravest of the Brave" along with three MVC's.

Ravi was a fully committed hands-on Commanding Officer (CO) who never shirked responsibility and never compromised on his convictions. I was fortunate to have him on my team and am fully appreciative of the way he led his battalion in war which remains the ultimate ambition of a motivated soldier. His courage and coolness under fire were his outstanding qualities which gave us our first victory and paved the way for our success in restoring the sanctity of the Line of Control (LC) and pushing the enemy back across the LC.

I was very saddened by his untimely demise and pray for his family to remain justifiably proud of his achievements.

Lieutenant General **Mohinder Puri** (Retd)

COMMONLY USED ABBREVIATIONS

GOC – General Officer Commanding

Col GS – Colonel General Staff

CO – Commanding Officer

2iC – Second-in-Command

RMO – Regimental Medical Officer

JCO – Junior Commissioned Officer

NCO – Non Commissioned Officer

ORs – Other Ranks

LC – Line of Control

CT – Counter Terrorism

HQ – Headquarters

RR - Rashtriya Rifles

LMG – Light Machine Gun

MMG – Medium Machine Gun

HMG – Heavy Machine Gun

AGL – Automatic Grenade Launcher

ATGM – Anti Tank Guided Missiles

SAM – Surface to Air Missiles

VrC – Vir Chakra

MVC – Maha Vir Chakra

RAJ RIF – Rajputana Rifles

GARH RIF – Garhwal Rifles

Coy – Company

Recce - Reconnaissance

ASC – Army Service Corps

KARGIL WAR: THE TURNING POINT

PROLOGUE

"Leaders aren't born; they are made. And they are made just like anything else, through hard work,"

– Legendary American NFL coach Vince Lombardi

"*Success has Many Fathers*" goes a popular saying; to it, one can add, *"Alas, Failure is a Bastard"*, especially when there are many consorts. Both imply the same - while the maternity is known, paternity is indeterminate, or worse, unknown!

The 2nd Battalion, The Rajputana Rifles (2 RAJRIF), came out with flying colours in the Kargil War- 1999, fought in the lofty mountains around Kargil in the Indian state of Jammu and Kashmir. Today, its spectacular success has many fathers. However, it may as well have found itself on the wrong side of the thin line that divides success and failure amidst the fickle fortunes of war.

But on one account, I had no doubt; whichever side the pendulum of fate swung, as the Commanding Officer (CO), I would be left holding the baby.

In those early summer months of 1999, as we moved into the Kargil Sector, one senior officer tried to pep up our morale, "You *are on your way to making history*!" I rued on what side of history I would land. Hopefully, not the kind that features in the military history question paper of Army's promotion exams asking examinees to list the leadership failures of commanders in battles that ended in defeat, and even worse, sheer disgrace!

This narrative is born out of my personal experiences in a war that was thrust upon our nation like a bolt from the blue. Today as we bask in the light of the success in battle, I must share this glory with those who can rightfully claim "paternity" to the success that 2 RAJRIF carved for itself among those deadly mountain tops.

A Combat Tested Outfit

As a combat outfit, 2 RAJRIF has few peers in an Army where units have competed fiercely to outshine each other in combat for over two centuries of their existence. When the fighting in Kargil broke out, the Battalion was engaged in intensive counter terrorism (CT) operations. The unit was in fine fettle, battle-hardened to a great extent by its Line of Control (LC) and later CT spell in Kupwara.

My three successive predecessors, Colonels VS Tavathia (later Brigadier), UK Dhar and KT Parnaik (later Lieutenant General and Army Commander), had fine-tuned the Battalion into a fighting machine, all primed up for a greater destiny when the opportunity came a calling.

Every soldier with more than three years' service in the Battalion had his own battle yarn to spin, describing his role in some tactical action or other. This proved a great asset as the men were realistic about their chances of survival under fire. Ironically, the credit goes indirectly to the Pakistani Army and their proxies, the jehadi tanzeems, for this battle inoculation that they had afforded to us!

The Foundational Force

Of course, the rank and file of the Battalion are at the top of my list. Never in my entire service[1] had I been privileged to serve with a set of soldiers more resolute in the face of adversity, remaining stoic in the face of mounting casualties, so full of commitment to their leaders and their subordinates, so ingenious in tackling the challenges they faced, so irreverently funny in dangerous situations and above all, a sense of *izzat* that only grew in intensity as the death toll mounted. In a nutshell, I was a lucky commander, going into battle with a courageous lot that could stare death in the eye and carry on with aplomb. Without these attributes, how else can one explain the combat performance of a unit down to about 60 per cent of its authorised manpower on the eve of the battle?

I will touch upon many individual acts of gallantry or dedication that I was a witness to or was informed of by others, once the dust of battle had settled down and we chatted during lulls in the fighting. I have scant doubt that for every reference that I make, there will be at least ten more that remain untold.

My Officers

The next on my list of approbation are the officers who led these exceptional men, themselves no less in courage and devotion. For me, this was a winning

[1] Col MB Ravindranath was commissioned on 07 June 1980 in 17 MADRAS but was transferred to the newly raised 21 RAJRIF in 1986, one of the mixed-class infantry battalions created by every Infantry Regiment after the 1984 mutinies in some SIKH battalions. He was selected to command 2 RAJRIF in 1997, one of the first of his course to have been granted command in the rank of Lt Col only. His combat experience included a stint in 19 Rashtriya Rifles, where he was in the raising batch of officers of this fine counter-insurgency force.

combination. We were, certainly under strength, inadequately trained and unprepared, both mentally and physically, for the awesome responsibility that was so suddenly thrust upon us, yet we prevailed. To their undiluted credit, the team of officers went on to lead with unbelievable maturity, a sense of dedication and a gay abandon.

Against an authorised strength of 21 officers, the Battalion had physically posted only 12 plus the Regimental Medical Officer (RMO). Of these, one officer was away on a course. Luckily, we were at the cusp of leave exchange (when both outgoing and incoming leave parties congregate at the Battalion Headquarters) when orders were received for the move to Sonamarg enroute to Drass. Major Sandeep Bajaj and Lieutenant Kenguruse returned from leave just as we inducted into Moghulpura in the Drass Sector. The arrival of Bajaj, my trusted Second-in-Command (2iC), was an immediate booster shot for my morale. Major Sandeep Kala, comfortably placed in the powerful corridors of the Military Secretary's Branch in Army Headquarters (HQ), did not hesitate for a minute in spontaneously answering the call to battle. Pulling just the right strings, he joined us and was to act as the 2iC during the war. Having served long in the Battalion, he knew the pulse of the men and provided the much-needed calmness when the troops got restive on being ordered for the second major assault after the capture of Tololing. Bajaj and Kala, along with Major Bhanwar Singh Rathore (a Regimental Commissioned Officer who had risen from the ranks), were the only officers who, in my opinion, had the requisite experience, maturity and training to conduct battalion-level operations at such short notice with almost nil preparatory training.

My four Rifle Company Commanders, the tip of the spear of the Battalion's assault waves, had service ranging from four to eight years; none had yet qualified in the Junior Command Course where a subunit commander learns the ropes of basic tactics, concepts and practices of handling an infantry company in combat. Four of the subalterns, who led the men into battle, had less than six months of service and were in their infantry attachment phase before assuming their service duty in their parent logistics corps - the Army Service Corps. While they had no clue about how to lead the men into a conventional attack, especially in super high altitudes, they could claim some counter-insurgency (CI) experience gained during our operations under 81 Mountain Brigade.

Some readers may complain that my narrative is overtly partial to the exploits of my officers; this does not mean others were not worthy, but then all my planning and execution of these plans hinged upon my discussions with my officers, especially those who were to lead these attacks. Every one of them, without exception, responded magnificently to my exhortations, accepting multiple responsibilities and roles as the dynamic ebb and flow of battle demanded. The bare fact that out of 13 officers who were present on the battlefield, four gave the ultimate sacrifice is proof enough of their commitment. I rest my case.

The Junior Leaders

2 RAJRIF is a seasoned old battalion (raised in 1817 as the 2nd Battalion of the 10th Regiment of the Bombay Native Infantry). Historically, the Junior Commissioned Officers (JCOs) have been the Battalion's spine, and this backbone remained unbending during the war.

Since there were never enough officers to go around, a great deal of load fell on the shoulders of my JCOs, and at times on tasks that were clearly beyond their pay grade. I place on record, without an iota of doubt, that a finer lot of JCOs I had never seen in any of the units I had served earlier - professionally sound, capable, with excellent physical fitness that would put to shame much younger soldiers.

So discerning was the selection system established in this old Battalion that every JCO carried the rank as a badge of honour with a palpable sense of pride on his selection. They enjoyed the respect of the Non-Commissioned Officers (NCOs) responsible for running the sections and platoons. The senior JCOs led with a deft touch, guiding their men through a judicious mix of advice sprinkled with some sharp barbs when needed and bouts of 'training' for those falling short of their exacting standards. There was little or no 'spoon feeding' by officers, as is prevalent in many other infantry units. And, I will let you judge as you read through my narration about individual actions conducted independently, laced with incredible courage and initiative.

The best compliment the Battalion received, in my opinion, was under the command of Brigadier (later Lieutenant General and Army Commander) HS Panag, a hard man to please. Panag, during one of his better moods, once remarked, seeing my JCOs in action, "Your *JCOs are as good as officers*!"

I hope my experience will correct the perception that has been gaining ground in the Indian Army that the JCO cadre, a relic of the British Indian Army, was more of a liability than an attribute, with ageing soldiers living out their service life enjoying the perks and privileges of their rank but falling short of shouldering real responsibilities. Just like officers, there are no good or bad JCOs or NCOs; it is their officers who hold this responsibility when they promote them and later invest in their training. I admit that many selections are done subjectively, catering to individual whims and fancies, and even worse, not correcting this mistake subsequently, which causes unit junior leadership to degenerate.

Leaders are Made, not Born!

Here, I unabashedly lay the credit for selecting such a fine lot of junior leaders at the doors of my predecessors. I was placed in command of 2 RAJRIF in September 1998 and can hardly claim credit for turning them into dynamic leaders in the short span of nine months!

Regimental readers would grasp what I am stating: it is the quality of the Ummedwar Cadre in an infantry battalion that is the foundation of its future junior leadership. Those soldiers who pass this critical gateway on their path to higher non-commissioned ranks are the ones who will run it in the future. It was common lore in the Battalion that the Ummedwar Cadres conducted during the command of Lieutenant Colonel (later Lieutenant General) OP Kaushik were the most exacting ones, and only the best and most deserving could make the cut. It is only a CO with a vision, an unerring eye to spot talent and the ability to mould raw human resources into battle worthy leaders who can produce the next generation of battlefield leadership; apparently, Colonel Kaushik was blessed with all these attributes, and I reaped the benefits.

The quality of good leadership amongst JCOs was not confined to a few isolated islands of excellence amidst superlative JCOs in prized battalion appointments and close to the command echelons; it was evenly spread. This was evident when I interacted with JCOs who commanded platoons in their routine activities. This quality came to the fore under the most demanding situations as sections and detachments went ahead with their independent operational task, controlled through nothing more than a tenuous radio link, under heavy fire battering their heads against well-dug-in foes where death was lurking round the corner. Without such leaders, success would have evaded us, leaving the Battalion in lifelong ignominy.

We had trained hard for three months at Gwalior, before being inducted into the Kashmir Valley. I have devoted a chapter to my training philosophy as it evolved with my experiences and study. Some readers may find it rather long, but while apologising to them, I have retained it for the benefit of future generations of combat leaders with whom I wish to share my experience.

Superior HQ: Blessing or Curse?

Last, my list includes my Formation Commanders under whom I passed through my baptism of fire in a conventional war. A battlefield commander shoulders the heavy weight of conflicting demands on his faculties during combat - trying to keep track of actions and locations of his troops, the deployment and angles of fire of support weapons and consequent safety, trying to second guess the enemy and attempting to divine his next move. No amount of peacetime simulation can prepare a commander for the real thing.

It gets worse in the mountains where the drag of logistics threatens to drown all operational insights; keeping the flow of ammunition and water ongoing can make the difference between victory and retreat. Amidst all this, the last thing that the CO needs is a higher Headquarters (HQ) that is sitting on his head, insisting on a 'running commentary' of events unfolding or, worse, unsolicited advice on an already complex tactical situation from the safe and comfortable environs of a well-sandbagged command post, without the benefit of a clear tactical picture.

The Battalion came under the command of Brigadier (later Lieutenant General) Amar Aul when the Kargil operations had already commenced, and there was little time for niceties. Both he and the Divisional Commander, Major General Mohinder Puri (later Lieutenant General), never asked for me on the B1 radio net (the brigade command radio link) more than thrice through both the major attack operations. Even then, the emphasis was on brevity, with just around ten sentences being exchanged. As the man on the spot, I had absolute freedom of action to plan and to put those plans into effect; if successful, the entire credit was placed in my account. The Brigade / Divisional HQ were steady in their support, pushing our demands in logistics forward to us perched high up in the mountains and stepping in with much-needed fire support when we asked for it in a tight corner; when we reached back for something extra, it was promptly provided without rancour or ill humour. I can never forget the sight of Colonel RB Singh, CO of the Divisional Ordnance Unit, personally visiting me with a pair of brand new DMS boots - somehow, he had come to know that I was walking around in a badly worn-out pair whose heels were threatening to separate from the sole! To date, I have not been able to unearth his informant!

My Motivators

In retrospect, I am convinced that my contribution was intrinsically driven by what I had imbibed through my various life experiences and interactions with people whom I had fortunately come in touch with; I did what I did, based on some previous learning.

Many people have moulded my life; some honed the professional aspect while others glazed the human side, and a few who impacted both. When embroiled in combat, I often experienced an eerie "**Slum Dog Millionaire**" kind of feeling that seemed to be pulling out the answers locked away somewhere in my past experiences, saving me from the ignominy of floundering for a tactical decision in a tight spot in front of my command. And the best part is that they worked.

Of these, my uncle was the first person who taught me to achieve anything worthwhile on my own steam and not expect to piggyback on others who are there to guide me. *'A road sign can tell you the direction and distance of the destination, but you can never reach the destination by sitting on this signpost; you need to walk it'*. He had figured out the '**Theory of Constraints**' all on his own. Once, while he was tilling the field in our village, I watched the neighbouring field being tilled with a lot of noise by another farmer. As a young city kid on a village vacation, I was mighty impressed by the energy and dynamism of the neighbour. I asked my uncle why he was so quiet and his oxen so steady, he replied, *'See, he has brought a new ox, and they are not paired well. One is strong and enthusiastic, the other calm and steady. So, he has to pull one back and prod the other to keep them going in a straight line. Soon, one will tire out from being restrained and the other by prodding and beating; the team will be forced to stop soon.'* By lunchtime, things happened as he had predicted. Then he remarked, *'When you must get work out of others, never pair anyone without matching competence and temperament. If they are unmatched, you can never get the best out of them. Probably you will end up losing both competences of the competent and temper of those involved for life'*. He had great insight into teamwork and the welfare of his family.

In every house (ours was a joint family), some are more capable than others, and it is in the best interests of the family if everyone is employed according to his capabilities and limitations. There is no use trying to insist on equal work from everyone, "*all fingers in the hand are not of the same length, yet every finger has its use singly and together,*" he said one day, and this stayed with me.

Another individual who had a defining influence on my thinking process was my first CO, Colonel (later Brigadier) V Mahalingam. A veteran of the 1971 Battle of Basantar and a war casualty to boot, he was fond of drawing out his companions into discussions during our long treks to forward posts in the mountains of Tawang, West Kameng District in Arunachal Pradesh. As his newly commissioned "*Intelligence Officer*", I was his frequent companion on these long hikes. He used to say, *'Guru, troops do not fight for you because you are an officer and giving correct orders. They fight for you only if they believe in you.'* He would encourage us to gain the soldier's trust by our personal and professional honesty and sincerity towards soldiers.

The Crucible of Battle

Kargil war was fought on an extended frontage extending from the Mushko Valley in the West to Turtuk in the East, a frontage of approximately 120 km. Pakistan had major intrusions in the Drass - Mushko areas and the Batalik-Chorbatla areas. Besides, there were minor intrusions in Turtuk and Kaksar areas.

The Attack on Tololing was psychologically challenging for me. When we entered the scene, the attacks of 18 GRENADIERS had been blunted with serious losses. Despite closing in with the enemy at a high cost in terms of casualties, including their Second-in-Command, the GRENADIERS could not dislodge the enemy from the dominating mountain tops.

The Army had been surprised by the audacious, if somewhat amateurish, move of the enemy. There was a prevailing sense of despondency and bewilderment. One could sense this, moving up from Srinagar to Sonamarg and into the battle zone. Interaction with officers and troops who were coming from the battle zone gave a picture of helplessness and fait accompli. The situation being painted in the transit camps by troops who had passed through the battle zone was enough to make even the fool-hardy and show-offs pause and think. Under these discouraging circumstances, how 2 RAJRIF raised itself to meet and best the challenge is what I will try and narrate.

With courage, determination, and some luck, this unit went on to register the first major victory of the Kargil War. A victory that set in motion a series of victories leading to the successful conclusion of the Kargil War. It is for this that '**The Battle of Tololing**' has been called the ***Turning Point*** in the Kargil War by many commentators, including by General Ved Malik, the then Army Chief.

There was a lull in operations in the Drass Sector till 28 June 1999. On the night of 28 June 1999, 2 RAJRIF, again, as part of 56 Mountain Brigade operations, attacked **Three Pimples Complex**, while 18 Garhwal Rifles (GARHRIF) attacked **Point 4700 - Tommy Complex**. 2 RAJRIF completed its task by the evening of 29 June 1999 and 18 GARHRIF by evening of 30 June 1999 had cleared the **Point 4700** Ridge Line. **Junction Area**, where the ridgeline from **Three Pimples** and the **Point 4700** ridge met, was secured by the morning of 02 July, bringing to a conclusion the operations of 56 Mountain Brigade.

For me, the *'Battle of Three Pimples'* was professionally extremely challenging. 2 RAJRIF planned and prepared for operations under extreme time pressure, unlike earlier battles where we were given the time, we had bid for. Ground reconnaissance threw up additional terrain and enemy friction, forcing us to continuously change our attack plans, thus making the task of preparation challenging. In the assault phase, we were unable to achieve the kind of surprise we had achieved in the '**Battle of Tololing**'. We faced one setback after another, yet in the end, pulled off another spectacular victory mainly due to the sheer tenacity of the rank and file despite mounting casualties and adverse tactical situations. It moved the Army Chief, General Ved Malik to suo-moto award '**Chief's Unit Citation**', the first Battalion in the Indian Army to be honoured thus during Operation Vijay.

I will try to communicate the professional challenges I faced, the desperation I felt at times, and the hopes I was nursing on that eventful night of 28 June 99 when, unknown to us, we had fought a manoeuvre battle, a rare feat in the mountains.

It was at this time we started hearing of reports of enemy withdrawal across all the intrusions. The units in contact and fresh units were inducted to pressurise the Pakistanis to vacate intruded posts. As a result of this continuous pressure on the ground and international diplomacy, the Pakistan Army was forced to retrace its steps to the status - quo - ante. Later, the Army Chief was reported to have said, '*It is not important how you start the war; it is how you end it*!' Kargil war, without any doubt, was a victory on the ground.

Some Generals uncharitably stated in private conversations that the war was won for India by the USA who compelled the Pakistani intruders to withdraw. By the time this happened, the Pakistan Army had lost all the features with direct observation on National Highway 1D. With this, their objective of '*To cut off supply lines to Siachen and capture it after it was sufficiently weakened*' lay in shambles. Nawaz Sharif, the Prime Minister of Pakistan, was sent by the Pakistan Army to procure a face-saving deal once it was internationally isolated with a clear message 'Return to Status-quo-Ante'. There is no doubt that Pakistan started withdrawing after President Clinton gave an unambiguous message to Nawaz Sharif. But it in no way means the Indian Army was not capable of reclaiming the territory by force. At that time, we assessed that we would be able to clear the intrusions by the end of September 1999, albeit with a heavy cost in lives. Hence, the comments of these uncharitable Generals can be put down to professional incompetence, professional jealousy, or both.

CHAPTER ONE

THE GATHERING STORM

Tashi Namgyal, a 36 years old shepherd from the tiny village of Gharkun near Batalik town, some 60 km from the District HQ of Kargil, wandered amidst the peaks looking for some lost yak in early May 99. He never imagined that what he witnessed would trigger a war.

On May 3, 1999, Tashi Namgyal, together with another shepherd informed the Kargil-based 121 (Independent) Infantry Brigade Group that they had seen intruders 'digging in' and 'building sangars' (stone bunkers) in the higher reaches of a remote portion of Batalik in Kargil district of Jammu and Kashmir. The following day, the Brigade HQ, with no idea who they were, despatched a patrol belonging to 16 GRENADIERS to investigate.[2]

As Tashi Namgyal narrated to Rouf A Roshangar of India Today,[3] "*On the morning of May 3rd, I had moved up with one of my friends some 5 km along Jubbar Langpa stream in search of my missing yak. I was scanning the mountainside through a pair of binoculars. And then I saw groups of men in Pathan attire and camouflaged Pakistani soldiers digging bunkers. Some were armed, but I couldn't ascertain their numbers. But one thing I was sure of - they had come from the other side of the LC. I came down and promptly informed the nearest post of the Indian Army. My information alerted the Indian Army, and they cross-checked and found that my information about the intrusion of Pakistani soldiers was correct.*"

The war which then commenced is better known as Operation VIJAY in India and Operation KOH PA (Operation KP)[4] or Operation BADR (as mentioned by General VP Malik) in Pakistan.

This was to become the first televised war in the Indian context, fought under the overhang of nuclear weapons in some of the most rugged terrain anywhere in the world. Soldiers battled each other, sometimes in deadly

---

[2] Dinesh Kumar, 'Kargil War 15 Years On', Tribune, Sunday, July 20, 2014, Chandigarh, India, http://www.tribuneindia.com/2014/20140720/pers.htm#1.

[3] India Today website- https://www.indiatoday.in/india/story/kargil-war-meet-shepherd-warned-army-1572296-2019-07-22 Kargil War: Meet the shepherd who warned the Army by Rouf A Roshangar, 22 Jul 2019.

[4] Zehra Nasim, From Kargil to the Coup, Events that Shook Pakistan,

hand-to-hand combat while struggling for every gasp of breath, over an icy, super high-altitude battlefield that stretched from Mushko Valley in the West to Turtuk in the East, a frontage of approximately 120 km.

The Intrusion

The plan for an incursion in Kargil had been cooking for a long time at the higher echelons of the Pakistani Army. There was the bitter taste of being outwitted by the Indian Army in Siachen in 1984, and under General Zia ul Haq, a plan was evolved. Kargil was chosen as the operation area since it was in direct view of and proximity to NH1, India's main supply route to Siachen. The plan envisaged a paradrop by a battalion worth to cut the NH1 through an undercover operation. These troops would hold down the enemy and isolate Siachen long enough for the troops to launch a ground attack.[5]

With the benefit of hindsight and based on war narratives written from the Pakistani side, it is clear that the Pakistani army had major intrusions in the Drass - Mushko and Batalik - Chorbatla areas. Besides, there were minor intrusions in Turtuk and Kaksar areas.

PAKISTANI INTRUSIONS IN THE MUSHKO - DRASS - KAKSAR SECTOR

As Nasim Zehra writes in her extensively researched book, "From Kargil to the Coup: Events that shook Pakistan,"[6] *Back at the Force Commander Northern Areas (FCNA), with the initial plan for Operation KP approved by the 10 Corps Commander Mahmud and the Chief of General Staff Aziz Khan in October, Pakistani troop movement across the LC had begun by late October. Headed for Drass, Brigade Commander Brigadier Masood Aslam was dropped from a helicopter in the Drass area, along with a Lieutenant Colonel and ten soldiers, for reconnaissance. They found the Marpola and Tololing areas unoccupied for miles. Lieutenant Colonel Mansoor, the Commanding Officer of NLI 6, then crossed the*

[5] ibid
[6] ibid

LC and entered the Drass area with his troops to occupy posts vacated by the Indian troops and to set up new ones. A limited logistics operation accompanied the initially limited NLI movement, the troops having merely taken off with basic supplies in their bag packs. The planners were confident they would not be discovered before summer and that their camouflage would carry them unnoticed into winter. However, within two months of the start of the operation, the FCNA commander believed the opportunity existed to expand the operation. Around the areas where Pakistani troops were ingressed, there were vast unoccupied areas across the LC with no Indian presence. In these areas, either the Indian posts had been vacated during winter or on those steep peaks, they simply had no posts. So, they went into mission creep, and by December 1998, the troops had begun to cross the LC from seven directions. This included areas West of River Indus, East of river Shyok, and from the top of Shyok Valley. For the Operation, around 200 troops were to travel for months, mostly on foot, to reach the Drass sector. There, the troops would occupy posts at Tololing, thereby reducing their distance to NH - 1 by almost three kilometres."

The assessment on the Indian side matches what Nasim Zehra's research has revealed from her interactions with the Pakistani brass. In his book, "*Kargil - From Surprise to Victory*,"[7] the then Chief of Army Staff, General VP Malik writes that the Pakistani top brass probably updated an old contingency plan just when preparations for the Lahore meeting were underway. The Pakistan Army was busy planning and carrying out recce and logistic preparations from November 1998 onwards for '**Operation BADR**' (the Pakistan Army's codename) to alter the alignment of the LC East of the Zoji La (pass) and denying the use of the Srinagar – Kargil – Leh highway in this area to India. Apparently, the planning and preparations were done only on the military side, with the political hierarchy kept in the dark. Northern Light Infantry (NLI) units shortlisted for the infiltration were brought up to strength. These soldiers were ideally suited for the rugged high-altitude terrain like our own Ladakh Scouts boys as they hail from the area, in their case, Gilgit Baltistan part of Jammu and Kashmir. The regulars were to masquerade as jehadi militants. General Malik writes, "*After carrying out further reconnaissance and establishing patrol bases from February to April 1999, the operation was to be launched in April – May 1999, under the direct command of Major General Javed Hassan, FCNA, to coincide with the melting of snow and the summer opening of India's National Highway 1D linking Srinagar to Leh via Kargil. General Pervez Musharraf and his team gambled on pulling off a 'Siachen type operation', i.e., pre-emption or occupation of tactically important heights before the adversary got to know what's happening.*"

7 Malik, VP, Kargil-From Surprise to Victory, Harper Collins, India

A somewhat complacent Indian command at the tactical level assumed it was some terrorist activity even though this area was so rugged that the Pakistan-sponsored tanzeems rarely operated in the area, except for making a few ill-fated attempts in infiltration in the past by small groups of terrorists. They were in for a big surprise when they sent lightly armed patrols to investigate. The first patrol recorded to have established contact with the intruders was from 4 JAT led by 22-year-old Captain Saurabh Kalia with five jawans.[8] The patrol, expecting a small, ragged group of terrorists, was caught by surprise on 15 May 1999 when it was ambushed by well-entrenched regular soldiers; there were no survivors. Allegedly, the patrol was captured alive once their ammunition ran out, and they were tortured to death in captivity. The bodies were returned badly mutilated.[9]

Troops were tasked to clear the ridges of what then was considered militant positions, but were utterly surprised to face defensive posts rather than holed-up militants. Soon, local formations fanned out to check out other winter vacated areas; this revealed that more and more ridge lines had been occupied.

The First Inklings

Most of us serving in the Valley, busy with counter-terrorism (CT) operations, were blissfully unaware of the storm that would soon engulf us. 2 RAJRIF, then under 81 Mountain Brigade, was deployed in the Kashmir Valley. Some of us involved in CT operations had been hearing 'langar gup' of some unusual activity going on in the neighbouring Drass/Kargil sector based on hearsay exchanges between troops and officers in Transit Camps, hospitals and HQs. The grapevine was that some intrusions had taken place, and troops on the ground were finding it tough to evict them. At this time, most of us were informally speculating on the causes and solutions.

On the night of 9–10 May 1999, heavy artillery shelling was reported near HQ 121 (I) Infantry Brigade Group in Kargil. It became clear that it was an artillery shoot being undertaken by a trained observer when the ammunition dump blew up after a direct hit. On 10 May, I was in Srinagar coordinating the logistics of a medical camp for the civilians of my area of responsibility with

---

8 India Today Web Story date 26 Jul 2019 https://www.indiatoday.in/india/story/capt-saurabh-kalia-story-of-first-kargil-martyr-1573838-2019-07-26

9 Ibid. The Kalia family has since been demanding that Pakistan should be brought to book and those responsible for the act be punished under international laws as the violence meted out to the six soldiers stood against the protocols of the Geneva Convention. Narender Kalia, who is over 70 years old, continues to make efforts and pursue the central government to move the International Court of Justice (ICJ) to pull up Pakistan, even after 20 years. He says he will continue the fight till the last day of his life.

the 15 Corps HQ staff and medical authorities at Base Hospital. I noticed some casualties arriving from 10 Garhwal Rifles. I found nothing unusual about it because casualties with gunshot and other battle injuries were common in the Base Hospital, which catered for the entire CT operations grid in the Valley.

Things began to get more frenetic by mid-May 1999, as casualties started arriving at the Base Hospital, either badly wounded or mortal remains being flown out in increasing numbers. It was clear that amidst mounting casualties, little headway was being made, and successive echelons of command were now staring at an intrusion on a massive scale. And worse, they were not even able to hazard a guess on how and what had happened. Little did I suspect that 2 RAJRIF would soon find itself in the eye of the gathering storm.

Things began to crystallise when, around the second week of May 1999, Brigadier (later Lieutenant General) D H Summanwar, Commander 81 Mountain Brigade, organised a closed-door session at the Brigade HQ where Colonel Angelo Mathews briefed us. The officer had come from the Kargil Sector and had a broad idea of the goings on. Coincidently, Brigadier (later Lieutenant General) Amar Aul, then commanding 56 Mountain Brigade, was also present in the briefing. We were to fight the Kargil war under his command.

Colonel Mathews briefed us on a map full of red dots splattered across all the ridge lines along the Line of Control (LC), indicating areas suspected to be under the control of the '*intruders*.' Apparently, he was on board a helicopter on an aerial surveillance sortie, which drew machine gun fire from one of the ridges. Clearly, the Colonel was sharing information on a '*need-to-know*' basis as he did not elaborate on what counter-action was being carried out by us. We, too, did not press him as we listened in rapt attention to the briefing with a sort of detached curiosity with no trace of premonition that in less than two weeks, we would spearhead the 'counter action'!

On hindsight, and based on my interaction with commanders at various levels after the battles, I can now safely conclude that by 15 May 1999, the jigsaw puzzle pieces were slowly falling into place. It was becoming clear at higher HQ that evicting the intrusion was way beyond the capability of local troops and formations. It was time to bring in the Big Battalions and the Big Guns from beyond the Valley.[10]

[10] Major Gen Ashok Verma, *Kargil: Blood on The Snow Tactical Victory, Strategic Failure: A Critical Analysis of the War by Kashmir Research Institute 2002 writes,* "In the initial period, it took more than a month for higher commanders in 15 Corps and Northern Command to believe what their troops were reporting about the strengths and degree of preparedness of the intrusions. By continuing to play down the lethality of the enemy confronting them, the higher commanders were undermining their own credibility. Fortunately, the steady buildup of Indian firepower and troops along NH IA turned the tide and the units in contact

As per John H Gill,[11] the operation seems to have experienced a degree of "*mission creep*" as it evolved. Junior commanders in the Pakistan Army, apparently pushed recce and security detachments into the unoccupied areas ahead of their positions and thus deeper into the Indian portion of Kashmir, expanding the incursion beyond its original scope as they exploited their initial success. John H Gill further states that mission creep and unit bravado may explain the extent of the advances in some instances, but cannot account for the breadth and depth of the entire operation. It seems more likely that from the beginning, the primary Pakistani goal in the Drass area was a penetration of at least sufficient depth to allow for observation and domination of NH-1D. By the time hostilities began, the infiltrators had built more than 130 positions up to five miles deep on the Indian side of the LC and equipped them with machine guns, antipersonnel land mines, man-portable air defence missiles, mortars, and, in some cases, light artillery pieces. The bulk of the force's artillery support, however, could only come from Pakistani guns emplaced in and around the Shingo River valley on the Northern side of the LC.

By 26 May 1999, India achieved a remarkable intelligence coup when it intercepted a telephone conversation between two very senior Pakistani officers. The transcript made it abundantly clear that we were dealing not with jehadis but with well-trained regular troops trained for mountain warfare.

The Indian Response

The range of options available to India at this juncture included an offensive (limited or full scale) to capture territory elsewhere, either across the LC or the International Boundary (IB), which implied escalation to a full-fledged war

---

themselves discovered the enemy's vulnerability by trial and error. On 10 June, the Chief Gen. V.P. Malik, during a visit to 70 Brigade at Handanbrok (near Chorbatla), asked the Brigade Commander, Brig. Devinder Singh, his assessment of the intruders in the Batalik sector. His answer was approximately 600: Maj. Gen. Badhwar, 3 Div GOC gave his as 400 and Lt. Gen: Kishan Pal, the 15 Corps GOC gave his as 45 militants. Both Devinder and Badhwar stated that the intruders appeared to be Pak regulars whilst the Corps Commander assessed these as militants. Here, it should be noted that by this time more than a month had elapsed since the intrusions had been first detected on 3 May. The Air Force had also been called in by 27 May for offensive air support.' Lt. Gen. Kishan Pal conceded in a television interview later that it was only after the first successful Indian attack on Tololing on 13 June, that he realized that with 8 universal machine guns captured on the objective, indeed the enemy were determined regulars and not militants fighting a hit - and - run battle. Such was the fog of war, but when at the end of it there was a resounding victory, it was all swept away in the euphoria. Fortunately, the fact was that the enemy had over - played his hand and the general arousal of the Indian units involved brought success.

11 Asymmetric Warfare in South Asia, Edited by Peter R. Lavoy, Cambridge University Presss,2009, Page 98

with Pakistan. As per General VP Malik, during the meeting of the Cabinet Committee on Security (CCS) held on 24 May 1999, the political-military strategy decided was that although India was a victim of intrusion and was exercising the maximum restraint, it was determined to get the intrusion vacated. As the military was not to cross the IB/LC, there was no formal mobilization or declaration of war.[12]

I guess it was then that the decision to move 6 Mountain Division into the battle zone was taken. I am sure the possibility of escalation weighed heavily on the minds of commanders at higher levels, and they decided to employ the troops available within 15 Corps first to attempt and evict the intrusion and, depending on the results, decide on the next course of action. Thus, units deployed in CT operations in the Kashmir Valley started moving out piecemeal into the Kargil Sector.

Luckily, the snow had been light the previous winter, and Zojila pass was opened earlier than normal, in fact a month earlier. Troops in the proximity of Zojila, along the Srinagar - Sonamarg Axis were the first to be inducted into the Kargil Area. 70 Mountain Brigade was moved to tackle the Batalik - Chorbatla intrusion, and 56 Mountain Brigade was to tackle the Drass- Mushko intrusions.

Barring the affiliated artillery units, no major redeployment of artillery was ordered. The intrusions, though massive in scale in terms of length and width, were probably considered weak in strength, both in numbers and ability to hold ground. It was reasoned that strong infantry patrols would unseat and scatter the squatters on the heights. This was predominantly the tactics followed in the Kashmir Valley to clear and push militants out of the dominating ridges. Insurgents can either stay put and fight, in which case they were mostly killed, or they disperse rapidly into the forest and lower reaches, ready to fight another day; invariably, the latter was their preferred course of action. This explains the initial forays by freshly inducted infantry units to clear ridges without much preparation.

The result of these operations was not on the expected lines. The enemy on the ridges was not budging. Moreover, he appeared to be well prepared. The commanders in charge of the situation were not ready to believe this. Hence, they kept chastising the subordinate commanders to act with determination and courage, many a times interfering in tactical movements for which the man on the ground was the best judge. Consequently, many a reputation of units and officers, who had otherwise formidable performances in CT operations, lay in tatters.

---

12 Malik, VP, Kargil-From Surprise to Victory, Harper Collins, India

Troops faced with unreasonable demands, where chances of success are slim and dangers extreme, act in a typical manner. They cease to try, for they can already foretell the results, and they tend to exaggerate the difficulties with a sure knowledge of the superior commander's inability to call their bluff. They do not mean ill; they expect their views to be considered seriously, for their lives are in the line of fire. But commanders, obsessed with their reputations and career prospects and their own infallibility in operational matters, rarely comprehend this. Increasingly, they insulate themselves in their make-believe world. Interpreting and reporting information, sometimes suppressing, to bolster their views, increasingly finding scapegoats for lack of success and covering up their follies by fudging and disowning. I believe this was what was happening in the area of operation.[13]

The only antidote to this operational meltdown is either to change the commander, the troops involved, or both. I think by around the end of May, it was becoming clear that the scale of offensive operations ought to be higher, and it was beyond the capability of 3 Mountain Division to conduct both offensive and defensive operations on a wide front extending from Mushko Valley to Siachen glacier.

HQ 8 Mountain Division, with its credo of "Forever in Operations", under the command of Major General (later Lieutenant General) Mohinder Puri, was in charge of the CT grid in North Kashmir. As the situation heated up in Kargil, he found his units increasingly getting sucked one by one into the neighbouring Kargil Brigade sector. General Puri consistently pointed to the induction of additional units without controlling HQ and offered his availability and willingness to move his HQ to the battle zone. This was accepted, and operational responsibility East of Zojila was reorganised. 8 Mountain Division with 56, 79 and 50 Parachute Brigade (inducted into Mushko Valley) was made responsible for the clearing of Drass- Mushko Intrusion.[14]

---

13 Harinder Baweja, A Soldier's Diary: Kargil, The Inside Story, Page 76. Ask Brigadier A.N. Aul, who came in later in May as Commander, 56 Brigade to conduct operations in Drass to show you his Brigade's After-Action Report if he will. It records what nobody in the army, right up to the chief, will ever tell you or show you. It says: "The intrusion was not considered a serious issue and it was felt that the intruders could be evicted with ease… On our arrival into the sector (May 22), the information available of the enemy strength and disposition was vague. The general information was that Tololing, Point 5140, 5100, 4700 and Tiger Hill were held. According to Headquarters, 3 Infantry Division, 400 to 500 militants were likely to be operating in the division sector with the majority of them being mercenaries."

14 Asymmetric Warfare in South Asia, Edited by Peter R. Lavoy, Cambridge University Presss,2009, Page 113 A new divisional headquarters was in place at Drass with three complete brigades under its command and more troops were on the way. In combat units alone, the Indians were able to move nineteen infantry battalions and six artillery regiments to the Kargil front in approximately three weeks, a remarkable achievement. To control this

This, I believe, was a crucial move that resulted in more comprehensive and coordinated operations in the Drass-Mushko sector. All the formations and units involved were fresh and did not carry any previous baggage of creating the current mess!

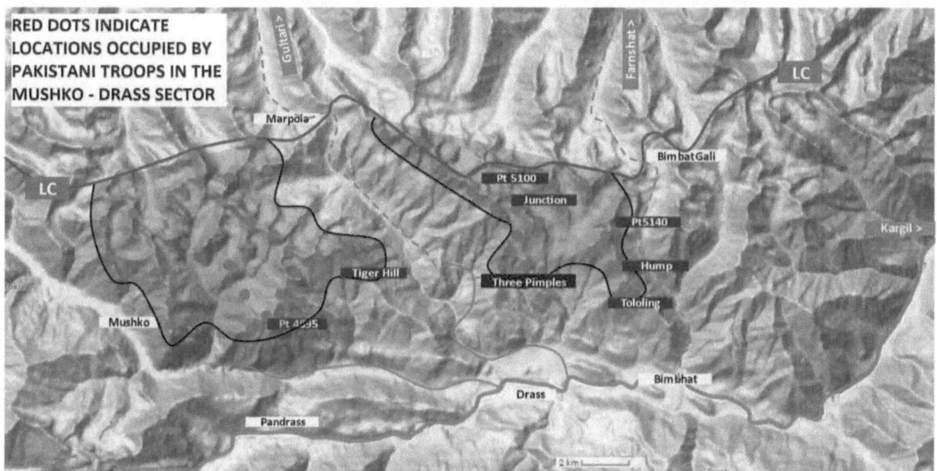

The Drass Sector

The Drass sector saw some of the most ferocious and gory battles during the Kargil Conflict. It saw the Indian Army rise like a Phoenix after the initial surprise and confusion to snatch back the lost peaks on which the enemy had slyly moved in.

The intrusions in this sector were the deepest, with Tololing being just four km crow's flight from Drass. These intrusions directly overlooked the NH 1D and interdicted all vehicular traffic in and out of Ladakh. It was imperative to evict the enemy from the sector on priority as it impeded the stocking and dumping activities that would resume as soon as Zojila pass opened in April/ May.

Recce and reports from patrols had indicated enemy intrusions at **Point 5140**, **Hump** and the **Three Pimples**. Further it was appreciated that he would be holding **Tololing**, **Hump** and **Point 5060** by a company each, and hence, the area surrounded by **Point 5060**, **Point 4700** and the **Three Pimples** was held in strength.

---

growing force, 15 Corps crafted an organizational arrangement placing the newly arrived 8 Mountain Division, drawn from the Kashmir Valley, in charge of operations against the Mushkoh and Drass incursions with 56 and 79 Mountain Brigades in the front line and 50 Para Brigade in reserve.

The mammoth feature of Tololing at an altitude of more than 16000 feet was five km crow's flight from Drass, directly dominated the NH 1D and made road movement extremely difficult. The Tololing Ridge comprised of **Tololing Top**, **Hump**, **Saddle**, going on along the ridge to **Point 5140**. The Tololing Complex comprised of **Point 4590** to the South West, **Barbad Bunker** to the South East, and **Tololing Top**.

Previous attempts by the Indian Army in May 1999 were thwarted by the enemy, effectively putting up such fierce resistance that a halt had been called in the attacks, allowing a consolidation of the initial gains. The stage was set for the next series of attacks.

The Deployment

The Chief of the Army Staff visited the Kargil Sector on 23 May 1999. After touring the area, he outlined a broad strategy of fixing and containment of intrusion in the initial phase, build-up of adequate force levels and supplies before the launch of any offensive operations subsequently, and finally eviction. Seeing the relative importance of sectors, he also laid down the priority for the capture of the objectives - Drass, Batalik-Yaldor, Kaksar and Mushko. The area of responsibility between both the Divisions under 15 Corps was shared by the 3 Infantry and 8 Mountain Divisions.

On 1 June, 8 Mountain Division had 56, 79 and 192 Mountain Brigades under its command. All these brigades had been inducted from the Valley. 79 Mountain Brigade with five battalions -17 JAT, 12 MAHAR, 13 JAK RIF, 2 NAGA and 28 RR (less one company) were deployed in the Mushko Valley.

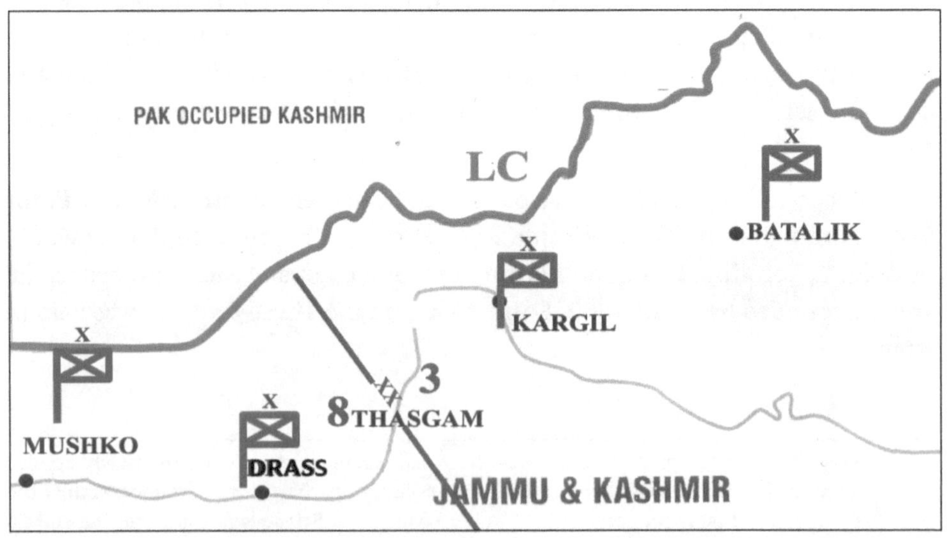

56 Mountain Brigade with four battalions consisting of 16 GRENADIERS, 18 GRENADIERS, 2 RAJ RIF, 1 NAGA and one company of the Indus Wing of the Ladakh Scouts were in Drass sub-sector. 192 Mountain Brigade would have 8 SIKH and 18 GRENADIERS placed under command for the attack on Tiger Hill and 3/3 GR and 1 Company 9 Para SF for the capture of Zulu Spur subsequently. 50 (I) Para Brigade (Army HQ Reserve), which had been deployed in Gumri on 12 June, was released to 15 Corps. It consisted of 1 PARA SF, 6 PARA and 7 PARA.

By the time the Kargil war came to an end on 26 July 99, the Kargil sector had a total of 2 Divisional HQs, 6 Brigade HQs, 52 Infantry Battalions and the equivalent of 16 Regiments of Artillery. In addition, there were the Engineers, Corps of Electronics and Mechanical Engineers, Army Service Corps, Army Ordnance Corps and Medical units. A total of nearly 80000 tons of ammunition and stores were consumed. 6 Mountain Division was moved from its location in Bareilly to Sonamarg and kept as reserve in case the need arose.

The intrusion picture was also getting somewhat clearer. In Mushko, the enemy had occupied Point 4689, Point 5113, Point 4342, Point 4388, Point 5063, Point 5368, Z spur, Point 4875 complex, Point 4040 and Point 5060.

In Drass, Point 5165, Tiger Hill, Point 4268, Marpola Ridge including Point 5240, Point 5100, Point 5060, Point 4700, Tololing, Point 5140, Three Pimples Complex and Point 5700 were under the enemy's control. This area was the most significant as the intrusions were the largest and closest to the single artery National Highway being roughly four to seven km from it. The Drass bowl was overlooked by Tiger Hill, Three Pimples Complex, Point 5140 and Tololing.

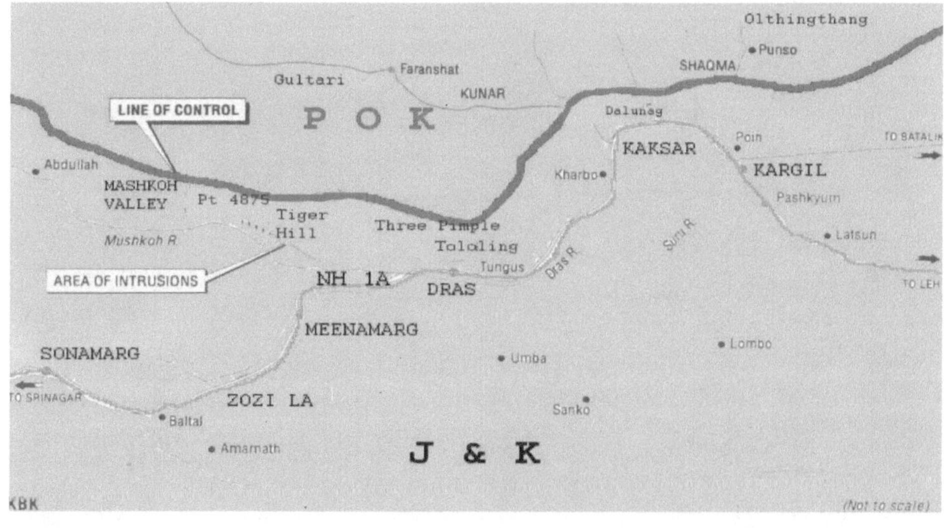

In Kaksar, the enemy had intruded in an area of 5 km x 4 km and had occupied Point 5608, Point 5605, Point 5280, Point 5270, Bajrang Post and Point 5405. Finally, in Batalik, the enemy had occupied most of the ridge lines emanating from the Ladakh ridge watershed including Jubar, Kukarthang, Point 4812, Khalubar, Churubar Sispo, Point 5203 and Muntho Dalo.

We were re-orbatted on 27 May 1999, as we bid goodbye to 81 Mountain Brigade and, from Kigam, Kupwara, moved to Sonamarg in preparation for our induction into the Kargil Sector. We then moved to Drass Sector, where we flirted with 79 Mountain Brigade for a few days before being transferred to 56 Mountain Brigade under whom we were to see the war through. On 04 June 1999, we were tasked to capture Tololing.

CHAPTER TWO

TRAINING FOR WAR

The force of those skilled in warfare is overwhelming, and their timing precise.

Their force is like a drawn cross bow, and their timing like a release of the trigger.

Even in the midst of the turbulence of battle,
the fighting seemingly chaotic, they are not confused.

Even in the midst of the turmoil of battle, the troops seemingly going around in circles, they cannot be defeated

Sun Tzu

Sun Tzu says there are many methods of winning a war, but one won without fighting is superior; the one by actual fighting is markedly inferior.

Yet actual fighting defines combat. Success is decided by numerous subunit-level actions, outcomes of which are directly decided by the quality of leadership at that level. Therefore, selection and training of subunit commanders is the most important responsibility of the officer cadre.

I would like to highlight a particular incident to underscore the importance of preparatory training for combat. When the battalion was in Gwalior, where I took command, the Divisional Commander was Major General AS Phatak. When our move for the Kashmir Valley became known, he emphasised counter-terrorism (CT) training for my battalion. Knowing the way the Army works, he supplemented this with an unambiguous order to his staff and formation commander that we should be relieved of all our commitments three months before moving out, that too in a busy peace station like Gwalior. With such backing, I was able to implement a few unorthodox methods in the conduct of training, which would have otherwise been considered outlandish and invited upbraiding by my bosses.

The battalion's performance in the war, the acid test of any combat outfit, justified this indulgence. "*Ravindranath, you have vindicated my view. If units are allowed to train by themselves, they will deliver,*" Major General AS Phatak told me after the war when I visited him in Leh, where he was the Chief of Staff of the newly raised Corps.

OODA Cycle for Infantry?

My orientation to operations and training was heavily influenced by Colonel Boyd's observation of combat mechanics. Colonel Boyd of the U.S. Air Force had studied air combat in the Korean War in detail. He observed that American pilots with slower and less capable F-86 Sabre jets could shoot down the Soviet pilots with faster and more superior MiG-15 fighters. He concluded that combat is a time-competitive activity in which each of the adversaries is continuously observing (O), orienting (O), deciding (D) and acting (A) in a cyclical manner called the OODA cycle. He correctly surmised that the one who gains time advantage in going through the OODA cycle would ultimately win the contest, the other either being eliminated or backing off. I had chanced up on this during my stint at the War Game Section of the newly raised Army Training Command (ARTRAC), where I was trying to understand the mechanics of combat for the purpose of developing a software model of warfare. I had gained a few insights that were to be useful.

At the lowest level, ***the tactical battle*** boils down to ***fire and movement.*** The purpose is always the same – hold, deny or secure a certain piece of ground; the method is the same – eliminate or threaten to eliminate by fire the one opposing the purpose of your action. At that level where physical force gets applied, there are few possible situations and responses that can be predetermined and practised. These are normally known as battle drills. Those teams and detachments adept at executing these quickly invariably gain time in the 'Action' part of the OODA cycle.

'***Decision***' at the lowest level mostly boils down to deciding which drill is the most suitable for a given situation and with what modifications. Once the broad type of operation and terrain are fixed, situations at this level have limited variety. One can reasonably predict the possible situations and the suitable responses. Training commanders at this level on the possible situations and the apt response can drastically reduce the decision time. The right decision depends on the right orientation.

'***Orientation***' is much more complex, especially in a dynamic combat situation. There are physical, psychological and informational influences that affect it. Improper orientation leads to wrong and/or delayed decisions, causing wasteful actions and time slippage, with all its consequences. On the other hand, proper orientation not only gains a huge time advantage but also ensures the economy of resources. Unfortunately, there is not much one can do to train people to orientate quickly in tactical combat; many a time, training impedes correct orientation; one has to *feel the situation.* However, one can help speed up the orientation by ensuring that an individual is in good physical shape. Physical strain impedes orientation: a tired soldier takes more time to grasp a situation than an alert one. Similarly, as a commander, you can contribute to quick orientation by ensuring clarity of goal – it provides the context in which all observations must be interpreted.

The ***factors affecting the flow of events*** differ depending on the operation and goal at hand. For instance, rain may affect the operations differently under different circumstances. For an attacker, it may impede movement but also allows surprising the defender. To a defender, it may enhance the defensive potential if the slopes become slippery, but reduced visibility may make him vulnerable to surprise. It may turn clayey soil to slush and desert sand to hard, firm ground. Acquiring these insights requires lifelong study and training.

Psychological acceptance of the 'need for action' and burning desire to make a difference must be imbibed. Without it, valuable time is lost at crucial junctures. Many a times, bringing about psychological acceptance is the hardest part. Depending upon the level of such acceptance or reluctance, an individual may not act at all, obey the orders without much inclination, or take ownership of the situation to go all out. The last state is the most desirable, the first the least and the middle is the minimum. These three factors, namely the physical, the informational and the psychological, work in tandem, feeding on each other. Command responsibility is to ensure that all three aspects are primed correctly before combat is joined. Of these, psychological orientation is the most important one; without it, nothing can be achieved. A commander must use every trick in his bag to ensure this.

Observation is taking in the raw environmental inputs. What one makes from personal observations and information depends entirely on the orientation at that particular instant. In combat, it is extremely advantageous to know what exactly to look for; it gains you the time advantage. It takes less time to take in the facts, leading to less time to orient and decide and more time to act. Enemy, Ground and Own Troops all need to be observed both in physical terms as well as psychological terms like morale and espirit de corps. Observation is an acquired skill that needs constant application to refine; combat, on the other hand, is a one-off activity, at least real combat. The challenge is to train the subordinate commanders to make mission-specific observations by themselves and to differentiate between an opinion and a fact when depending on others for informational input. Wrong observations lead to incorrect interpretations, which always results in faulty orientation. Faulty orientation leads to inappropriate decisions and wasted actions. Observation and orientation feed off each other, the accuracy of which depends more on how one accepts the situation rather than trying to fit it into some pre-conceived concepts.

The swift and correct OODA cycle by the section and platoon would give the company and battalion commanders a great time advantage. This would enhance tactical effectiveness and lead to the overall success of battalion operations. Operating the OODA cycle quickly and accurately requires highly motivated troops.

Lessons on Motivation

History matters in building esprit de corps in combat units; old battalions have plenty, but it can cut both ways. It is said that we must '*Take from History its Embers, not its Ashes*'.

I was commissioned into 17 MADRAS (Cochin), a battalion that had a torrid time in the 1965 War with Pakistan. There were many factors for this - lack of training, shortage of weapons and equipment, inexperienced officer cadre, the unfortunate bombing of the train they had arrived in at the disembarking station, and inept conduct of the advance operation by the brigade, to name a few. But the battalion had shrugged off its fouled-up combat performance in 1965 and did wonders during CT operations in Nagaland just two years later. Throughout my four and half years in the unit, I discussed their 1965 war experiences with the veterans of those operations; without exception, all accepted their mistakes but concluded that this had driven them to improve and excel. Their experience ingrained in me the value of training for success in war.

2 RAJRIF had completed 182 years when I assumed command. The unit's battle history is a regimental lore, and we all have been fully tutored in it. As the 20 Bombay Native Infantry, it fought in Iran in 1856 as part of a British Expeditionary Force in the Great Game played with Tsarist Russia of those days. While a British officer was awarded a Victoria Cross during the campaign, two equally deserving Viceroy Commissioned Officers, Subedar Major Mohammed Sharief and Subedar Peer Bhatt, were turned down as that exclusive medal category was then not open to Indians. Later, in the Great War, the battalion was unfortunate to be part of an inept and megalomaniac General Townshend's campaign in Mesopotamia. Under Turkish siege for nearly six months at Kut-al-Amara, the troops were taken captive when the unit was ordered to surrender. Thereafter followed the infamous 'death march' to Turkey. In all this, the redoubtable Subedar Major Kitab Gul emerged as a hero who refused to abandon the Jat and Rajput troops despite Turkish threats and enticements.

In India's first war after independence, the 1948 Kashmir war, the battalion fought in the final link-up operation with Poonch and was awarded one Mahavir Chakra and ten Vir Chakras. In November 1998, when we celebrated our Battle Honour for Poonch, Major Acharya and Subedar Kuldeep Singh conducted a light and sound show of the campaign, with Major Acharya narrating the story line in his deep and sonorous voice as the eternal '*Samay*' (Time), a take we had borrowed from the popular TV Serial Mahabharata. At the end of the show, there was pin-drop silence, and there wasn't a single dry eye amongst the audience. That is the power of history on the psyche of people. Could our movement to Kargil be yet again the hand of destiny creating fresh history for this great Battalion to gift to future generations?

I was fortunate to have laid my hands on a small book '***How to Motivate People***' by the little-known consultant Andrew Sargent. This masterpiece had a practical and common sense approach to the subject of motivation. Sargent overturned my earlier understanding of motivation that "*happy troops are motivated troops.*" He says, "Research has failed to show a consistent correlation between employee satisfaction and performance --- job satisfaction may reduce – absenteeism, grievances (*improve discipline and happiness*) - not necessarily increase productivity" – italics mine. On the other hand, the relation between motivation and performance is obvious, he states and adds that the relationship between motivation and performance was mutually reinforcing. What impressed me most and changed my approach to motivating my command were some precinct observations.

Value of Self Worth. "*What is work without pride? Is not work an expression of self-esteem? Shouldn't people feel proud of what they do*?" he asked. It implied that people must be professionally respected and tasked, not personally patronised. Had we over done the '**Bhola Ram**' routine (that the soldier is an uneducated village bumpkin who needs to be carried along), I asked myself? I had personally experienced the capabilities of jawans, NCOs and JCOs when professionally tasked with a worthwhile task, contributing to the success of their section / platoon / company – during my stint in CT with 19 Rashtriya Rifles (RR).

Job Competence. Andrew Sargent observed that people who know how to do their jobs are motivated. Therefore, he opined that the selection of people for a job and subsequent training is an important component of motivation. I understood that I was responsible for ensuring that people with the right attitude and skills were selected and trained for their expected roles. We had done a pretty decent job on both counts as far as CT operations were concerned; we had selected and trained troops for the role and not the rank. It was to be seen how this selection and training would hold up under different circumstances, especially in conventional combat.

Motivation is Effective Communication. Another profound observation was that '*motivation is communication*'. The crux is the ability to communicate the goal with clarity and the purpose with passion. But continuous communication till the goal is achieved is effective communication. Andrew Sargent observed that one can communicate effectively with only 10 to 15 people, not hundreds. Effective communication is a two-way flow of facts, ideas, and emotions at the individual level. "*Most successful teams have eleven to fifteen players*", he observed, "*not 40 or 50*". It meant that I, as a battalion commander, could not effectively motivate everyone in the battalion and, therefore, I had to select a smaller group to communicate effectively. That made immense sense. I was new to the battalion and hardly knew anyone, so I adopted it. My 2iC, Subedar Major, Company Commanders, Adjutant, Quarter Master, Regimental Medical Officer, and Caste JCO (senior most JCO of the Rajput and Jat Caste responsible for managing the interests of their respective castes) was the team I had decided to focus on. While Town Hall meetings like '**Sainik Sammelan**' were used for communicating the broad intent and the like, actual control and directing was through this team. That worked wonderfully. Would it work in the emerging situation?

Subunit Cohesion

Effectiveness in the execution of the OODA Cycle requires the complete subunit to act as a single coherent entity.

I had chanced upon an article in the U.S. Infantry magazine on the lessons learnt from the Vietnam War. It had extensively quoted Stephan Solarz's work on the causes of the American debacle in Vietnam. The lack of subunit cohesion was the primary cause of high casualties in operations, which was attributed to the '**Tour of Duty**' syndrome. The troops were rotated in and out of operational units for a fixed tenure. During their tenure, they were part of various operations on a roster system to ensure that all duties were equally shared, much like our '*Working Party*' system – fatigue duty for mundane area upkeep. This had led to a different set of people going out for operations from the bases each time, due to which, while there was acquaintance, there was a lack of intimacy. When such teams came under an adverse situation, their overall effectiveness was marred by miscommunication, lack of predictability and mistrust, leading sometimes to disastrous results. Mutual understanding, trust and bond leads to subunit cohesion. Intimacy in groups, subgroups and teams comes from working together for a long time towards a common goal.

Sometimes, sub-groups form amongst the troops that act independently and to the detriment of the overall goal. This was brought home tellingly in a Gregory Peck movie '*Twelve O' Clock High*' based on the working of a U.S. Bomber Group during the bombing campaign of Germany. Gregory Peck, the hero, is posted to a unit taking in many casualties in air battles. Soon he finds out that individual pilots are breaking formations to go out to help a close friend in trouble, thus exposing the rest of the group to the greater danger of decimation. The movie portrays how he goes on to rectify this and emerges as a successful Group in operations. The movie was part of a leadership series during my cadet days at the Indian Military Academy, Dehradun and had left a deep impression.

Sub-unit cohesion is extremely important for success in operations. First, it helps by speeding up the OODA cycle tremendously and second, by linking goals to subunits, it ensures there is ownership by everyone in the subunit. Throughout my service, I had tried various methods to bring about subunit cohesion, but none had given me satisfaction. I hit upon the solution as a company commander with 19 RR. It came from solving an administrative problem.

Leave as an Element of Morale

In the semi–feudal society that the army is, granting leave at times becomes a sort of patronage to the vassals. Planning leave of company personnel and its execution is a challenge a company commander regularly faces, granting emergency leave - unplanned and stress-inducing for soldiers - being the biggest. It is always difficult to assess the veracity of the emergency the soldier is facing at home. The only satisfactory solution from the soldier's point of view is being granted leave, which is not always feasible. Not granting leave sometimes has led to stressed individual soldiers committing suicide or running amok. If assessing the claim's veracity was difficult in a regular battalion, where a soldier's past is well known, it was many times more challenging in the floating population of an RR Company.

After failing to secure leave from you, the soldier would ask for the Commanding Officer's interview. The battalion commander did not have any additional inputs than the company commander except perhaps more experience. If the CO granted leave, the Company Commander's stock would stand reduced in the eyes of the soldier; if not granted, the soldier squarely held the Company Commander responsible. Either way, it was a bad result for the Company Commanders. The success, or otherwise, of the soldier's quest for emergency leave depended upon his ability to plead his case or the effectiveness of those who could lobby his case with the Company Commander or the

Battalion Commander. These lobbyists were the '*go to*' persons if someone wanted to go on '*out of turn*' leave. Such persons are always alternate centres of power, and a challenge to the command at any level. Bad decision-making denied leave to the deserving, leaving the individual sullen in the least. At the same time, the undeserving manipulator got leave, putting a question mark in the troops' minds regarding the company commander's ability to judge. Such decisions always resulted in lowering of the esteem a commander was held in. If one were in close contact with troops, they would always let it be known that you had erred.

Democratising the Process. I wanted to ensure that while genuine cases got badly needed leave, the manipulator was denied his extra leave. I reasoned that the best information and correct assessment of the genuineness of the leave request would be available at the section level. If I could involve them in the decision-making process for granting such leave, I could ensure genuine cases got leave. To do this, I decided to outsource the leave granting responsibility to the Section (the 10 men squad of an Infantry Platoon). For it to be effective, I had to ensure that the Section members were as permanent as possible, that they had quota fixed for leave, and that the authority to grant leave rested with the Section Commander; the Company Commander merely provided documentary support. This took care of the planned leave. For emergencies, we did a small innovation. We parked an additional leave vacancy for the platoon with the Platoon Commander and kept an additional vacancy per platoon at the Company Commander's level. This additional vacancy would be granted on an emergency basis with the proviso that the vacancy would lapse back to the pool with the first person who returned from leave from that subunit. This worked like a charm. The section and the section commanders were deciding on the sequence and duration of leave amongst themselves. In case an individual required leave emergently, the section decided on re-sequencing leave amongst themselves, and the Section Commander and Platoon Commander negotiated the extra leave vacancy to cover the gap till the first person from their subunit returned. The Section Commander became the 'Go To' person for the section from a non-entity and the arbitrator within the section. In emergencies, he emerged as the champion of the soldier's leave needs, not the Company Senior JCO, Company Havildar Major, Company Clerk or Company Commander's buddy. In short, the Section Commander emerged as a power centre. This had many side benefits that were more useful than losing my power to grant leave to the soldier. The main benefits were that the section worked as a 'Band of Brothers' and the Section Commander emerged as their undisputed leader. The Platoon Commander's relationship with the Section Commander became cooperative rather than coercive. I, the company commander, was relieved of the potentially risk-prone venture of deciding on a soldier's emergency leave requirement and could concentrate on my operational responsibilities. From here, channelling this newfound group dynamics for tactical purposes was easy. Soon, we had sections well-versed in tactical drills to meet all challenges in CT operations. Sub-unit cohesion in CT operations had been brought around by providing real authority to the section commanders.

I had learnt my lesson. If one wants subordinate commanders to be effective, then giving them responsibility alone does not suffice; they must also be given authority. Authority implies discretionary control over dispensing some object of want of subordinates. Centralisation of Authority and Decentralisation of Responsibility do not go together, however compelling the argument for such an arrangement. Decentralisation of leave sanctioning powers to Section Commanders and permanency of troops within a Section was one of the first things I implemented after assuming command of 2 RAJ RIF.

Training Junior Leaders

An effective OODA cycle requires effective sub-unit commanders. Umpteen official operational reviews had indicated the failure of junior leadership as one of the causes of concern in the army. While everyone understood and talked about the importance of junior leadership, few attempted to compile guidelines for training them. We had a plethora of training manuals and notes for various operations, syllabi, training, and examinations for promotion - testing skills and knowledge, but never practical guidelines on how an officer must select and train people for the command of sub-units.

All our command courses, namely Junior Command (for Captains and Majors), Senior Command (for Lieutenant Colonels approved to command a battalion) and Higher Command (selected Colonels who have excelled in unit command), concentrate on the tactical and administrative aspects of command. I had learnt the hard way that performance in such professional courses (while my course record was impressive) mattered little in winning acceptance by your subordinates as a leader. What mattered was how I could challenge, train, and help them perform the tasks I allotted to them.

How does one use this insight to train junior leaders? I came across the book, "*Small Unit Leadership: A Common Sense Approach*" by Colonel Dandridge M Malone of the U.S. Army, which impressed me with its practical approach. As soon as I had assumed command of 2 RAJRIF, I purchased this book and translated it into Hindi. '*Skill + Will = Kill*', the book highlighted and gave a practical methodology to train a leader to enable him to lead his sub-unit successfully. Major Acharya reviewed this book and educated all of us, especially the JCOs, on the methodology and its implementation. We adopted some of the methodologies in our preparations for CT operations. The results appeared to be quite effective in the limited time we had in CT operations. Would they continue to do so under different circumstances was dogging my mind?

Finding and Training the Right Sub Unit Commanders

During my stint at the War Game section in ARTRAC, I came across the writings of Colonel Trevor N Dupuy on the effectiveness of different armies during the war, mainly in World War II. Given the same type of resources, he had empirically proved that the German Army always generated more combat power than its adversaries. Analysing the reasons in his book '*Genius for War*,' he identified the excellence of the German section commander over his contemporaries as the main reason; the famed German General Staff was considered an additional contributory reason. The German General Staff firmly believed that a good section commander could take ten normal soldiers into operations and return successfully, whereas an incompetent section commander could easily lead ten good soldiers to death. Their belief in this dictum was so strong that when Hitler tried to reduce the training period of section commanders from one year to meet the increased requirement of troops during the Russian Campaign, it was opposed vehemently. The allied armies had found that even when they had operational breakthroughs, tactical mopping up of scattered German subunits consumed more time and troops. The main reason, Dupuy observed, was the difference in the professional competence of sub unit commanders of the adversaries. The German General Staff had built an operational edifice on the foundation of sound sub-unit tactics executed by section commanders who were selected and trained with utmost care. During the command of my company with 19 RR, I experienced the truth of this concept first-hand.

After assuming command, I discussed the role of section commanders with my team of officers. I asked them to identify one competent commander for each sub-unit in the rifle companies - 36 section commanders and 12 platoon commanders. Increasing the number of ranks at all levels purely to ensure enhanced financial remunerations has undermined the command structure. Therefore, if required, I permitted them to dump the rank structure requirement to find a competent sub-unit commander.

To identify these commanders and ensure that the available talent was equally distributed among the sections, we hit upon having an Inter-Section Competition. The rules were simple. Each section was to be represented by a Section Commander and six other ranks; each section was to undergo four tests: kit inspection, firing, point-to-point march by day and night, and obstacle course. Based on the ranking in each of these tests, the sections were to be finally rank ordered. The sum of each section's rank score was the company score. The company with the lowest score was to be the winner. There is nothing like an inter-company competition for priming a company for action. This galvanised the company commanders and platoon commanders to assess, sort out and redistribute the personnel in their respective companies. This was not a gladiator sport wherein few selected stalwarts represented the company, and all efforts went to prepare them. Everyone was involved in the company; no one wanted to suffer the ignominy of being left out of the section. One could see the soldiers within the section pushing each other, helping each other, and dressing down the laggard – even if it was the section commander – to complete the task. It was very satisfying to watch the best man for the job emerge within the section for the role at hand – for instance, map reading – and to see the section's personnel coaching each other in rifle firing. It was also very satisfying to see the section, platoon and company commanders investing huge effort to plan, train, motivate and lead their respective commands to give their best.

One incident from that period is still etched in my mind. There was a scramble to get a firing range allotted by the sections and platoons. After one such firing, I received a report from Charlie Company Commander that a bullet was stuck in the barrel of a rifle. I could not fathom how it had happened and everyone insisted it got stuck during firing. If that were to be the case, there had to be a bulged or burst barrel, so I knew there was more to it, and I insisted on knowing the truth. The company personnel and the commanders were sticking to their stories, and I was poking holes into it. Finally, Subedar Dharmveer Singh spoke out honestly and revealed that while emptying the chamber, the bullet had been detached from the brass cartridge case and remained stuck in the breech. In their effort to extract it, they pushed it further down the barrel, hoping it would come out from the muzzle end. I appreciated the honesty of the JCO. It was a good opportunity to make it known to all junior leaders that I, as their battalion commander, made decisions based on their reports. False reporting, I told them, could lead to wrong decisions on my part. Even worse, since they knew that my decision was based on false information, they would be reluctant to obey or implement it, which would lead to a vicious cycle of lies, mistrust and misinformation. In active combat, this could spell disaster.

Culturally we have always associated people with the news they bring. We have numerous stories where harbingers of good news/tidings are awarded, and those of bad news are either punished or branded as inauspicious people. It is common practice in organisations to keep the Boss ignorant of unsavoury happenings until they manifest themselves dramatically. Thus, we are conditioned to fall into a pattern of passing on good news or successes with great speed while suppressing the bad news or failures as long as possible. This is bad for any organisation but worse in combat.

I insisted to my core team that they must fearlessly share their opinions and information. From my side I promised them I would not hold them responsible for consequences of actions on my orders or those done in good faith, nor associate them personally with the information they reveal.

The result of this hectic activity, which lasted about a month and a half, was that we had cohesive sub-units led by competent leaders; leaders and their men knew the strengths and weaknesses of each other. We also communicated candidly at all levels with no one taking offence when their mistakes were highlighted. The empowering of section commanders with leave granting power had yielded companies with well-balanced and spirited sub-units where the writ of commanders was accepted willingly. The challenge for me then was to ensure that this 'chain of command' was strengthened and sub-unit commanders trained.

Maximising the Training Strength

It helped that we were in the pre-induction phase for CT operations, a time window of about three months before the battalion was operationally committed. Dissipation of strength in administrative duties, some necessary and unavoidable and others not so, was the bane of unit training. Subunits at training were always under strength.

My first objective was to maximise the numbers for training at the company level. The major chunk absent from training at the company levels were detachments on guard duties - the standard Quarter Guard, ammunition and armoury guards, a few watch and ward guards and patrols to prevent movement of civilians and stray animals. They used to be equitably distributed amongst the companies, thus resulting in reduced and ever-changing people available for training. Thus, the training was neither complete in the spread nor in depth.

I nominated a company as a Duty Company in rotation and allotted the responsibility of all guards in the unit to that Company Commander. Secondly, I suspended the practice of Duty Officer and Duty JCO. Thirdly, all duties were allotted to sub-units, not *ad hoc* groups, and it was up to the sub-unit commander to execute the task with his sub-unit. This immediately made the complete strength available for training on the days they were not the Duty Companies. The Company Commanders could now focus on training their commands.

Historically, guarding important places had been allotted to subunits, and their commanders were responsible for execution. But the ceremonial aspect, especially in the Quarter Guard, had become more important somewhere along the line. Military bearing, good looks, and drill took precedence over the ability to guard against real threats. As a result, the selection and dress of these selected few got greater attention at the cost of those not selected. This type of nurturing gladiators, I had always felt, led to breaking the chain of command, neglecting the average Joe, and favouritism and bickering. Though it earned the appreciation and kudos of the powers that be in peaceful times, it mostly resulted in inefficiency, ineffectiveness and huge losses when faced with challenging situations requiring a military response.

The flexibility with which an organisation can respond to dynamic and uncertain situations is a product of the competence of its chain of command system and the quality of people manning these posts. Flexible actions guided by the overall goal or aim are the only way to handle the confusion that prevails in the fog of war. Our decision to allot duties and tasks only to sub units yielded many immediate benefits. All troops got a chance to be on duty at the Quarter Guard; the section commanders learnt and trained their commands in mounting a guard. Every work, even routine fatigue duties, to be done in the battalion was allotted as a task to companies; the responsibility of analysing the task and deciding on equipment, the quantum of troops and the method of execution was left to the Company Commander and his team. The Company Commander, with his platoon commanders, became responsible for tasks allotted to them; thus, they were on their toes planning, coaching, checking, and supervising. As a result, commanders at every level were getting to observe their troops and assess them. The chain of command was being trained and exercised daily in the art of 'Decision Making and Implementation'.

Training with Special Forces

Now that the entire chain of command was involved in training their commands, my duty was to ensure that what they taught was tactically sound and in harmony with our expected role in CT operations.

When I was in 19 RR, 9 PARA (Special Forces) always used my company base at Kakrosa in Kupwara district whenever they operated in the forests of Hangnikut and Haphruda. We sometimes provided them with terrain guides, and I was highly impressed with how their sections conducted their tactical manoeuvres. I ordered my platoon and section commanders to befriend the Special Forces troops and learn their tactics. I used to request their Company Commander to demonstrate and teach us some basic section-level moves, which he would oblige. The result was that soon, my company in 19 RR had become quite adept at moving as sections through the forest in militant-infested areas undetected and carrying out small unit actions. Soon, the newfound skills were producing results, and 'kills' started happening. Seeing us, couple of other company commanders followed suit. Our ascendancy over militants in the Vilgam – Kakrosa - Haphruda – Hangnikut – Magam belt was gratifying.

I wanted to replicate this in 2 RAJRIF. I sought the help of 9 PARA (Special Forces) once again. I wrote to the CO of 9 PARA (Special Forces) requesting him to train 12 NCOs from my battalion in the fine art of small unit tactics and drills in which they were highly adept. Colonel John Britto responded positively and added his request, '*Could I spare some of my best men to join his unit*?' I immediately responded by offering to send my complete Ghatak Platoon with a promise that anyone who chose to join his unit was his, to which he readily agreed. In a month, I had my 12 NCOs trained in small unit tactics, and in three months, my whole Ghatak Platoon was trained and tested by 9 PARA (Special Forces). Out of the 18 who had gone as part of the Ghatak Platoon, four decided to join 9 PARA (Special Forces). With the arrival of these 12 NCOs, training standards at the platoon level went up a few notches; the commanders knew how to react in what situation and trained their commands to respond correctly.

Realism in Training

Section drills are good for ensuring quick response of the sub unit commander and his team, but they have a lacuna. They do not teach the commander or his team how to assess the situation and decide the response. One can do situation training to improve this. It is easy to create the confusion of battle at higher levels of command by forcing decisions under incomplete, at times conflicting, information. The physicality of the situation is progressively less relevant as the level of command increases; however, at the section level, it is a totally physical situation that is relevant. Every tree, fold-in the ground, and boulder has a bearing on the decision. So has the perceived or actual location of the enemy, the location of individuals, his section, time of day and weather. At this level, the observation, orientation, and decisions are to be made in seconds, unlike higher-level commanders who are physically in less challenging positions and whose time frames for observation, orientation and decisions are longer. Trying to train them by painting a situation takes more time than the time spans he is required to observe, orient, decide and act. Thus, the time pressure that needs to be created to make training realistic at his level was difficult to achieve.

Field exercises are a great improvement, yet they lack the effect of fire, which is the most potent and meaningful influencer at that level.

I had worked with the Infantry Weapon Simulator System (IWESS) equipment during my tenure with the War Game Section. We had carried out trials using this equipment to carry out Hit-Rate Analysis of infantry direct firing weapons - Rifles, Light Machine Guns and Medium Machine Guns – in defence. In this system, the bullet was represented by an Infra-Red beam shot out from a weapon. The targeted soldiers had strapped on IR detectors, which could simulate a 'Hit' by continuous beeps that would stop only when the soldier lay down. The trial was fun and highly educative. The results were astonishing. The troops became excited as if they were in actual combat.

The potential for training using the IWESS was huge but where was this equipment? For some unfathomable reason, this equipment was allotted to the Infantry Regimental Training Centres, which trained recruits in the basic skills of soldiers. I contacted Brigadier PS Choudhary, the Centre Commandant of The Rajputana Rifles Regimental Centre (my regiment). Brigadier PS Choudhary had been my CO and was very fond of me. He held this particular equipment but did not have the authority to lend it to me. The Regimental Centre was under the Western Command, and the battalion was under the Central Command. Anyone familiar with the workings of the Indian Army would appreciate the bureaucratic maze one would have to negotiate to get hold of the equipment; at that time, I did not have the luxury of time. I pleaded and cajoled, using all the reasons and emotions I could muster; finally, he agreed. I knew Brigadier Choudhary had taken a huge professional risk that could mar his career if found out. I promised him that I would keep this a secret from my superiors.

Once we had the equipment, the enthusiasm in training went up manifold and so did the dexterity with which our section commanders were handling their sections. Improvement in stalking was spectacular; fire and movement became smooth. The speed with which the sections would try to outflank each other was heartening, and the prognosis for CT operations was good. I then understood the remarks made by Lieutenant General (Later General and Chief of Army Staff) S Roychoudhary, GOC-in-C, ARTRAC. During the conduct of hit-trial data for tanks using SIMFIRE equipment in Mahajan Field Firing ranges, he had said, "*As far as crew training is concerned, 20 km of this has more value than hundreds of kilometres of Exercise Digvijay (a huge scale field manoeuvre carried out by the Indian Army in the early 1980s).*"

What was left for me to complete the training of sub-units in battle drills was the feel of real fire. During our pre-induction training at the Corps Battle School, we had insisted on our training methodology, much to the chagrin of the Officer in Charge of the Battle School. The section would be put inside the trenches in the firing range, and various small arms would be fired over them;

they had to guess the weapon, its distance and how close the shot had passed. The troops enjoyed it, and after some practice, they had become quite adept at it.

Our training was tested when we were inducted into CT operations in the highly active Kigam area of Kupwara. In the month and a half in the CT grid, in an area considered to be low in militant density and actions, we had initiated many encounters. I would like to believe it was mainly due to the small unit tactics we adopted and the high skill levels of the sections in tactically traversing through a variety of terrain that is in North Kashmir. But, we had only one success till then, our inability to convert each encounter to a kill had been traced to our poor hit rate in firing from the hip. When a split second is available in close combat, this skill gives you that time advantage in executing an action. We were making a practice range in Kigam when we were called out to move to Sonamarg.

The opportunity to train my battalion for CT operations and conduct CT operations helped me to ease into my command smoothly. I was greatly assisted by the fact that the battalion had a robust leadership culture, nurtured successively by numerous Commanding Officers who preceded me. The JCOs and NCOs were highly spirited, took pride in their rank, and were not afraid of pulling it when the situation so demanded. It also helped that the troops were drawn from Jats and Rajputs, both have a cultural acceptance of patriarchal authority, which differs in many social characteristics.

Preparing for Command

A word about my own personal preparation for my unit command, an event that is the most cherished dream of any soldier, would not be out of context.

During my pre-departure interview, Colonel HC Marwah, my boss at the Army School of Mechanical Transport, had advised me to "seep" into the battalion and not "barge" in. The battalion was old and must be doing something right to have survived (and done well) for so long, he had said, and I should not be in a hurry to change things. Like most aspiring Commanding Officers, I had my bucket list ready. But cautioned by Colonel Marwah's sage advice, I refrained from blindly and mindlessly implementing this list.

CHAPTER THREE

INDUCTION INTO THE BATTLE ZONE – MOVING TO SONAMARG

Changing Gears

It was around midday on 25 May 1999, and I had just seen off Major General Mohinder Puri, the GOC, at the helipad near my HQ at Kigam, near Kupwara. The GOC had flown in to congratulate the Battalion on its first "kill" in a CT operation we had successfully carried out in the Sadganga bowl of the terrorist-infested Kupwara District.

Even before the dust raised by the chopper's rotors settled, I saw Lieutenant Praveen Tomar, my officiating Adjutant, rushing towards the helipad. Brigadier DH Summanwar, Commander 81 Mountain Brigade, wanted to meet me urgently. At the Brigade HQ, he explained that I was to move to Kargil at short notice and gave me blanket sanction to plan my movement. The Brigade Major, Major Raja Subramani of the GARHWAL RIFLES (Now Lieutenant General and Army Commander) and I sat down to plan our operational relief, which was done without much fuss.

The speed at which things were moving gave me a sense of foreboding, of being pushed into something bigger than what it seemed. The battalion was lacking many vital crew-served weapons (we had only one Automatic Grenade Launcher (AGL), only two tubes of 81 mm mortars and four Medium Machine Guns (MMG) against the authorisation of four, six and eight, respectively). This shortage did not matter in our CT operations as the primary weapons were rifles and light machine guns (LMGs); a full-out assault was entirely a different bowl of fish! Thankfully, there was all-round cooperation and our shortcomings in the heavier support weapons were promptly made up by transfer from our sister battalions in the Brigade - 3/3 Gorkha Rifles and 3 RAJRIF.[15]

[15] Harinder Baweja, *A Soldier's Diary: Kargil, The Inside Story*, Page 45. This is best illustrated by the experiences of 2 Raj Rif Col Ravindranath and his men who arrived in Sonamarg on May 29. He received the Warning Order (WO) for movement to Operation Vijay on May 25. Till February, the unit had been in Gwalior. After a month's pre-induction training at the Corps Battle School at Khrew from 10 March to 10 April, the unit moved to militant-infested Kupwara for counter-insurgency operations, under 81 Mountain Brigade. Before they could

We had been inducted into the CT grid about a month back and were deployed along the ridge lines leading to the Kashmir Valley hinterland from the Kalaroos area. The rifle companies were all scattered in independent company operating bases equipped with small arms and light equipment to match the terrorists in mobility. All heavy weapons and equipment were stored at Pattan near Baramulla.

As mentioned earlier, I had some inkling of a serious situation developing in the Kargil Sector after what I witnessed during my short trip to Srinagar and the useful briefing of Colonel Angelo at HQ 81 Mountain Brigade with his pockmarked map with red dots indicating 'terrorists' sitting on nearly all the tactically important terrain features. This was totally out of character; terrorists were known to occupy tactical features when an opportunity offered them and bring down fire, but they rarely held ground when seriously challenged. What was reported from the Kargil Sector was unusual. Though unsure about our impending task, I guessed correctly that it would be some offensive action.

This situation had come at a most inopportune time for me personally; I was keenly looking forward to a spot of leave, having last met my family in November 1998. Major Sandeep Bajaj, my 2iC, was on some well-deserved leave, having led the unit advance party into our new operational area, and my leave was tied to his return sometime in June 1999. I had made some lovely plans for the leave, bringing the family (my wife and two daughters) to Srinagar, where I had served earlier and then visiting Leh and Himachal Pradesh with them. They were to start their journey on 27th May 1999 - after two days; the first thing I did was to put all plans of a family holiday on hold indefinitely.

---

settle into their counter-insurgency role came the message telling them to move to Drass in the Kargil sector. While acclimatising at Sonamarg, Ravindranath also tried to make sense of what was happening in Kargil. His 'After-Action Report', finally signed on September 11, tells a hair-raising story. They were trying to assess what their likely task in the war would be on the basis of 'rumours'. Presuming that 2 Raj Rif would be used in an offensive role to evict the intruders, Ravindranath had quickly put together three teams of officers, JCOs and NCOs to work at the following: (a) Evolve an assault methodology to be adopted for attack by the unit in view of the exposure gained by other units. Team to collect information about enemy tactic, their weapon strength and deployment. The team was told to arrive at a tactical doctrine to overpower the enemy. (b) Assess the administrative requirements in terms of equipment and food articles. (c) For physical fitness and acclimatisation, the team was to select routes and work out a schedule so the unit could stand the stress and strain of the operations ahead. They had heard the horrifying stories of how 1 Naga and 8 Sikh had been pushed into the mountains with no warning, acclimatisation or fitness drill. The units had arrived with incomplete armouries. 2 Raj Rif was luckier. In the three and a half days between the receipt of the Warning Order and the Movement Order which came at 1400 hours on May 28, the unit had identified all items it would require for High Altitude Area (HAA) operations. Shortage of special weapons and equipment had been made up from 1/3 Gorkha Rifles and 3 Raj Rif and the unit had also carried out rehearsals bunker bursting and section assaults.

On the drive back to Kigam from the Brigade HQ, I succeeded in getting through to my home from an STD booth enroute and, in a short and crisp message to my wife, told her, "*Cancel your journey.*" Obviously, I could not say anything more on a public line, and I guess it left my wife bewildered and concerned. Meanwhile, a warning order to be prepared to move to Sonamarg at 24-hour notice was waiting for me at my HQ.

The urgency of the situation required that we move out of our company operating bases in broad daylight, not a smart move in terror-impacted areas. This was an open invitation for terrorists to, at the least, ambush our convoys or place improvised explosive devices (IEDs) on our routes. More seriously, they could attack our posts when they were thinning down and rendered vulnerable. I tried to stagger this change, moving out the most vulnerable companies at night while letting some movement occur by day where there was no habitation nearby.

26th May 1999

By 1000 hours on 26th May 1999, transport for our movement was rolling into Kigam and the place was a bedlam of activities - packing of heavy stores, sorting of baggage and loading of trucks as they arrived. Collection parties to make up for the shortfall of ammunition and stores were despatched to the nearest Ammunition Point and to the Ordnance Depot at Srinagar. Major Madan, Bravo Company Commander took the advance party to Sonamarg on the same day. By evening, the entire battalion was packed, loaded and ready to move when 'stand down' orders were received. Tired and frustrated, we unloaded the trucks, and the empty transport returned to Kupwara under escort.

Just then, one of our intelligence sources came in and reported the presence of terrorists in a particular house in Kigam. I consulted my officers, Vivek, Acharya, and Mohit. Tired from all the activities since morning but undeterred, there was not a moment of hesitation in completing the task that could lead to an encounter; such was the spirit and professionalism of these young men. At about 2300 hours, the cordon was in place around the target house, but the birds had flown the coop by this time. Mindful of our primary task, which had not been cancelled, I reluctantly called off the operation.

27th May 1999

The next day, I decided to optimise the load tables since we had been allowed a break in our movement. The company loads appeared overly heavy towards administrative requirements. With the battalion moving into actual operations, either offensive or defensive, in the tough terrain around Kargil, the companies were asked to pare their loads accordingly and to prepare load tables more suitable for attack/defence in the mountains.

Defensive operations did not pose as much of a challenge as offensive tasks. In the mountains, this invariably results in attacking along a ridge line and clearing the opposition preventing you from establishing yourself on a tactically dominating ground. Such tactically important ground is also invariably well protected with strong bunkers. Hence, capturing such tactically relevant features, if the enemy cannot be forced to vacate it through ruse or manoeuvre, will invariably come down to clearing the bunkers by sections.

My section commanders had proven themselves capable of offensive manoeuvre in CT operations. If I could enable these section commanders to effectively lead their sections in clearing these bunkers, we knew we could successfully attack. The company and platoon commanders' task would then be reduced to preventing the enemy in mutually supporting positions from interfering with these section commanders. To achieve this, I tasked Subedar Ram Kumar Lamba, who had been an instructor in the Platoon Commanders Wing of the Infantry School, to organise a lecture demonstration. This was done with professional excellence on the afternoon of 27 May 1999. In my closing remarks, I communicated to the troops the possibility of going into attack and the requirement of preparing themselves tactically, physically, and mentally. I asked them to practice these drills on their own until every section commander was satisfied that he could execute it day or night with the passage of minimum verbal instructions.

There was another reason I had organised the lecture and demonstration. My working knowledge about our impending operation was scant and was culled from radio and TV broadcasts, conversations with Army Service Corps (ASC) drivers who were making frequent trips to the battle zone and staff at higher HQ who could reveal little on telephone lines. Not surprisingly, it was sketchy and mostly hearsay, but whatever little there was, it was hardly encouraging.

During CT operations, the battalion Ghatak Platoon had been organised from Reconnaissance and Surveillance and the Pioneer Platoons, with few Signal platoon men incorporated. Tasks of the Ghatak platoon required high-level skills in scouting, recce, sabotage, surveillance, communications and personal weapons skills, including sniping. Besides these skills, they required a high degree of physical and mental endurance and the ability to operate singly or in small groups inside militant-dominated terrain. These skill sets and mental and physical abilities had great commonality with those of the Recce and Surveillance Platoon and the Pioneer Platoon (they handled explosives, obstacles, traps, etc.). We retained them as such. Mortar Platoon, which had been assigned the role of CO's Quick Reaction Team, was reverted to its original role and asked to polish up their mortar drills and get their equipment ready.

28th May 1999

By the afternoon of 28th May 1999, we received orders to concentrate in Sonamarg by the next day.

Securing the Rear Base

We were moving with only our combat elements, leaving behind the bulk of our offices, clerical staff and some of our tradesmen, in all about 30 all ranks. They were to guard all the personal and organisational equipment and hold onto the camp measuring 600 metres by 300 metres. It had forests on three sides where militants could approach as close as 20 metres unobserved during the day. The village of Kigam was around 300 metres on the fourth side, and the road leading to the camp passed through it. Given the militancy situation, I was worried for the safety of the troops staying back. Already low on strength, I could not spare combat troops to secure these assets. Hence, all the assets were ordered to be placed in the central barracks. Subedar Sashidharan, the Battalion Head Clerk, was nominated as the Rear Base Commander.

It was decided to hold the security posts on the outer perimeter during the day and withdraw to an inner perimeter during the night. Barracks in the inner perimeter were selected to provide all-round protection; they were strengthened with sandbags. During the day, all effort was made to depict the presence of many troops and patrols were planned along the lines of outermost buildings. The gut feeling was not good, given the fact that there was a high concentration of terrorists in the Lolab Valley just across the ridge and the fact that we had many an encounter on the ridge above the camp. But under the circumstances, there was nothing more I could do.

An Astrological Hurdle

While I was resting after dinner, our Religious Teacher (RT) or 'Panditji', Subedar (RT) Bisht, came to see me. He said 0600 hours was not an auspicious time for the unit to move. I had never heard of this type of reasoning in my service life; I think real-life danger does evoke such apprehensions. I could grasp the import of what he was saying and was unaware of how many others he had shared his apprehension. Under such tense situations, men would want all things to be favourable to them; it has a great psychological impact, mostly for the adverse. I do not believe in such things, and I fail to comprehend why God would sometimes nominate windows as good or bad; our actions and intentions make them good or bad. But commanding troops with very high religious belief, I could not be blind to their feelings or fears, real or imagined.

As a way out, I convinced the Panditji that since my command element was leaving the location at 1030 hours, we could take that as the time of departure of the unit, even if, due to operational compulsions, other subordinate elements were departing at staggered timings, before and after me. The Panditji, who too appeared to be looking for a compromise, promptly agreed, saying, "*To thik hai sahab. Jab mukhia prashthan karte hain, usko paltan ka prasthan ka samay mana jayega. Woh ghadi shubh honi chahiye*" (It is alright. The time the head leaves is considered as the time the unit has left. In fact, that is a very auspicious time"). I breathed a sigh of relief, a near miss!

To ward off any such inconvenient astrological interventions in future, I cautioned Panditji that the operational situation may impose a selection of timings in the coming days that may not conform to his auspicious astrological calculations. When such a conflict arose, he must immediately discuss the matter only with me and not anyone else. "*You should also come with 'Dosh Parihar' (Counter Measures) strategy as you are both an expert in finding the 'Dosh' as well as an expert in executing the counter-strategy,*" Panditji nodded vigorously, happy to be a cog in the battalion war planning process!

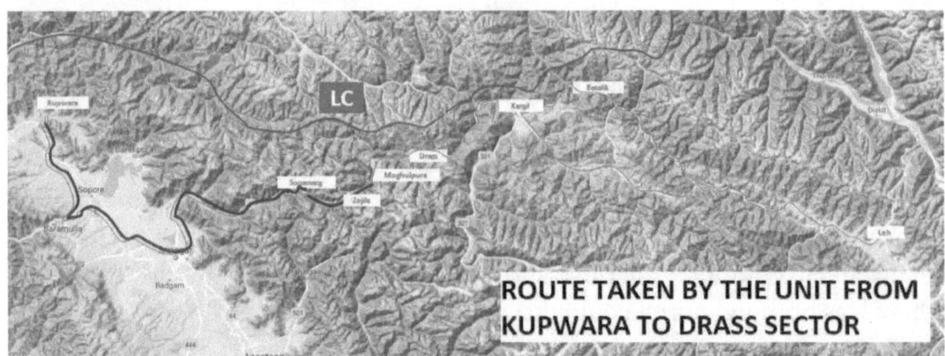

ROUTE TAKEN BY THE UNIT FROM KUPWARA TO DRASS SECTOR

29th May 1999 - The Movement to Sonamarg

The movement did not commence well. We were in for a shock when Civil Hired Transport (CHT), commercial goods carriers commandeered for military operations, started arriving in driblets. Road movement of army units is carried out in a controlled manner in the form of tightly regulated convoys. A convoy, for operational purposes, consists of tactical subunits capable of fighting by riding military transport driven by trained military drivers who can react appropriately to the commands of the convoy commander. One cannot expect the same from untrained civil drivers. Besides, military operational transport normally has four-wheel drive and can traverse cross-country if required. CHT is generally used to move bulk administrative stores or units under non-operational conditions along paved roads. But CHT had its advantages too; CHT could move on roads without a road securing party in place and was unlikely to draw the attention of terrorists or their spotters, especially if they moved at night.

The civilian contractor for the CHT was a burly and jovial Sardarji from Jammu, who handed bundles of currency notes to the company commanders for filling fuel enroute, since he could not be present with every package that was departing at different timings. Despite the package movement, all CHT reached Sonamarg without a hiccup, another plus point for CHT drivers' acumen for moving over difficult terrain independently with little guidance and fixing minor repairs on their own. ASC drivers, on the other hand, are stranded with the slightest breakdown.

I was unable to sleep well, with the rumbling of CHT arriving through the night till late morning keeping me awake. We despatched the first lot of vehicles to Pattan and the Old Airfield location in Srinagar to pick up ammunition and ordnance stores around midnight with personnel of the Quarter Master Platoon and some security. We decided to move in company columns with staggered timings for ease of command and control (as well as not to attract the attention of local militants and their sympathisers).

The first column left at 0600 hours on 29 May. We did not have maps of the area; hence, I decided to go via 8 Mountain Division HQ to pick them up. I also hoped to pick up some solid information from there or at the 15 Corps HQ.

After seeing off all the companies, I left for the Divisional HQ located at Sharifabad. I first met Lieutenant Colonel Ugrasen, an old friend and the General Staff Officer Grade I (Intelligence). It was apparent that the Division had as much (or as little) information as I had. All that Ugrasen had to show me was a large-scale map of the Drass area with many red dots on different ridge lines, little different from what Colonel Angelo had frightened us with. I demanded maps of the area, but he had none to spare as it was not their area of operation so far. But he was kind enough to write an authority letter for the Intelligence Branch of HQ 15 Corps to meet my map request.

Similarly, Brigadier Roychoudhary, Deputy GOC of 8 Mountain Division, had little more to add to my scanty information cache. The principal players, the GOC and his Colonel General Staff (Col GS), were unavailable; everybody was cagey about their whereabouts, so I did not persist and departed for HQ

15 Corps after a hasty lunch with Ugrasen. Knowing that I was unlikely to gain much information here either and running late, I collected my two sets of maps and proceeded to Sonamarg.

A Sightseeing Column!

Driving along Gupkar Road and Dal Boulevard towards Sonamarg, when we reached Nishat Garden, I was in for a shock. Our convoy, in all its glory, was neatly lined up on the road with few souls in sight and even scantier security! As per our route planning, the convoy should have taken the Srinagar – Leh Road through Qumarwari - Safa Kadal and would have been in Sonamarg by now, according to the time and space, much before the road opening parties were lifted around 1700 hours; it was already nearing 1600 hours.

Obviously, they had taken the Srinagar Bypass and wasted time. I was aghast at the utter ignorance of the dangers lurking in the terrorist-infested urban space of sprawling Srinagar. The situation was fluid; no one knew what Pakistan was up to. If they had opened a front in Kargil to ease pressure on groups of terrorists operating in the Valley, the terrorist groups would have been specifically tasked to engage troop convoys headed for Kargil. Here was my convoy, a sitting duck waiting to get on the next day's newspapers and headlines for all the wrong reasons.

The Valley was experiencing very high-intensity terrorist activities in the early days of 1999, and I was apprehensive about getting safely to my final destination, wherever it was. I had done a stint in Srinagar during the high tide of insurgency in 1989-91 and knew first-hand how dangerous it was for the troops as exposed as my unit was right now. My orders to the convoy had been explicit - clear Srinagar as quickly as possible.

Furious at this clear breach of my orders, I interrogated the few men near the vehicles. To my utter amazement, I was told the troops had stopped to visit the nearby Nishat Garden, a tourist hotspot of Srinagar! A single sniper could wreak havoc on the stationary convoy, and the unprepared troops would naturally have retaliated blindly, inflicting grave collateral damage in the narrow streets. Suffice it to say, Major Vivek Gupta, who happened to be the first to come in my sight, got a belly full, and that energised all concerned; we were back on the road in flat 15 minutes. I decided to bring up the rear to prevent any more surprises.

We were crossing the area where the highway joins the main Srinagar - Leh Road, and I heard bursts of automatic fire. Since nothing seemed to be coming in our direction, we kept moving, and soon, we were out of the congested, built-up areas of suburban Srinagar and heading towards Ganderbal.

It was already 1930 hours as I neared Gund, but I was happy to see the road-securing parties still deployed. I stopped to exchange a few words with them and was relieved to be informed that they would only be reeled in once our convoy had cleared their stretch of the road safely. To my delight, I found the boys to be from 19 RR, a battalion of which I was a member of the raising team between April 1994 and February 1997. It was still being commanded by Colonel VK Singh, under whom I had served. The unit HQ was at Gund, where I stopped briefly but found that the CO was out. The troops, of course, received me with much pleasure and hospitality.

Just short of Sonamarg, our ammunition vehicle broke down, and our EME repair team was put in to repair it. Since I had operated in this area in my earlier tenure, I was reasonably sure they were safe. I continued towards Sonamarg and reached safely around 2030 hours with no other adventure. It appeared a good beginning to what was to be a long journey, barring the "sightseeing" at Nishat!

Confusion Galore

Major VK Madan, who, along with the advance party, had been camping in Sonamarg for two days, appeared agitated. "*The situation up forward is very bad. We must somehow get out of this*, Sir," he blurted; my heart sank, but retaining control, I ticked him off. Fortunately, other officers had not overheard our conversation. Gathering the officers together, I ordered the men to be fed and organised for rest at the Transit Camp for a night halt. However, if orders arrived to continue with the movement, they should be prepared to depart quickly.

While waiting for our dinner to be laid out in the Transit Camp Officers' Mess, Major VK Madan quickly brought us up to date. His information was not officially sourced but was based on hearsay rife in the Transit Camp, not a very reliable source. The gist was that the heights around Drass were held strongly by the enemy, and so far, any attempt to dislodge the enemy had been beaten back with prohibitive losses for the assaulting troops. Clearly, we were heading for this meat grinder, which was not a pleasant thought. The OC Transit Camp had no orders for us or our further destination.

After dinner, we anxiously watched the news on the solitary TV in the transit mess. The newscasters' reports were even more shocking - unknown to us; events had been moving at a dizzy pace. The Indian Air Force (IAF) had begun airstrikes on the intrusions on 26th May, avoiding crossing the LC. On 27th May, we lost a Mig 21 due to a missile strike and a Mig 27 to an engine flare out, killing Squadron Leader Ajay Ahuja. Flight Lieutenant Nachiketa, it was reported later, was captured. On 28th May, an armed Mi-8 helicopter was shot down by a Stinger missile while engaging enemy positions on the ridge line near Drass, with many fatalities. Mr. George Fernandes, our Defence Minister, who had assured the nation a couple of days earlier that the intrusions would be cleared in 48 hours, was now offering a safe passage to the intruders who showed little inclination to take on his offer.

To add to the general confusion, the Pakistani newspapers were surprisingly silent while a media storm was brewing in India.[16]

All these battle indicators were clear signs that the situation was far graver than a few "terrorists" occupying some heights, as was being projected by the military hierarchy in the Valley. I met some COs from the 6 Mountain Division infantry battalions at dinner. They gave no reason for their presence, pulled out from their peacetime locations, nor did I embarrass them by asking. Primarily an offensive formation trained for mountains, their presence meant an offensive was on the cards. This was an undeclared war but a confused one where orders were hard to come by.

For any commander, there is no greater danger than his command getting into a feeling of despondency even before a single bullet has been faced, being done in by rumours. The only sure cure is action; action of preparation to overcome possible future challenges. Firstly, this positively engages them with the situation as it emerges, and secondly, it indicates to them that safe delivery from the situation is in their hand - in their acts of preparation. Looking back, these practices contributed to the success of subsequent operations.

The human mind is a great piece of wonder; it can churn up great hope or despair out of seemingly innocuous pieces of information. From what I could sense, the Transit Camp was full of juicy gossip. Neither the narrator nor the listener bothered to think about the veracity of what was being transmitted. Under these circumstances, I needed to isolate my unit from the Transit Camp. I also needed to ensure the officers were in close contact with their troops. My officers were young and enthusiastic, very impressionable and lacking in experience. I needed to ensure they did not pick up some damaging impressions as Major Madan had probably done.

---

16 The Daily Dawn issue of 31 May 1999 made no mention of the intrusion but vaguely referred to it as an ongoing freedom struggle. "*There is no terrorism going on in Kashmir; it's a freedom struggle," Gen Musharraf said. "People have risen against India; let that be very clear.*" This after an Indian Mig 21 had been shot down and its pilot killed on 27th May, allegedly after he had landed safely on the ground, and one Mig 27 crashed the next day due to engine failure and its pilot captured, both over Batalik sector. On 28th May, a rocket firing Mi-17 helicopter had been brought down, killing four of its crew. Speaking at a book release ceremony on May 31, Prime Minister Nawaz Sharif was quoted as saying that "people India brands 'infiltrators or intruders' are in fact Kashmiri freedom fighters who are struggling for their right to self-determination given to them under the United Nations."

Fears of an Air Attack

Deciding to pitch camp at Sonamarg till further orders, we closed in for the night. But I was uneasy, with the shooting down of aircraft indicating that the air battle was joined. Sonamarg, being a wide valley and a base for moving into the Drass Sector, was an ideal target for enemy air strikes. My unit vehicles neatly lined up nose to tail along the road would be easy pickings, as would my men billeted in the exposed transit camp barracks.

My darkest thoughts floated back to the experiences of 17 MADRAS, the battalion into which I had been initially commissioned in 1980. In the 1965 war, 17 MADRAS were moved by train under cover of darkness to Gadra Road in the Barmer Sector for an attack on Pakistani-held Munabao. At daybreak, Pakistani Sabre jets came screaming down, and the ammunition wagon received a direct hit and blew up mightily, causing casualties and giving the battalion a bad jolt even before they had joined the battle. The shock effect was to last and had a telling effect on subsequent operations and the troops' performance. Scarred by their war experience, I recollect that during every exercise, the veterans of this battle were fanatic about troop dispersal when halted in an open area.

These two factors - physical safety from possible air strikes and fear of possible psychological undermining of my command prompted me to decide on the need for dispersion. After dinner, I gathered the Officers and JCOs, brought them up to the situation, and frankly shared with them the need to disperse. I ordered the battalion to disperse in company groups towards the base of the mountains, South of the road, along with their vehicles. Lieutenant Tomar, the Adjutant, was ordered to tuck in the battalion HQ in some nondescript central location. This was to be completed by 0400 hours.

Satisfied with the situation, I tried to catch some sleep, but with so many thoughts racing through my mind, it was impossible; a medley rebounded in my head, apprehension mixed with helplessness about the situation. Anticipation and excitement come automatically when one is on the verge of something very important and dangerous. Lack of instructions or tasking was leading to confusion on what I ought to be doing; an unknown future fuels fear. I dug into my past experiences for cues on what I should be doing; I had never faced a similar situation. I had experienced anxiety in CT operations when one patrols the jungles of Kashmir at night, knowing that danger could lurk ahead. But, one experienced relief as soon as one heard a bullet because the spur for action and clarity in a situation comes with it. Irrespective of whether the outcome was a success or a failure, it released coiled-up tension. I anticipated a series of assaults to clear militants from ridgelines, uncharacteristically holding to fixed positions. I hoped for clear orders in time to plan and supervise these clearing operations personally. The emerging situation required a full -blooded assault by my young and inexperienced company commanders working independently in the constraining terrain.

An Un-blooded Team of Officers

A word about our state of officers would not be out of place. We had 12 officers posted against an authorisation of 22. However, only nine accompanied me into battle, excluding the Regimental Medical Officer (RMO), Captain Somanath Basu. Major Sandeep Bajaj and Lieutenant Kenguruse were on leave till 01 June. Lieutenant Kenguruse, Lieutenant Praveen Tomar, and Captain Vijayant Thapar had been commissioned into ASC in December 1998 and were on infantry attachment. Likewise, Lieutenant Rautela was commissioned in March 1999 and joined us in end March 1999. Major VK Madan joined us after completing his staff appointment at the end of April 98. Major Vivek Gupta joined us from Infantry School in November 1998, and Major Mohit Saxena returned from the Mortar Course in October 1998.

I assumed command of the battalion at the end of September 1998. It was my eighth month in command, and I did not know my officers well enough. Of the four officers who had been with me since I took over command, Lieutenant Vijay Ramanan was out on Young Officer's course, Major Rathore, the Quarter Master, and Major Sandeep Bajaj had moved out with the advance party at the end of November 1998. Major Acharya was the only officer I had worked with for the longest time, barring a month's leave when he went to drop his wife, who was expecting.

In November 1998, we organised the Golden Jubilee of the Battle of Poonch on a grand scale in which the Battalion won 1 Mahavir Chakra and 11 Vir Chakras. Sandeep Bajaj, Rathore, Acharya and Vijay Ramanan had an active role in organising it, and as a result, I had fairly intense interaction with them. Acharya and Rathore were the Adjutant and Quarter Master respectively, at Gwalior; thus, one had a chance to observe them closely. Bajaj was our most qualified officer, and I had leaned on him heavily on all professional matters.

My knowledge about the rank and file was sketchy at that time, as my acquaintance with the troops was limited to eight months, during which time I got to know the JCOs and some NCOs, especially Section Commanders, fairly well. This was a spin-off of reorganising and training the unit for CT operations.

My observation and experience in CT operations with 19 RR convinced me that success in tactical-level operations depended on two critical elements:

accurate intelligence and small-unit action. This was how the Special Forces were more successful than others. Success in small unit actions depends heavily on the ability of the Section Commander, the skill sets of individuals and the cohesion within the section. I had personally invested a lot of energy and thought into this in the run-up to our induction into CT operations. We successfully identified suitable commanders at the section and platoon levels. These efforts made me confident that the battalion could execute its tactical plan.

In his 'Manoeuvre Handbook', William S Lind states, "*Tactics combines two basic elements, techniques and education*". The JCOs and NCOs were trained, had mastered the techniques, and were capable of executing various drills, but the education of my company commanders, with barely four to six years of service, was not enough for handling operations at the company level. They were first-time Company Commanders who had trained their commands for small unit actions well. Their professional training was limited to tactical planning and handling platoons in CT operations; they, however, lacked training in planning company-level offensive operations in the High-Altitude mountains. When faced with a tough tactical challenge, such officers push themselves to the front to compensate for their lack of tactical acumen honed in training by personal example. Results many a time are disastrous, resulting in unnecessary casualties of sub-unit commanders and their command going to ground / withdrawing.

Such were the thoughts that were haunting me and making me nervous. What was going to happen? What type of tasks would we get? Were we capable of executing the tasks allotted; this was no training exercise; it was for real. Would my battalion be able to deliver? Would I have the confidence of my subordinates? Would I be able to deliver or fail? Would I be blamed and shamed? Would I come out of all this with my honour intact? Would I come out of it alive and without being maimed? The fear was gripping and almost numbing.

CHAPTER FOUR

MY EXPERIMENTS WITH FEAR

As I lay on my bed that first night at Sonamarg, I fought a battle deep within me. Many emotions were swirling around, but the most overwhelming one was pure, unadulterated fear. It was not as though one faced physical danger for the first time. I had experienced many encounters in CT operations, had some lucky escapes and was happy to be alive. I kept telling myself I needed to get hold of myself and calm down. Alone with myself, my mind was darting here and there; no amount of self-talk was helping to steady my mind, and I gave up trying. I lay blankly on the bed, not knowing what to do next.

From somewhere within the depths of my mind, the memory of my conversation with Brigadier VK Verma, my Brigade Commander in Gwalior, floated up. It was the farewell interview before we left Gwalior for CT operations. "*Ravinder*," he said (like most North Indians, he called me Ravinder instead of Ravindra), "*you are going into CT operations. Your superiors will task you and expect it to be executed somehow; you cannot refuse your orders. Remember you are everything to the unit: father, mother, brother. It is you who must think and look after the safety, welfare, and honour of your command. Your superiors will not do that for you. You must create the best chances for the battalion to perform. It is you who must ensure minimum cost to your battalion. You should do everything in your power to do this.*" he had advised. "*To get the battalion to deliver is your sole responsibility*", he had concluded. Getting the battalion to deliver was my responsibility, and it hit me hard and jolted me. Here, my battalion was in unchartered territory, uncertain of the future, of possibly great danger under my responsibility, and all that I was worrying about was coming down to my name, my fame, and my life.

'*Karmaṇy evādhikāras temā phaleṣu kadācana*' (करमण्येवाधिकारस्ते मा फलेषु कदाचन), a shloka from Bhagvadgita, advising us to follow the path of '*Karma*' came to my mind. We have only the Right to perform our prescribed duty, but not to the fruits of our actions. It was my duty (*Dharma*) to act. I realised I was not afraid of attempting my task; I was not even seeking fame but was afraid of failing. I knew there was nothing wrong with fearing failure; it keeps you alert and goads you to greater effort. The fear of failing was becoming debilitating because I was more worried about the consequences of failure to my name and fame than focusing on the task itself.

Under such mental turmoil, I decided to do what I could, to the best of my ability, without bothering about the consequences over which I had no control. With this, the whole perception suddenly changed, and calmness returned. I could see that my attachment to success made me fear failure; this fear was all-pervading, influencing every thought of what I should be thinking and doing. Now that I had snapped the link between the result of my action, success or failure, and the action process, I could focus very clearly on the task at hand. The fear had vanished. It was clear to me that I did not influence the current situation, that my ability to influence the situation was limited to what I could get my battalion to do and that I had no control whatsoever on the outcome of my actions. Once I accepted this fundamental truth, everything started falling into place like a jigsaw puzzle solved.

I have reflected on this after the war deeply to understand this shloka. The word '*Adhikar*' has often been interpreted as Right, hence the interpretation "*We have only the right to perform our prescribed duty, but not to the fruits of our actions*". Without the Right to the fruits of our actions, we can have a scant motive to act, and this would lead to inaction. The motive for action is a desired end state, the goal. One may not attain it, but that is a different matter. One cannot be denied the right to choose a goal. Without a goal, all actions become meaningless and mechanical. Inaction is better than mindless and goalless action. A second part of the shloka is rarely quoted or interpreted in context. It says, '*mā karma-phala-hetur bhūr mā te saṅgo 'stv akarmaṇi*' (मा करमफलहेतुरभूरमा ते सङ्गोऽसत्वकरमणि॥) It is normally interpreted as "*Never consider yourself the cause of the results of your activities, and never be attached to not doing your duty*". The first part had manifested slightly differently that night at Sonamarg. I had realised that I was not responsible for events beyond my control. But there is something not right about the second part. How can one be attached to not doing one's duty?

One can have attachment to an idea, a person, a result of actions, and even action, but attachment to inaction is absurd. This does not make sense. The word '*Adhikar*' has been interpreted as Right in the first part, but it also has a meaning equivalent to power or control. If one uses this meaning, then the shloka could be interpreted as "You have control (*Adhikar*) over your actions (*karmani*) only but never (*kadācana*) on the results of your actions (*phaleṣu*). Never attach (*saṅgaḥ*) yourself to the results of your actions (*karma-phala)*; it will cause (*hetuḥ*) inaction (*akarmaṇi*)." This makes good contextual sense.

Arjuna was pleading on many accounts about why he did not want to fight, and Krishna was motivating him to fight.

Arjuna is worried about the casualties he would cause and the near and dear ones he has to fight with; this has led to a situation of inaction on the part of Arjun. To contextualise, Krishna separates cause - action – result. He persuades Arjun with the logic that one should not attach oneself to the result of one's actions because it can lead to inaction, a disastrous situation in war. Further, Krishna persuades with the logic that one cannot control the result of one's action; one can control one's action. Therefore, he is asking Arjun to rise above his attachment to the results and focus on the action; for someone going into the battlefield, that advice is very sound. At another place in the Gita, it says that a true soldier is "*neither overjoyed in Victory nor despondent in Defeat*", which becomes possible only if you can detach yourself from the consequences of your action to yourself: name, fame, and safety. Without this detachment, however, temporarily, one cannot focus on the task at hand. I had to get my act together, not worrying too much about the consequences. Worrying too much about the consequences would lead me to inaction and even worse consequences. I decided to get my act together.

Next was to figure out my actions; here, I was guided by the '**Chetwode Code**'. Chetwode Hall is the sanctum sanctorum of the Indian Military Academy, Dehradun. On the wooden wall of the pulpit are inscribed the timeless words of Field Marshal Philip Chetwode that must guide an officer of a national army.

Chetwode Motto

The safety, honour and welfare of your country comes first, always and every time. The honour and welfare of the men you command come next. Your own safety, honour and welfare comes last, always and every time.

It meant that my duty to the nation must guide my actions; in doing so, I have to ensure that men under my command have the very best chance to deliver what I ask them to. While the Bhagvadgita showed that action was the route, the '**Chetwode Code**' showed me the path for my actions. I decided to do everything within the limits of my capability to ensure that. In other words, I was to separate myself from my body and my mind, and mind from the inner me, and inner from actions, and actions from consequences. In a nutshell, practice detachment, being in the thick of the situation without being in it, made sense. Professional decision-making requires clinical thinking with a cool mind, keeping all fears and apprehensions irrelevant to the task out of the equation. I promised myself to be professional and not get distracted by extraneous influences.

Actions without purpose achieve little; they cannot be mindless, and they need to have a goal. In a confusing situation, one cannot get a clear goal for various reasons, from confusion and incompetence to broken communications, to name a few. I was in that situation. Brigadier Shamsher Singh, from the Corps of Signals and my boss at War Game Section, ARTRAC, once narrated his experience in the Indian Peace Keeping Force (IPKF) in Sri Lanka. He was posted to the HQ IPKF to help out on some special requirement, and when he reached there, the commander and staff there had no use for him, and he was without a task. He could have sat back and passed his time happily doing nothing; he chose otherwise. He scouted around the HQ and found no organised method of handling casualties, so he set about doing it and streamlined it. He had said, "*Ravinder, we are officers. We cannot be waiting for orders and sitting on our haunches. If there are no orders, we must create one ourselves*". I decided to prepare my battalion for attack in High Altitude.

With that, what was expected of me was crystal clear under the circumstances. I resolved to focus on the success of my battalion without getting distracted by the 'what if' of my actions. My duty was to ensure my battalion had the best chance of success in whatever task it was to be allotted. Uncertainty, suddenness and volatility of the situation had unnerved me and undermined my confidence. It is fascinating how detaching one's action, the only thing you can influence, from its consequences, which one cannot fully control, and resolve to do what you can clears all the mental confusion. Fear, founded or unfounded, leads to anxiety, and anxiety clouds thoughts. Therein lies a good leadership nugget: subordinates will be more than willing to do your bidding if you are ready to absolve them of the consequences of their actions.

For me, this was the turning point of the war; I had won a challenging internal struggle and emerged with a clear perception of my path. I was happy and confident. I was ready for the challenge; I would meet it with unfettered professional action and resolve. I then took mental stock of the state of our training, equipment, and preparedness, both physical and psychological.

CHAPTER FIVE

OUR SOJOURN AT SONAMARG – PREPARING FOR BATTLE

30th May 1999

The morning came, and there was no air strafing that I had feared the previous night! I contacted the Colonel General Staff (Operations) at 15 Corps HQ for further orders. I was told to stay put at Sonamarg, and further orders would follow.

We had spent the night in a dispersed state, but since our stay in Sonamarg was likely to be extended, the men had to be made more comfortable. As usual, the cook house was the first to come up and industriously prepared lunch. The sky was bright and blue; the sunlight had lit up the valley of Sonamarg in shades of green. Beyond the road to the South was the River Sindh, from where the bare ridge lines rose majestically, looking dark and ominous. A beautiful sight, that is why Sonamarg ranks high on tourists' itineraries. Everything was so beautiful and calm, but anxiety dominated my mind, and of my men too.

Tackling Uncertainty

If there is anything that causes the greatest amount of anxiety to humans, it is uncertainty. Uncertainty is that twilight state where one is unsure of a potentially dangerous future. This impairs decision making on how to prepare for the emerging circumstances. The loss of the ability to act, and inability to control causes anxiety. Under these circumstances, those who can bring in certainty or promise certainty command attention and obedience.

To quell some of that anxiety, I held a conference with my officers and JCOs around 0900 hours in the open to enjoy the lovely day. Acutely aware that I was under intense scrutiny, I nervously began my briefing, gathering confidence as I progressed. I started on a positive note by giving a '*shabaash*' for our movement from Kigam, wherein we negotiated safely through a terrorist-infested area. I indicated that the situation remained unclear and orders were still awaited. I would update them as soon as the situation got clearer but gave no timelines. I suggested we share everything we have observed and heard to assess the current situation.

Everyone hesitated to speak; they probably expected me to give my views first. In uncertain circumstances, where immediate action is not required, the leader must not express his opinion upfront unless one is sure, as it invariably leads to the colouring of opinions. Soon, everyone was animatedly involved in the discussion to assess the current situation. Slowly, information started flowing, which I kept summarising so that others could add or negate.

What emerged from our 'pooling of langar gup' was that apparently, the heights around Drass and Batalik had been occupied by the enemy (Pakistanis or militants, no one was sure then). Our actions to evict them had been beaten back with a bloody nose, making it amply clear that the "terrorists" were holding dominating ground with some strength and were determined and well-fortified.

The most damaging information, however, was about the enemy. It was rumoured that they were occupying 'concrete bunkers'; that they had ingeniously piled up cement bags, riveted them with long-angle iron pickets and poured water over them, and the whole thing had cast itself into a solid bunker immune to our fire. Firing ports had been created, covered with sliding metal plates. As regards enemy tactics, unlike irregulars, he was displaying *"fantastic fire control"* it was rumoured, allowing our assaulting echelons to approach very close, then suddenly sliding open the firing port covers to spray our troops with heavy automatic fire. As per the statements made by troops who had been fighting the 'intruders', these were no ragtag terrorists holding on to hastily prepared defences. Clearly, they had been in occupation of these dominating heights for some length of time which we had failed to detect. The outcome was evident in the '*massacres*' that were taking place when our men launched clearing operations.

It was clear that we were taking casualties, although the numbers fluctuated widely as per the fears and anxieties of the teller; there were no official updates, so the rumour mill was running at full speed.

I had some experience constructing defences in high-altitude areas; it was back-breaking work. Every single piece of material required had to be humped up on our backs. Construction itself was never an easy task. Preparing mortar, aligning stones, placing reinforcements, and pouring mortar were strenuous and time-consuming activities at 9000 feet and above. The snow and vagaries of weather make construction and subsequent maintenance of defence work extremely tough. Were the reports of such superior defence works true or just fantasy of some fertile mind we had no means to judge? With progress in building material technology, the question of whether the enemy could surprise us was on my mind.

The reports of the enemy being in the positions for some time and remaining undetected were intriguing. How would that be possible? Besides troops on the ground, we had air and satellite surveillance; someone should have picked it up and reported, given the rivalry amongst the competing intelligence services to project themselves in a favourable light.

I assured the group that our resources were rapidly being mustered and moved forward for application. So, we were not alone but a cog in a giant machine slowly and laboriously gathering pace. Even our Air Force had joined in, although they too, had suffered some losses.

The administrative picture was equally depressing. Under these confused circumstances, logistics elements were at a premium. No civilian porter was available, and the fighting men were humping all the loads. I had gathered this from other units whose Quarter Masters had tried to muster local porters from the Sonamarg Valley but found that fear had driven them away; the first arrivals promptly gathered the few who had lingered behind. We all agreed that off-road administration of troops would be a challenge. We needed to make necessary administrative preparations.

To lighten the mood, I quipped, "*We are sitting here in Sonamarg not to watch the India-Pakistan cricket match*" (The Cricket World Cup was underway in England). Everyone laughed. "*What do you think our task will be?*" I asked. "*We will be inducted into the operational area,*" someone said. "*To do what?*" I queried. There was silence for some time; I let it hang. "*To occupy some defences,*" replied someone. "*For what purpose?*" I posed. "*To prevent further ingress,*" was the reply. The conversation was not going where I wanted it to. "*Is that the only task we can get?*" I persisted. There was a long silence, and I let it persist, and one could feel the tension in the meeting. "*We could be asked to attack,*" said Subedar Ram Kumar Lamba, Senior Junior Commissioned Officer (JCO) of Bravo Company. I quickly grasped the chance and posed, "*Does anyone disagree?*" I asked, and there was silence. "*Now that we all agree that we could be asked to attack, what do you think is that one key element in defence that will prevent us from capturing a feature?*"

Remembering that we had practised Bunker Bursting Drills in Kigam, I said that well-sited and coordinated bunkers formed the framework of defensive positions, and destroying one or two was the key to breaking the integrity of a defensive position. In response, a few voices spoke in unison, "*Yes, if we can clear one or two key bunkers, we will be able to engage the enemy in close combat; in close combat, superior numbers prevail.*"

So, the discussion progressed, debating on the strengths needed, the type of weapons to be used, the selection of approach for the attack, etc. Observing that we were on weak grounds as we had not refreshed our training in offensive operations in mountains, I concluded the discussion by emphasising the evolving drills to close in with an entrenched enemy without incurring casualties. This also gave me time to organise my thoughts on attack operations.

The army teaches you an effective technique for planning the next course of action. Whatever the final goal, immediate action emerges by asking, "*How far can I plan now?*" The answer was, "*Till I receive the next order*". We decided to use the time available to evolve the techniques to close in with enemy defences along a ridgeline, acclimatise ourselves for high-altitude operations, and prepare administratively for off-road operations.

Mountains: A Peculiar Beast for the Assault!

Ridge lines in high-altitude areas are generally very narrow, at times no more than five to 10 metres wide at the top and often rocky. This is both a challenge and an opportunity. The enemy understands these ridge lines are the most likely attack directions, and defences are always biased towards ridges. He can concentrate all his surveillance and weapon systems on the few possible avenues of movement. The terrain is full of rocky outcrops, and traversing them quickly is difficult; sometimes, special rock craft is required to traverse. It is akin to a mountaineering assault on a peak with enemy opposition added in.

I dug into the memory cells of my tenure as an Instructor in the Mortar Wing at the Infantry School, Mhow. One of my regular assignments for all courses was a lecture on "*Effect of Large Apex Angle on Ranging.*" Conducting 81 mm mortar shoots for students in the field firing ranges of Mhow, I had watched with astonishment how civilians, old and young, darted into the target area, while it was being plastered by mortar fire to pick up the brass and metal shrapnel unscathed, which fetched a pretty price in the grey market. The local police are supposed to keep them away, but it is almost impossible, especially when the firing is on. My impression that field and medium artillery guns would be more effective in keeping such metal scavengers off the target area was belied when I attended a fire power demonstration at the School of Artillery in Deolali. I explained to my men the degree of difficulty that our artillery would face in providing effective support. We may have to depend entirely on our ingenuity.

Geometry of Artillery Fire

I explained how, in mountains, long-range indirect fire through artillery guns and mortars is quite ineffective. The fire of these is generally applied statistically, and where 50 per cent of the fired ammunition falls is called a '**Belt of Fire**' indicated by a square - an artillery field battery (six guns) has a 150 X 150-metre **Belt of Fire**. In contrast, a medium gun battery with the same number of guns will spread 250 X 250 metres. In reality, the geometry of this '**Belt of Fire**' is skewed - the spread is larger along the direction of fire and shorter along the direction perpendicular to the direction of fire. The angle of fire influences the ratio of spread between the two directions; flatter the trajectory, the greater the ratio. The spread is generally a function of range. Artillery fire planning essentially boils down to matching the geometry of the targets with the geometry of the belts of fire of various artillery units.

A section in attack perched on a ridge in the open has a geometrical signature of about 10 –to - 15-metres X 100 metres. So, what are the chances of engaging this section effectively with a Field Artillery battery in broad daylight, even if the target is ranged and the centre of a belt of fire matches exactly with the centre of the section? Let us also assume that the enemy battery is in line with the ridgeline. The conditions are most favourable to the artillery and most unfavourable to the infantry section. If 100 artillery rounds are fired on this enemy section, only 50 are expected to fall within a box of 150 metres X 150 metres. The width of the target is 10 to 15 metres. Taking the higher figure of 15 metres, it is still $1/10^{th}$ of the effective zone. Assuming the spread of rounds in the beaten zone is uniform, which it is not, we would have five rounds falling within the axis along the ridge. The spread of the section along the ridge is 100 metres, which is $2/3^{rd}$ of the effective zone. The probability of a round falling on the section reduces by $1/3^{rd}$, leaving three to four rounds. This is a highly simplified explanation, and there are many mathematical infirmities; the actual figure may be around six to seven in the most ideal of cases. Punch in other factors like an altered line of fire, improper ranging, the effect of weather and visibility, the probability falls drastically.

Artillery fire kills or maims by shrapnel, scraggy rocks both enhance and diminish the effect of fire. It provides protection if on the lee side, else the stone debris of the blast enhances the splinter effect. One hundred rounds is a lot of ammunition for a battery to fire, and in high-altitude mountains, it is even more difficult to provide logistically. In a nutshell, I told them the indirect fire of artillery is not likely to be a potent force to stop a determined section from advancing along a ridgeline.

The conclusion was that the answer lay in a greater number of our own direct firing weapons like the trusted 84 mm Carl Gustav Rocket Launcher and Medium Machine Guns (MMG).

Automatic Weapons in Mountains

While engaging section-sized targets along ridgelines, MMGs have their shortcomings. As a 2nd Lieutenant in 17 MADRAS, I was part of a recce team to site a company for defence in the high altitude Tawang Sector. The team was led by Major Raghubir Singh, the most practical soldier I have met. '*Defence of the Duffer's Drift*' by Ernest Swinton and Major Raghubir Singh taught me about siting and fighting defensive battles at the tactical level, much more than all the formal training I had undergone in various tactical and battle schools.

We would start from the top, and Major Raghubir would ask my team and me, with full section kit and wearing red jackets, to go down along a ridge line up to about 1500 metres and come back up. "*If you can go down, then it is possible to come up along the same ridge line, approach along what is viable for the enemy,*" he would say. While we went down and returned, he and his team, located at different points where he intended to place weapons or locate trenches, would record the locations where my team was visible and where it was not. On our return, he would put all this information together, providing the ground state where we were not visible. With this comprehensive input, he would decide which positions were most suited to keep the visible areas under direct fire and locate his machine guns. He would mark areas not under observation for indirect weapons, booby traps and trip flares.

"*We need to know the enemy is there before we fire our weapons. Otherwise, it will be a waste of ammunition*", he had explained. He would mark areas of easy going and open areas for minefields and constricted areas for obstacles and booby traps, "*We need to keep him longer in the zones where we can engage him with our direct fire weapons and stop his movement in restricted terrain*", he added. "*These machine guns have a trajectory, and the terrain contour does not exactly match the trajectory. Hence, there will always remain areas which are dead to our fire,*" he had pointed out and added, "*so we either prevent the enemy from using that ground or we must have that area under observation so that we can switch weapon position or its fire to bring it under fire. Firing without observation is firing in the air; it may appear threatening but will not be effective.*" I therefore knew that even on a ridge line covered by machine gun fire, there would be areas where enemy fire could not reach. That left us with the challenge of traversing areas where enemy MMG fire could knock us down.

While in the War Game section of ARTRAC as a Major, I was asked, "*How many rounds of small arms fire does it take to cause a fatal casualty?*" by the civilian programmers developing computerised war games. I was stumped; I had never considered battle in such statistical terms. We researched to find an answer, and we chanced upon a statistic that put the figure at one casualty for every million rounds fired. They had taken the figure of those killed in World War II due to gunshot wounds and divided it by the reported expenditure of small arms rounds that were fired. That meant practically no chance of being hit. Definitely, all the casualties had not been chance events in statistical terms so I had suggested we conduct a '**Hit Data Trial**' under a live situation to arrive at this figure.

All those present had looked at me strangely, thinking I was suggesting a tactical exercise with troops with live fire. Infantry Weapons Effect Simulator System, IWESS for short, had arrived recently for use in training tactical subunits in a realistic manner, whose working I have explained earlier (*Chapter Two*). I suggested we use this equipment to get the data. The suggestion was taken up, and Infantry School was tasked to conduct a '**Hit Data Trial**'; I was a member of the War Game Section and Major Amul Asthana[17] was representing WARDEC, the organisation overseeing the computerised war game model development.

The trial was conducted near Mhow and yielded interesting insights into combat mechanics. A platoon was assaulting a section post in a two-up formation, each wave being separated by 100 metres. To keep the variables low, the terrain chosen was rolling and open plain with no cover for assaulting troops. Day and night trials were conducted, and both sides were fitted with IWESS equipment. The assaulting troops were constrained to move steadily, holding their formation and passing through the defences. The defenders were to fire from their trenches and cease-fire when the attackers reached 30 metres. The first-day trial was a disaster; there was just one hit. I discussed it with Amul Asthana, and we went over the manuals again and found that we had to calibrate the IR emitter with the sight. We recalibrated all the weapons and fixed the primary and secondary arcs of fire and the fixed line for LMG and MMG. The second trial threw up hit patterns. We conducted six more trial runs; the sixth was under drizzling conditions. Subsequently, we repeated this trial at night. We then collated the data and plotted the locations of hits for each trial on an enlarged map.

The pattern that emerged was that there were about seven to eight casualties; 50 per cent of casualties occurred at a range of 50 metres or less, and

17 Incidentally, Amul Ashtana, a friend, was the Second – in- Command of 2/11 GR in the Batalik Sector.

the casualties in the 150 to 250 metre range were mainly by machine guns. There were no hits beyond 250 metres. The casualty percentage was around 20 to 25 per cent of the platoon strength. Our historical data study found that a 10 per cent casualty rate at unit or sub-unit level leads to mission failure. Interestingly, the hit rates dropped drastically in the rain by around 80 per cent. Even more interesting was that the hit rate was reduced to an average of one in the three night trials; no illumination was used. This data pattern of hits and ranges fitted in with our experience in firing ranges where hits reduced as the range increased.

I shared these deductions with my subunit commanders in more simplistic terms. I asked them to develop a drill to exploit these factors limiting the effectiveness of the enemy's indirect and direct fire. The aim was to get as close as 50 metres to the enemy bunker without getting hit. I told them that we would have the winning formula if we could achieve this. At 50 metres, the Bunker Bursting drill would kick in, and the battle would degenerate into fighting through the objective, where superior numbers of the attackers would start undermining the defender's ability to hold on to his defences. I chose Major Vivek Gupta, Charlie Company, and Major Acharya, Alpha Company, for this task; they were to be seconded by Subedar Ram Kumar Lamba of Bravo Company and Subedar Sayar Singh of Delta Company with a section each. This way, there was to be representation and a sense of involvement from all assaulting companies, and it would be easy to take the technique back to their respective companies.

The Men are Fully Involved

After the conference, I relaxed in the sun with "*Pillars of the Earth*" by Ken Follett, set in medieval Britain amidst the churn between the Church and the Royalty, putting up a façade of an unfazed and calm commander. In the background, I could overhear animated discussions as different teams huddled together to chalk out plans as per the tasks that I had assigned them.

Ravindranath (fifth from left) with unit officers at Sonamarg

While others dispersed for lunch, I heard Vivek and Acharya discussing something, with Subedar Ram Kumar Lamba and Subedar Sayar Singh joining in now and then. They had been tasked with finding a solution for attack along the ridge line. My curiosity took the better of discretion, and I joined the discussion. Their solution was to advance to the closest feature to the enemy position on the ridgeline that was beyond effective small arms fire and establish a fire support team. Under its cover, sections were to leapfrog using fire and movement until they had closed into the range of effective personal weapons fire, which I had nominated as 50 metres. I thought it was workable (later in battle, this model worked).

High Altitude Acclimatisation

Sonamarg is located at a height of 9100 feet; the ranges around rise to 13000 feet. Zojila Pass, at 11650 feet, was around 30 km from Sonamarg. Major VK Madan, Bravo Company, assisted by Major Mohit Saxena, Delta Company, was given the responsibility to organise acclimatisation. Senior JCOs of Alpha and Charlie companies were also co-opted into this planning. The objective was to climb the hills around and spend as much time as possible at that altitude. We utilised our stay in Sonamarg for acclimatisation.

D Company troops acclimatising on the Sonamarg Heights

Logistical Challenges

We had no clue as to the administrative difficulties ahead of us. The rumours indicated that fighting troops were finding it hard even to get meals; why the well-established supply chain that sustains infantry battalions even under the worst circumstances had collapsed was a mystery, a worrying one at that. We decided to stock up on some ready-to-eat items. Our Rajput and Jat boys come from a hardy rural stock and can stoically bear great hardships; in times of shortages and droughts in their native villages, they have historically survived on roasted gram and 'gur' (jaggery). I passed orders to procure both items in substantial quantity.

But how to sustain these forces logistically if operations got extended? The Battle of Dien Bin Phu in the First Indo-China War (1948-1954), which our generation was very familiar with because it was in our promotion exam syllabus when we were Captains, came to my mind. This is where the Vietnamese forces soundly beat the French colonial power. The valley of Dien Bien Phu is located 250 km from Hanoi, in the highlands close to the border with Laos, which the French had developed as a logistics base with an airstrip. Holding the surrounding heights, the Vietcong were exposed to the overpowering firepower of the French dug down in the valley around the airstrip, making an assault suicidal. Then, they started digging trenches from their dominating positions towards Dien Bin Phu. Soon, they slowly crawled forward to occupy areas from where they could bring the airstrip under effective machine gun fire and, more importantly, logistically maintain the troops in such advanced and exposed positions. With their logistics cut off as the airstrip was rendered unusable and under constant fire from the encircling ring of trenches, the fate of the French garrison, comprising some of their best fighting units like the PARAs and the Foreign Legion, was sealed.

I wondered if we could take a leaf from the playbook of General Võ Nguyên Giáp and his innovative warriors. With the seed of an idea planted in the minds of the company commander, we closed the discussion. Later in the day, Vivek and his team came up with a plan for sections to advance with sandbags, which, as they crawled forward, they would use to build a wall, building successive walls to negate the enemy's aimed fire. It sounded doable, but I wanted to try it out on the ground in an exercise, my worry being would soil be available on Kargil's barren, steep slopes.

As I was halfway through my book, there was a flurry of activities; the warning order for our movement had been received.

31 May – 01 June 1999

Over the next two days, I observed animated discussions by the rank and file on the nitty -gritties of closing in on the enemy. I was happy that my troops were positively engaged. On 30 May 1999, the companies tried their versions of the drills for closing in. On 01 June 99, in the morning hours, Vivek and Acharya were ready to demonstrate their attack drill on a sharp ridge line North of Sonamarg at around 11000 feet.

While I was moving to the demonstration location, I saw a jeep careering down the mountain road, with the Officer Commanding of the Convoy Ground, an ASC Major on board. Breathless, he informed me that I was being searched for as my battalion was to report immediately to Matayen, where HQ 8 Mountain Division had been established. Our brief but fruitful sojourn at Sonamarg ended abruptly.

CHAPTER SIX

MOVING ACROSS ZOJILA INTO DRASS SECTOR

01 June 1999

On 01 June 1999, we quickly struck camp and departed for Matayen around 1400 hours, reaching Zojila around 1600 hours. It was pleasing that my old comrades from 19 RR were guarding this vital gateway into Ladakh. We continued and reached Moghulpura by 1700 hours.

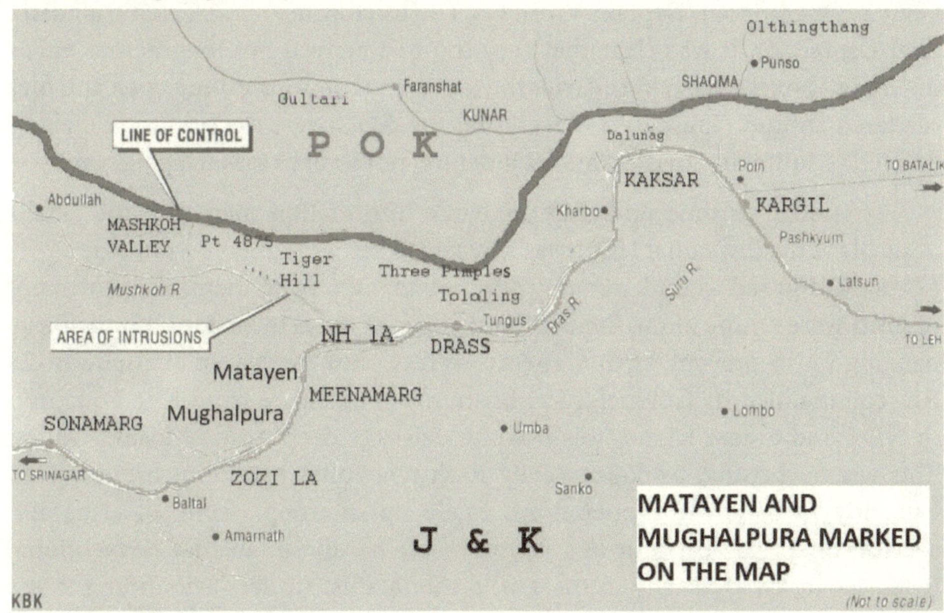

Moghulpura is a small, picturesque grazing ground with Drass Nala running through it and adequate sharp cliff faces surrounding it. An ideal place to tuck in the Battalion with adequate water and cover, I ordered the battalion to halt there while I moved to Matayen, approximately four km ahead.

A Worrying Outlook

While we were organising ourselves at Moghulpura, a three-vehicle convoy with artillery ammunition from Kargil stopped near us. The ASC JCO in charge asked me where he should deliver the ammunition. Having no clue, I asked him to follow me to the Division HQ, where someone would surely guide him to his destination. He was a bit shaken, having closely survived some very accurate artillery fire as his convoy was crossing Drass.

Around 1730 hours, I reached HQ 8 Mountain Division. We would have surely missed it, but for two Chetak helicopters (Aérospatiale Alouette III) parked by the roadside, a most unusual sight. The pilots, hanging near the aircraft, indicated to me a small cluster of vehicles: the Division HQ.

As I entered the Operations Room Tent, the Colonel General Staff (Col GS), Colonel AS Chabbewal (Later Lieutenant General), greeted me like a long-lost friend. I was relieved to see a face that reminded me of jolly Santa Claus with his peppery beard and a wide genial smile. After three days of living in a suffocating vacuum, finding a comforting source of authority was a huge relief! Colonel Chabbewal had his operational staff with him, including Major Prasher, GSO 2 (Operations), Captain Virdi, GSO 3 (Intelligence) and Captain Kadam, Staff Captain Q. It was clear that they too had arrived not long before me as document boxes were lying all over the tent with their tops gaping open and files scattered around. These four officers and the GOC were the sum total making up HQ 8 Mountain Division at this juncture, not a very reassuring picture.

I wasted no time updating my battle information map with the details available at the divisional HQ. I was shocked to see large areas on our side of the LC marked in red as under enemy occupation. Opposing them, an assortment of units were strung along the Southern edges of these intrusions, precariously hanging on to prevent further enemy ingress onto the National Highway. 28 RR, commanded by Colonel S Krishnan, my coursemate from Kilo Squadron in NDA and a dear friend, was holding defences deep inside Mushko Valley. This was surprising, as conceptually Rashtriya Rifles battalions are designed explicitly to handle CT operations. Made up of troops from all arms and services on a two-year tour of duty, they were hardly suitable for conventional defensive tasks, especially in these wild mountains. No less astounding to me at that moment was the 16 CAVALRY, an armoured unit similarly employed on the Pandrass Ridge overlooking the National Highway. It was obvious that everything on hand was being thrown in to contain the Pakistani ingress!

I was relieved to see that closer to the intrusion areas, regular infantry battalions were holding fort - 17 JAT and 12 MAHAR on the Southern slopes of the massive **Point 4875** feature dominating Mushko Valley and 8 SIKH on the Southwestern and Eastern slopes of **Tiger Hill** as also South of **Point 5100** much further to the East and totally detached from the main forces. There were deployments of 16 GRENADIERS and 1 NAGA marked along enemy intrusions and some from the Ladakh Scouts. 18 GRENADIERS occupied the Southern slopes of **Tololing**. HQ 79 Mountain Brigade (Tral) and HQ 56 Mountain Brigade (general area of Ganderbal, South of Wular Lake) had moved to Mushko and Drass respectively.

Apparently, there was no clear-cut plan, and troops were hazardously thrown into the breach as they arrived. The Operational Staff at HQ 8 Mountain Division made it clear that it was probably the Corps HQ at Srinagar or 3 Mountain Division at Leh that was handling the situation till this juncture. A crisis of an immense magnitude was brewing and could burst over at any moment!

Major General Mohinder Puri received me; this was only the second time I had met him. Upon his enquiry, I quickly updated him on my battalion's activities. He ordered me to stay at Moghulpura till further orders and prepare to clear the ridge lines in Mushko Valley, a task on which I shall receive my orders from Brigadier RK Kakkar, Commander 79 Mountain Brigade. Having passed instructions to my unit to get line communications through to the Division telephone exchange, our sole source of information, I moved back to Moghulpura.

I was delighted to see Major Bajaj, my 2iC, who had fortuitously returned from leave and had speedily fetched up to Moghulpura with young Kenguruse in tow. Briefing the officers, I ordered a dispersed company-wise deployment. The training that had been interrupted at Sonamarg was to resume immediately. Still wary of surprise air attacks, we dug slit trenches if caught in the open. Three companies and the Battalion HQ were deployed North of Drass Nala and Bravo Company was to the South beside the bridge. The Regimental Police (RP) Post was established at the bridge.

Camp set up at Moghulpura

Moghulpura was located at about 10500 feet, ideal for second-stage acclimatisation. The overlooking heights were around 13000 feet, suitable for the next acclimatisation stage. I exchanged notes with Major Bajaj, sharing the situational update and my apprehensions about the lack of clarity. The professional that he is, he calmly heard me out and did not seem disconcerted at all. That did wonders for my morale! We listed our "**To Do**" tasks in the order of priority - training, acclimatisation and morale building - while we awaited formal orders from the higher HQ.

02 June 1999 - The Fog Dissipates… a Little

The next morning, around 0830 hours, I met Brigadier RK Kakkar, Commander 79 Mountain Brigade, at the makeshift helipad next to the Division HQ. As a young Captain, he had been my instructor in Kilo Squadron in the National Defence Academy, Khadakvasla. For some reason, he took a liking to me and was instrumental in placing me on important cadet appointments at different stages of my Academy days. I had last met him at his HQ at Khrew.

After exchanging pleasantries, he quickly briefed me on the latest operational situation and my broad task, ending with, "*Ho jayega na?*" (Will you be able to do it?). I could not resist the temptation and replied, "*Sir, Ab pata chalega ki aap ne mujhe kya sikhaya hain*" (We will come to know what you had taught me). He laughed out, "*You Badmash!*" (Scoundrel)

The helicopters were ready, and soon, we were airborne for my first aerial recce; things were moving fast! Above the din of the rotors at around 18000 feet and about three km South of Drass Nala, Brigadier Kakkar indicated the massif North of Pandrass Ridge, whose Southern slopes were held as I had seen marked on the map by 28 RR and 12 MAHAR. He asked me to see if I could detect any movement. At five kilometres, it is hardly possible to see the details of the feature, let alone people in the open; at that distance, a 100-metre-long space occupied by an infantry section is just about 1 degree wide and extremely difficult to spot through a binocular in a vibrating helicopter struggling to stay aloft in the thin high-altitude air. We asked the pilot to close in with the massif for a better, more detailed look. He informed us that their orders were not to fly North of the line he was holding, given the shooting down of a Mi8 helicopter of the Air Force a few days earlier.

This brought home to me the limitations of aerial recce and the vulnerability of the pilot as an airborne observation post. He cannot close in too much or hold his position too long for fear of being taken on by handheld missiles and other weapons. I suggested to Brigadier Kakkar that foot recce, the tried and tested method of Infantrymen, would get us more relevant and reliable information.

He concurred and asked the pilot to return. We decided that I would move with my recce parties to Mushko Valley and execute a recce plan that his staff would finalise. I returned to the unit around lunchtime, with no further inputs.

On the way, I stopped at 18 GARHRIF, where Colonel SK Chakravarty, the CO, though my senior by a year, was a friendly acquaintance. We had both operated under 8 Mountain Division in the Lolab Valley. His battalion was converting from a mixed-class battalion, where the troops belonged to four different castes / regions, into a single-class battalion with troops from the Garhwal region in the Himalayas. He was to be withdrawn from operations and given adequate time to ensure mass migration and rebuilding of the new team.[18]. For a battalion under reorganisation to be moved into operations further indicated the desperation driving our response. Colonel Chakravarty had gone to Drass for recce, and I met other officers and the Deputy Assistant Quarter Master General (DAQMG, colloquially called DQ) of 79 Mountain Brigade (a Major) who happened to be visiting. "*As far as I am concerned, the LC has been permanently changed,*" I heard the DQ holding forth. That shocked and shook me greatly, and not wanting to hear any more of this, fearing that my resolve would weaken, I quickly excused myself from there.

On reaching the Battalion, I told Major Bajaj to organise the recce parties, which were to leave around 1600 hours. I also warned him that many negative stories were circulating and that we needed to insulate our officers and men. He said he would locate himself at the RP Gate, screen the visitors, and oversee the training simultaneously. At that time, we were unaware that destiny had different things in store for us. Unbeknown to us, things were moving in different directions; Mushko was not to be our objective, and Tololing was about to happen.

Around 1500 hours on 02 June 1999, I received a call from Colonel AS Chabbewal, the Col GS who informed me that 18 GRENADIERS were assaulting Tololing that very night and that we were nominated as a reserve. We were to be ready to move at short notice. With little more information, we were tasked as a reserve for an action we had little clue about. Not surprisingly, we were on tenterhooks the whole night.

---

[18] Mixed-class battalions were an experiment in national integration in the aftermath of Operation Blue Star in 1984. These battalions were raised in 1985 by drawing troops from four different regiments in equal proportions. During this experiment, I was shifted from 17 MADRAS to 21 RAJRIF along with the troops of South Indian origin. After 15 years of dithering, the Army had decided to undo the exercise and revert the troops back to their original class-specific regiments.

03 June 1999 - A Task at Last

Around 0500 hours at daybreak on 03 June 1999, Colonel Chabbewal gave me the distressing news that the attack had failed with grievous losses; Lieutenant Colonel Vishwanathan, the Second – in - Command of 18 GRENADIERS, had been killed (awarded a posthumous Vir Chakra later); the battalion had already lost Major Adhikari (awarded posthumous Mahavir Chakra) earlier. We were asked to be prepared to attack **Tololing**, and I was asked to meet Major General Mohinder Puri at HQ 56 Mountain Brigade, at Drass at 1100 hours. I asked the battalion to stand down and called for an Officer-JCOs conference at 0800 hours. The situation was rapidly changing and getting grimmer by the hour!

We convened in the tent designated as our makeshift Operations Room, where I was told that Major Madan was *hors de combat,* having slipped in the bathroom tent, badly spraining his ankle. This was disappointing because I needed every single officer of mine, especially a senior one like Madan. I brought my command element up to date. They were to continue with the acclimatisation and the assault training while I got detailed orders from the Divisional HQ.

I started for Drass around 0900 hours. As I crossed Matayen, the Division HQ location, a Field Regiment was deploying near the bridge across the Drass Nala. I came across 1 NAGA Regiment strung across the road, and troops appeared tired, weather-beaten and demoralised. It was obvious they had been through the meat grinder.

Further ahead towards Drass, I came across the board that informed me that Drass was the second coldest inhabited place on earth; not a pleasant piece of information when you are likely to go higher up the mountains! The Drass village consisted of a few huts on either side of the road and seemed completely deserted; driving through the ghost village was eerie. At the end of the village was a military camp where HQ 56 Mountain Brigade and the battalion HQ of 16 GRENADIERS were located. One could see clear signs of heavy artillery shelling; one barrack was completely burnt, and other structures were heavily pockmarked with splinters.

According to my map markings, all the mountains surrounding us were supposed to be occupied by the enemy, and I wondered as I looked up whether enemy artillery observers had us in their sights from their mountaintop perches - the accuracy of fire did indicate good observation. It surprised me that despite the artillery domination, there was a clutch of vehicles parked haphazardly and a large congregation of officers awaiting orders.

Top Brass at HQ 8 Mountain Division

I only knew Colonel Chakravarty, CO 18 GARHRIF; all other officers present were Captains and Majors. We were soon joined by Colonel Alok Deb, the CO of 192 Field Regiment of Artillery, the regiment nominated for close support to the 56 Mountain Brigade. From Colonel Deb's conversation, one could make out that he had come out of the underground operations room to fetch me and Colonel Chakravarty. As we started towards the operations room, he said, "*Do not accept a task you cannot execute.*" I was taken aback, but the advice stuck in my confused brain.

As we descended into the well-lit underground operations room bunker, an animated discussion was underway on the map board. We unobtrusively took our seats in the last row. Lieutenant General HM Khanna, the Army Commander, and Lieutenant General Krishan Pal, the Corps Commander, were in a discussion with Major General Mohinder Puri; Brigadier Amar Aul, Commander 56 Mountain Brigade, was attentively listening in. All faces were grim, and the atmosphere was eerie. One could sense that the situation was grave, and everyone was trying to make sense of the uncharacteristic tactics of the 'terrorists' stubbornly clinging to the heights, such behaviour had not been encountered before. The Army Commander and the Corps Commander were, to my utter amazement, discussing redeployments of infantry sections (10 men squads) of 8 SIKH, presumably on the slopes leading to Tiger Hill!

Then the discussion veered off to a meatier subject- the capture of the **Tololing** feature, in which we figured rather prominently. 2 RAJRIF was to attack **Tololing** from the South, and 18 GARHRIF was to attack **Point 5140**, located further to the North on the **Tololing** ridge, from the North.

Major General Mohinder Puri made a point that 18 GRENADIERS, who had invested so much effort and lives in Tololing, which was tantalisingly close to their grasp, must be given one last chance to capture it: this was agreed to. But, Major General Puri was asked to ascertain from the CO 18 GRENADIERS whether his battalion could take it on. We were sent outside to wait while a decision was taken.

As we waited, Lieutenant General HM Khanna, the Army Commander, emerged and stopped to shake our hands on his way to his waiting Alouette. "*All the best, remember you are writing military history,*" were his parting words. One was aware we would be involved in operations, but *creating military history* was a bolt from the blue for me; the stakes were getting higher by the minute, an eventuality I had still not grasped. Military history is written after wars, not for '*CT operations*,' I pondered. More irreverent thoughts joined in with an image of some old and bearded person scribbling history on a thick scroll; it was a throwback to "*Samay*" of the TV serial Mahabharat. While shaking hands and mumbling my thanks, I began seeing visions of a promotion examination sometime in the future for a military history paper featuring the question "*List the reasons for the failure of 2 RAJRIF's attack on Tololing highlighting the shortcomings in the Leadership Qualities*? (30 marks)" It was enough to make any man break out in a cold sweat!

No sooner had the helicopter with the Army Commander taken off, as if on a cue, shells started screeching down, landing mostly on the other side of Drass River, to my considerable relief. This being my first exposure to artillery shelling, while all others around me appeared to be cool, I asked one NCO, "*Don't you get into bunkers when the shelling starts?*" He calmly replied, "*Sir, gola us paar hi jata hai, ek aadh nala ke is paar girta hain.*" (Most rounds fall on the other side of the river, and very few land on our side). I appreciated his courage and nonchalance and proceeded to the mess, hoping the NCO's assessment of the enemy's accuracy was correct.

The mess hut overlooked the river, and I must admit it was a sight for sore eyes. Crystal-clear waters gushed amidst the white and grey stones polished by years of erosion. Greenery on the other side was rendered even more magnificent with the majestic backdrop of rising mountains. All the windows had been fortified with sandbags to prevent shell splinters from coming in.

There were a large number of officers, mostly Majors and Captains from the infantry units, in contact or being brought in as reinforcements like us, Artillery, Services and assorted others who were visiting Brigade HQ and had joined in hoping to get a quick bite courtesy of 8 Mountain Division. Tactical discussions galore were in progress with gay abandon and options flung around, thick and fast, on how to evict the intruders. These ranged from the absurd to the pathetic! An especially talented young Captain was enthusiastically going on about heavy, concentrated air strikes while major forces surrounded the intruders, cut off routes of maintenance to the LC, and starved them into surrender once the winters set in (still half a year away!) I felt like I was in Alice's Wonderland - Generals were deploying sections while Captains were planning operational-level manoeuvres! Here I was faced with a seemingly insurmountable task and not getting anywhere, while all around me people were finding solutions for problems that did not concern them even remotely.

After lunch, my eyes were following Major General Puri. My task had been held in abeyance; it was a neither-here-nor-there situation. I noticed Major General Puri was talking on the telephone, apparently to CO 18 GRENADIERS.

I was standing about 10 metres from him. He spoke at length, but due to the surrounding din, I could not make out a single word he spoke. Near the end, he paused, looked directly at me and quizzically raised his eyebrows; I nodded acquiescence.

This is how I was offered the task of capturing **Tololing**, and I accepted it.

CHAPTER SEVEN

THE ATTACK PLAN FOR TOLOLING

Tololing, as seen from Drass

03 June 1999 - An Idea Takes Root

The intrusions in the Drass Sector were the deepest, with **Tololing** just a four km crow flight from Drass. These intrusions directly overlooked the National Highway 1D and theoretically interdicted all vehicular traffic in and out of Ladakh.

After lunch on 03 June 1999, I met with General Puri and Brigadier Aul in the operations room alone. I was asked about my course of action. I told them I would gather as much information from people in contact for the rest of the day and formulate further courses by evening. General Puri asked me to brief him at the Division HQ on my way back to the battalion after gathering the information.

First, I looked up Major Ajit of 16 GRENADIERS, who had led a patrol to **Tololing** on 23 May 1999. He gave me a graphic description of the feature, describing its four smaller bumps. He had reached the forward most area between these bumps under the enemy's direct domination. These 'bumps' were 10 to 15 metres higher than the ridgeline approach, so he could not discern the enemy's presence on them; coming under heavy fire, he had to withdraw to cover quickly. This was one of the first patrols to check out the 'intrusion' in the Drass Sector once it had come to light. Based on this information, 18 GRENADIERS had been launched to secure **Tololing** on 25 May, a costly attack that had finally ground to a stalemate.

I then met Captain Manish from Ladakh Scouts. His detachment had been located on the Western slope of **Tololing** and had been ordered to fall back to their parent unit. He explained that the Western slopes were steep and without cover, dominated by the **Top** held by the 'terrorists'. I met Major Mohanty, the Brigade Major and updated my map on the deployment around **Tololing**; I also got to understand the operations of 18 GRENADIERS since 25 May.

My First Impressions

18 GRENADIERS appeared to have attacked in an intelligence vacuum. One approach was probed at a time, which was shifted to the next one when held up, till all three approaches had been unsuccessfully exhausted with casualties. The third attempt along the Southern Spur to an area called '**Barbad Bunker**' reached as close as 40 metres from the objective. A desperate attack to evict the intruders was launched at night but was beaten back along this third approach. Led by the 2iC, Lieutenant Colonel Vishwanathan, he had been killed while leading the assault. I could not comprehend how an attack that was so close to the objective had not succeeded in at least establishing a foothold; it would have given me a launch pad to exploit. With all three approaches so strongly defended, I was at a loss as to how to get to **Tololing Top**. I needed something different, but no new ideas were forthcoming.

I shared my thoughts with Brigadier Amar Aul and suggested that instead of banging our heads against **Tololing Top**, we should attack **Hump**, a feature just North of **Tololing Top**. I thought that the sustenance of **Tololing Top** came through the **Hump**. But Brigadier Aul, who had done a recce himself right up to the mortar position of 18 GRENADIERS, ruled out the possibility of attacking **Hump** and insisted we must go through **Tololing**. Not convinced, but not wanting to contradict without a ground recce, I told him I would visit 18 GRENADIERS to get more information. Around 1600 hours, I left for Bimbat, where 18 GRENADIERS had its battalion HQ.

As I approached 18 GRENADIERS, I prepared myself for the emotional impact of meeting troops who had just undergone the adrenal rush of an assault but were beaten back with casualties - it could dent my confidence and drain my resolve. I forced myself to remain calm and not come to any conclusions until I saw the ground. I did not want to be swayed by the experiences of others, good or bad. I would make decisions based on my assessments without thinking too much about the outcome. I applied a principle that has worked well for me so far, '*think hard, decide, act and never regret a decision, for that is the best you were capable of, accept the consequences with equanimity*'.

Bimbat is located around 10 km from Drass. The road loops around a feature known as TV Hill, as it has a local TV transmitter and micro-wave repeater station atop. I reached 18 GRENADIERS around 1630 hours. This was not the best moment to be a visitor; the mortal remains of their popular 2iC, Lieutenant Colonel Vishvanathan[19] had just been carried down from the heights. I saluted him. The CO 18 GRENADIERS was with the Ghataks up on the Southern slopes, so my innumerable questions remained unanswered.

Considering that I had to take on from where Lieutenant Colonel Vishvanathan had left, the task was daunting and unnerving. After coordinating the guides to lead my recce parties to the locations held by Majors Dasgupta and Rathore of 18 GRENADIERS along the SW and SE approaches to **Tololing** respectively, I left around 1730 hours for the Brigade HQ.

As we drove back with my driver Naik Vidhyadhar, the Intelligence Section NCO, my Radio Operator, and my buddy Babulal, a million questions raced through my mind. The enemy had beaten back a full battalion attack launched from multiple directions, as per the training pamphlet, inflicting heavy casualties. Without the crucial surprise factor, the task was nothing short of sheer suicidal, and my gut reaction was one of helplessness; I could taste the bitter bile in my mouth. I had to find an alternative, and **Hump** seemed to provide one.

We were approaching Drass, and we had just emerged from behind the TV Hill onto the hairpin bend, and suddenly, we were bracketed by a salvo of artillery shells exploding all around us. Jolted out of my reverie, and before I could say anything, Naik Vidhyadhar, in a remarkable display of nerves, gradually increased the speed and calmly drove through the curtain of falling shells as if he was driving through a curtain of rain, not high explosives.

---

19 I had met Vishvanathan about two weeks earlier in the Commanding Officers conference at the Division headquarters. He has impressed me with his assured manners and quick wit. Now, to see him lifeless was shocking. This was the first battle casualty I had come face to face with in this war.

We drove into the Brigade HQ, quickly disembarked, and while my boys sought shelter in the nearest bunker, I headed to the Operations Room.

To my astonishment, Brigadier Aul was standing outside his room, calmly gazing at the massive **Tololing** feature, oblivious of the shells peppering the area of the Brigade HQ all around him. Stoic is the word that flashed in my mind along with "*a typical Gurkha*," the regiment to which he belonged. When I wished him, the Brigadier looked at me briefly before returning to his unperturbed contemplation of the scenery while asking, "*Have you made your plan?*" Keen to get out of the shelling as I did not share his degree of comfort out in the open, I blurted out, "*Sir, what are you doing so far ahead in all this shelling?*" Slowly, he turned his head in my direction, as if reluctant to pull his gaze away from **Tololing**, the mountaintop that was evidently causing his preoccupation, and replied sardonically, "I *am here to make sure that you guys go ahead*!" Of course, he had a point.[20]

In most dangerous situations, for all the bravery and sacrifice talk that abounds under less strenuous conditions, we all need a solid push to move ahead, not so much physically (although with some, a physical push may also be called for!) but more psychologically. His display of determination and courage must have inspired the staff at the Brigade HQ to continue performing their duties calmly, and visitors from forward units would not envy the safety that a rear-located HQ routinely enjoyed. I, for one, would have done it slightly differently by tucking the HQ into the folds of the slopes, away from the direct observation of enemy OPs perched on the mountaintops. Getting blown up by an artillery shell is not the most heroic way to go down fighting.

We went into his room, and I shared my plan to conduct a recce the next day. He shared with me the disposition of **Tololing** from the **SE Approach** and reiterated that that was the way to attack. He spoke with confidence, having climbed along the approach up to the Mortar Position established by 18 GRENADIERS. For a man pushing 50 years, it was no mean feat of physical endurance and determination to climb up to 13000 feet. His stock in my eyes went up a couple of notches, even though I did not agree with his insistence on **Tololing** and **Tololing** alone. But prudently, I held my counsel till I had something better to offer. He asked me to report back after my recce the next day. I contacted Major Bajaj from the Brigade HQ and asked him to have a

20 Vijayant at Kargil, Thapar & Dwivedi, Penguin e bury Press, 2020, Page 122. The headquarters of 56 Mountain Brigade, commanded by Brig Amar Aul, was located in Drass, from where one could hear and see the shells exploding and the machine guns firing. Some NCOs who had been there said that the scene made their blood run cold. Brigade headquarters had been a target of enemy guns.

sketch of **Tololing** and Hump and the O Group ready for the next day's briefing on my return.

On my way back to the battalion, I decided to update Major General Puri. He was relaxing in his Shaktiman-mounted caravan, reading the latest issue of India Today. I shared with him my apprehension of attacking **Tololing** and my view that it would amount to reinforcing a failure. Attacking **Hump** would be equally effective in ensuring the fall of **Tololing** and with a greater chance of success, as the enemy would be surprised. The GOC concurred with my viewpoint and asked me to elaborate. I told him that I would be carrying out recce in the next 36 hours to evaluate the options and evolve a plan of attack for the capture of **Tololing / Hump**. He mulled over it for some time and asked me to update him after the next day's recce. I then shared with him all the rumours that were floating around and the loose talk that was going on. If this continues, we will be left with demoralised troops and a demonised enemy, making our task as battalion commanders extremely difficult. He promised he would have it taken care of. Later, I learned he shared this with the Corps Commander, and relevant instructions were passed to the Transit Camps to explicitly brief the transient troops from rumour-mongering or falling prey to it. I left feeling a bit more confident as I had some support for exercising the **Hump** option.

The Recce Plan

By this time, a rough plan for the recce was taking shape, the objective of which was to have an attack plan to capture **Tololing**. I reached back to my training at the Junior Command Course in the College of Combat, Mhow. The emerging recce plan bore an uncanny resemblance to the one I had made during the course when we were planning the attack on the hill feature near Manpur; all that was left to do was fill in minor details here and there. By the time we drove into our camp, I was ready with my recce plan.

I had already decided that we would give it our best try without being influenced by the general mood prevailing around us, I told myself that I would be extremely careful of what I said and how I said it. I did not want my command to blindly accept my attack plan like a set of automatons, especially when, in all probability, they were being marched to their death. My nearly two decades' worth of experience in the Army had convinced me that our rank and file were more competent than we tend to credit them with. In tough situations, your men are not hanging on to every word you, as their leader, are saying; they are assessing whether *you believe* in what you are saying. They would follow you blindly if convinced they can trust you and are not being taken for a ride. I earnestly wanted my determination to percolate down to my command so they were focused on their part of the task, which would achieve the overall mission. We do not have the luxury of time and inclination to waste it on peripheral issues.

I went straight to the operations room tent and had the sketch marked with all the details I had gathered. While that was happening, I had an informal chat with the officers and JCOs to elicit what they were up to during my absence. It was reassuring that they had focussed on acclimatisation and discussed and practised the drills for attack along a ridge line. The general mood was of keen anticipation, which I found very encouraging. Their spirits calmed my fears as I sought comfort in their confidence, especially after my visit to forward locations blanketed with despondency and fear. As I started my briefing, I felt somehow rejuvenated. I decided to stick to bare facts, which all could verify, and follow the standard recce briefing format taught at the Infantry School. This is how the briefing went: -

a) **Information of Enemy.** The enemy has occupied the **Tololing Ridge**, including **Tololing, Hump** and **Point 5140** Complex.[21]

b) **Own Information.** 16 GRENADIERS is holding defensive positions at Bimbat Gali, Rattan and Niyaz. 18 GRENADIERS attacked **Tololing** along SE, South, and SW approaches between 25 May and 02 June. All attacks have been repulsed, and 18 GRENADIERS have firmed up along each of the approaches. 18 GARHRIF has been tasked to capture **Point 5140** attacking from the firm base provided

---

21 Vijayant at Kargil, Thapar & Dwivedi, Penguin e bury Press, 2020, Page 125. Pakistan had prepared strong defences at high positions that gave them an advantage and had stocked those well. Tololing was the deepest incursion in India's area. As per a Pakistani officer's account, they had named it Azam Post. By the time they had reached Tololing, they were 24 kilometres away from Bunyal near Gultari, their headquarters across the LoC. As per this account, Capt Iftikhar and Maj Azam had established these posts. The going was terribly tough for them but they had established good positions. The Tololing ridgeline consisted of Tololing feature, including Point 4590, Tololing Top, a flat area between the two called Flat, Barbad Bunker and then echeloned northwards was a feature called Hump. Beyond Hump were a series of hillocks along the ridgeline serially named Hump 1 to Hump 10. North of that was the most dominating feature of this area, Point 5140. There were two main approaches to attack Tololing from Drass — one along the south - western ridge, which led right up to Point 4590, and the other along the south - eastern ridge, which led to Tololing Top. Initially, 18 Grenadiers had been tasked with clearing Tololing. Their operations began on 22 May 1999, supported by 16 Grenadiers, who were part of the Holding Battalion. 2 Naga simultaneously commenced operations against Point 5140. These attacks did not succeed due to abysmal intelligence, leading to incorrect assessment of enemy strength and inadequate artillery support. The repeated attacks resulted in many casualties, including Maj Rajesh Adhikari and Lt Col Ramakrishnan Viswanathan, among others. These setbacks resulted in despondency among the Indian troops. The commanding officer (Ravi) gave instructions to all the officers to keep the men busy, to talk to them and to go to the temple to seek strength.

by 16 GRENADIERS. 2 RAJRIF has been tasked to capture **Tololing** attacking from the firm base provided by 18 GRENADIERS. In the end, we could attack **Tololing** along the SW and SE approach simultaneously; or capture **Hump** and Attack **Tololing** from the North.

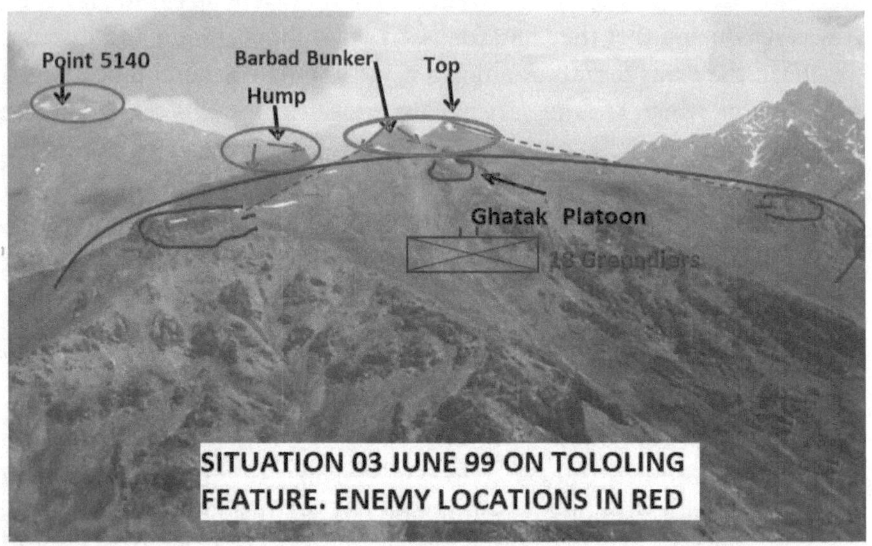

c) **Mission.** The objective of the recce is to evolve an outline plan for the capture of **Tololing** and **Hump**.

d) **Method.** Four recce patrols will conduct recce from 04 June 1999 to 05 June 1999 to gather the required information.

Recce Patrol 1. Company Commanders Charlie Company (Vivek) and Bravo Company will recce along the **SE approach** to evolve an attack plan for the capture of **Tololing.**

Recce Patrol 2. Company Commanders Alpha Company (Acharya) and Delta Company (Mohit) will recce along the **SW approach** to evolve an attack plan for the capture of **Tololing.**

Recce Patrol 3. Lieutenant Kenguruse will assess if **Hump** can be assaulted from the **Eastern Direction** with Rattan location as a firm base.

Recce Patrol 4. Subedar Karan Singh will assess if **Hump** can be assaulted from the **Western direction** with Niyaz as a firmbase.

e) **Tasks.** Recce Patrol 1 and 2 will get the following information

- Enemy defensive positions layout, automatic and other support weapons on **Tololing** and likely enemy strength on **Tololing.**
- Enemy defensive positions and support weapons at **Hump** and **Point 5140.**
- Suitable Forming Up Place (FUP), company and platoon release points along the nominated approach.
- Availability of covered approach up to the selected FUP.
- Location of Firm Base and support weapons available from 18 GRENADIERS.
- Location for Fire Base to support the assault along the respective approach. Subedar Ram Kumar Lamba of B Company and Subedar Man Singh of A Company to be responsible.
- Approach route to enemy defences from the firm base and enemy interference along these routes.
- Assessment of movement time to Firm Base, FUP and Objective.

Recce Patrol 3 and 4 will get the following information

- Enemy defensive positions layout, automatic and other support weapons on Hump and likely enemy strength on **Hump** and **Point 5140.**

- Location of Firm Base and Support weapons available from 18 Grenadiers.
- Approach route to enemy defences from the firm base.

e) **Timing and Coordination**

- Patrol 1 and 2. Carry out recce on day of 04 June. The guide will be available at Road Head at 0600 hours.
- Patrol 3 and 4. Carry out day recce from **Rattan** and **Niyaz** locations, respectively. Carry out a close recce of **Hump** on the night of 04 / 05 June.

Traditionally, Delta Company and Bravo Company had been the leading companies for assault in the battalion. I had intended to follow the precedent, but the absence of Major Madan (Bravo Company Commander) put me in a quandary, and I decided to lead with Charlie Company. To attack along a ridge line, a fire support base of direct and indirect fire weapons had already emerged as a basic requirement for the troops to close in with enemy defences and start close combat. From what I had gathered, most of the attacks had gone in without such intimate close support planned. If we were to succeed, a Fire Base would be the key. I made special efforts and nominated the senior JCOs of probable reserve companies (Bravo and Alpha Companies) to recce for this task.

After finishing my briefing, I cautioned them about what they should concentrate on. "*We are not on a fact-finding mission on how the attacks till now have failed*", I warned them. "*We will get all the information required to execute our task. Just concentrate on it*," I advised. "*See to believe, record what you see, ask specific questions to troops on the ground to get answers I have asked of you. Observe and absorb the tactical situation and keep yourself above the emotional situation*," I told them. "*Don't pass any judgment on how others should have done their work or how well you are going to do*", I warned them. "*We will leave at 0400 hours tomorrow*," I said and bid them goodbye.

I was confident that information for planning an attack would be gathered, but I was apprehensive about what kind of interaction they would have with the troops on the ground. I wanted to ensure they extracted all the information required while not getting influenced. Exaggeration is typical of troops who are only humans, whether after a victory or a failure. In failure, the difficulties and the enemies' capability is amplified manifold, whereas our superior abilities are trumpeted in success. There is no surer way of failing in war than exaggerating or ridiculing enemy capability. Circumventing the influence of the emotional state of troops in contact and forming the relevant question without appearing accusative or threatening is only possible if there is a cogent recce plan. If we were to attack **Tololing** successfully, 18 GRENADIERS could make it happen by pointing us in the right direction; we could not antagonise them with boorish or dismissive behaviour. I conveyed these thoughts to my command.

First Sign of Trouble with Major Madan. With that done, I enquired about Major Madan since he was absent. Major Bajaj had met and spoken to him, and Captain Basu, the RMO, had attended to him; the injury was minor, and he had a second opinion from the 308 Field Ambulance. Both reported he would be fine.

04 June 1999 – The Recce

Around 0400 hours on 04 June, it was already twilight. We had gathered near the Operations Room tent; Major Madan was missing. Given the situation, I expected him to be present, at the least. His absence caused me great unease. I ordered the RMO to get an opinion from the surgical specialist from the Forward Surgical Centre.

As we were on the cusp of a high-risk operational task, getting a grip on the discipline of my command was paramount. I intended to send a message that I would not accept this type of shirking of responsibilities and hoped to jolt Major Madan out of what I could see as "*pure funk*," a natural reaction to extreme danger but which soldiers must learn to control and overcome.

The recce parties left at around 0400 hours. Patrol 2 and Patrol 4, which were probing the SW and Western approaches, were dropped at Drass. They started the climb just next to the battalion Tactical HQ location in the empty house that had been occupied. The parties left a little early as they had to traverse a patch in the open under the direct observation of the enemy. The patch was often bombarded by enemy artillery fire and was probably a registered target for them. I had personally briefed both Major Acharya and Major Mohit to leave early. I did not want any untoward incident right at the planning stage. It was about a five-hour climb to where Major Dasgupta of 18 GRENADIERS was camping and had established a Firm Base that was in contact with the enemy. The climb was steep, but all the troops were physically fit, motivated and, more than anything, eager and curious to find out details of the objective area. I told them to spend the complete day on Top at the Firm Base location, gather as much information as possible from 18 Grenadiers, observe the movement, if any, check the possible directions of attack, and try to formulate a plan. I even told them to make sketches of the objective area so they could explain the objective in detail to me on return and to their troops.

Lieutenant Kenguruse also departed early with his Ghatak team. His recce report was the one I was most concerned about, as I wanted to exploit the **Hump** approach to capture **Tololing**. He had to climb through the nala towards **Hump** to either identify an approach towards **Tololing** or establish a stop location at **Hump**. The Nala led to a saddle that was midway between **Hump** and **Tololing Top**. It was the only approach that the 18 Grenadiers had not exploited.

The rest of us reached Bimbat around 0630 hours and met with the guides deputed by 18 GRENADIERS. My guide was from the Ghatak Platoon and had an ample beard. This beard was a carry-over from CT operations, where it helped in covert operations. Customary hospitality was insisted upon and accepted. We had breakfast of 'Aloo Puri' and sweet tea and set off for **Location Rathore**.

Here, let me update you on the importance of the **Tololing** feature. At 15000 feet, it was the deepest penetration of the enemy forces, approximately seven km from the LC. It was the Southernmost tip of the **Tololing Ridge** running South from the LC, and had **Point 5140, Hump** and **Tololing Top** as its three main features. To its East on the LC was **Bimbat Gali**, held by 16 GRENADIERS. Bimbat Nala, which originated thereabouts, runs parallel to the ridgeline at a distance of approximately 1000 - 1500 metres, clearly dominated by the ridge line. It made me wonder how the post at Bimbat was surviving with its supply route so thoroughly dominated and how 18 GARHRIF would build up for the assault on **Point 5140**. 18 Engineer Regiment was already working on a safer track for linking Bimbat Gali. To the West were the ridge lines of **Point 5100**, **Area Junction**, **Point 4700**, and **Three Pimples** around three to four km away, these battles were still in the womb of time and unrevealed to us.

At the base of **Tololing** was the Srinagar – Leh Highway, open only in summer, the sole supply line, jugular if you like to call it. At this juncture, one was not aware of the enemy's design. Possession of **Tololing** allowed him to roll down with a major force and cut off the highway at around 10000 feet. He could get across the Drass River and occupy Umbala Ridge to get a peep into Suru Valley. As it is, just holding what he had gave him multiple options for interdicting the highway. He could interdict it at will with artillery at multiple locations, especially the stretch from TV Hill towards Bimbat, which was on a flat piece of ground and an ideal target for artillery, a taste of which he had dished out to my party earlier. He could inject ambush teams that could physically interdict the traffic on the highway anywhere, almost at their choosing. The urgency, therefore, of evicting the enemy from **Tololing** was clear as day to a tactical commander.

Bimbat location is around 10500 feet, and **Location Rathore** is around 14000 feet and four kilometres away as the crow flies. Having briefed and seen off Lieutenant Kenguruse to **Location Rattan**, we started our climb to Location **Rathore** around 0700 hours along a well-beaten track, under the observation of **Tololing Top** for most of the approach. Range restriction was our only protection; we were out of their infantry weapons and too small a group to be considered lucrative enough for a snap artillery engagement. The enemy had gotten accustomed to a hive of activity on our side and even perhaps took pleasure from it. We posed no significant threat to him even if his Observation Posts (OPs) had their binoculars trained on us.

By around 0900 hours, we reached the **Mortar Position** of 18 GRENADIERS, a Section with three tubes occupying the small flat piece of ground. From here, I could see what Brigadier Aul was trying to communicate about **Tololing**; I made a rough panorama sketch in my diary. I enquired about the ammunition status from the Mortar Section personnel and found that they had 10 – 12 rounds per tube. That allowed them to carry out ranging and engagements with five-round effective fire twice. Knowing the challenges of using mortar fire, especially in the mountains, I realised how inadequate that quantum of fire would be. I learnt that lugging ammunition was the biggest challenge. One person could carry two bombs in a trip that took two hours to climb. This way, they fetched up 6 - 8 rounds per tube daily. I realised that I needed to find a mortar position that could be easily supplied with ammunition.

Further, on our way to **Location Rathore,** our guide indicated a place from which the enemy fired a Heavy Machine Gun on the company trying to approach **Tololing**. That weapon emplacement was about two kms from the highway and could have easily engaged moving vehicles with accurate direct fire. They had been pushed back, he added.

We continued climbing and were at a distance of 1500 metres from **Tololing Top** when we came to a sudden drop of about 100 feet, which further rose by another 300 feet about 500 metres from us. We made quick progress in this patch unobserved and climbed up to **Location Rathore**. My team of Radio Operator Naik Rajinder, Intelligence NCO and my buddy Naik Babulal Saran with Subedar Ram Kumar Lamba was received by Major Rathore and we waited for others to catch up. Once Major Vivek caught up, I chided him that I had been quicker than him in climbing, and he revealed he had loose motions. He appeared tired but continued without giving up. We were guided to different vantage points by Major Rathore for briefing.

He gave us the maximum possible information about the enemy and described the attacks launched by 18 GRENADIERS and the hurdles they faced while moving up. He also indicated the likely locations of the bunkers from where the enemy had engaged the attacking troops. I realised that the entire company was under the open sky with barely three to four pup tents where the boys used to go and sleep on a rotation basis. It gave me first-hand information about the objective area. I made a few sketches of **Tololing Top** in my diary.

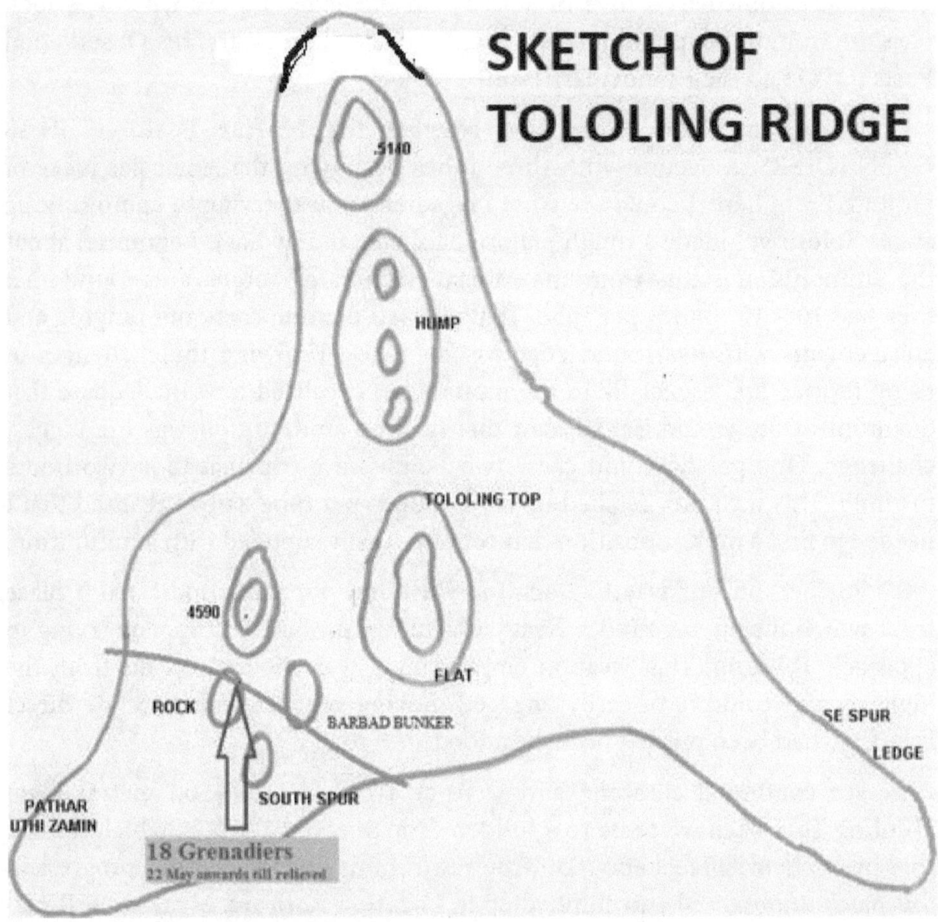

We started back from Location **Rathore** at around 1700 hours. It was a three hours descent. By 2000 hours, I had reached the battalion HQ. Major Bajaj received me and updated me about the whereabouts of the recce teams who were on their way and would reach within an hour. I told him to get the recce teams directly to the operations room for debriefing. By about 2200 hours, all the teams had shared their observations and findings.

Recce Results

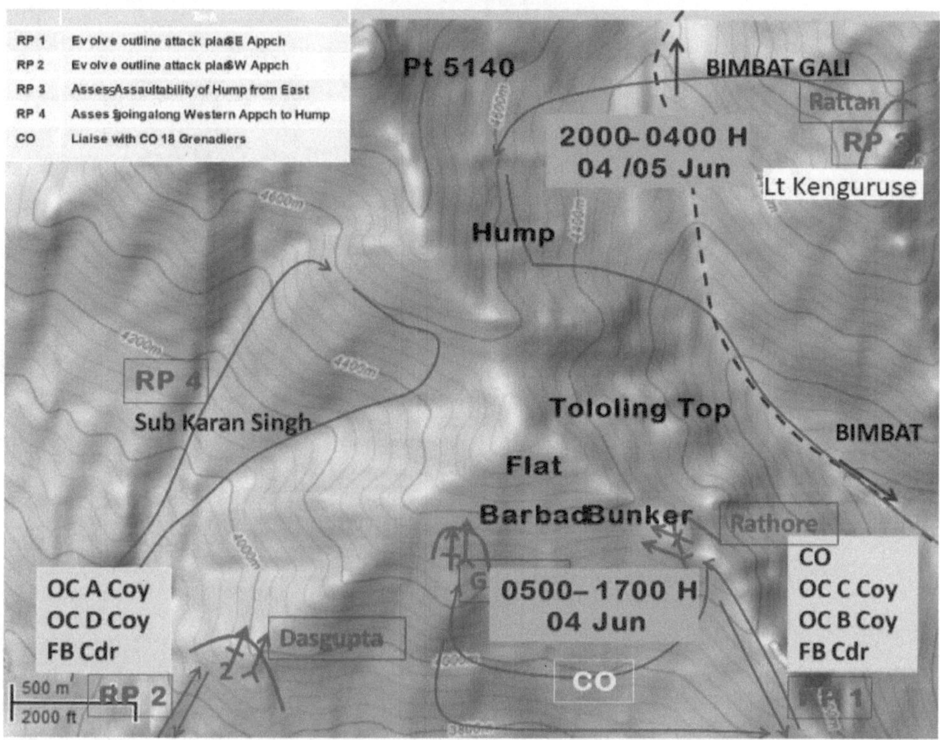

What emerged was that the troops of 18 GRENADIERS were in the open at the firm base. They sat behind the rocks that provided them cover from enemy fire and the weather's vagaries. Their bodies and faces had sunburns, their hands were rough and tanned, their clothes emitted a foul odour, the troops' morale was low, and the place was stinking. Combat situations are tough! They shared information about the likely location of enemy bunkers, types of automatic weapons fired by them, and the movement of enemy troops, which was scantily available. The company commanders had made free sketches of the objective, the likely approach and a tentative attack plan. Lieutenant Kenguruse informed me that the route to the **Saddle** was a steep climb and was dominated by the enemy both by observation and fire. It could be mined, though no concrete information emerged. The ground did not permit the movement of a company group through the Nala to attack from the Northern side of **Hump**. I told my officers to brief their companies about the objective.

Recce Report and Conclusions: 2 RAJ RIF

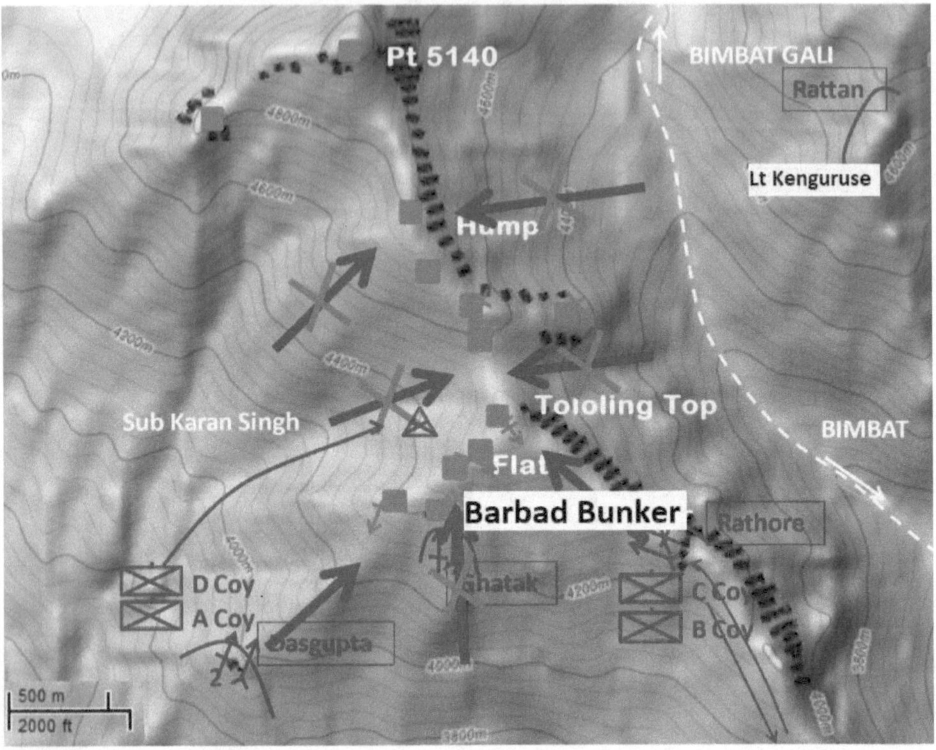

Enemy Disposition

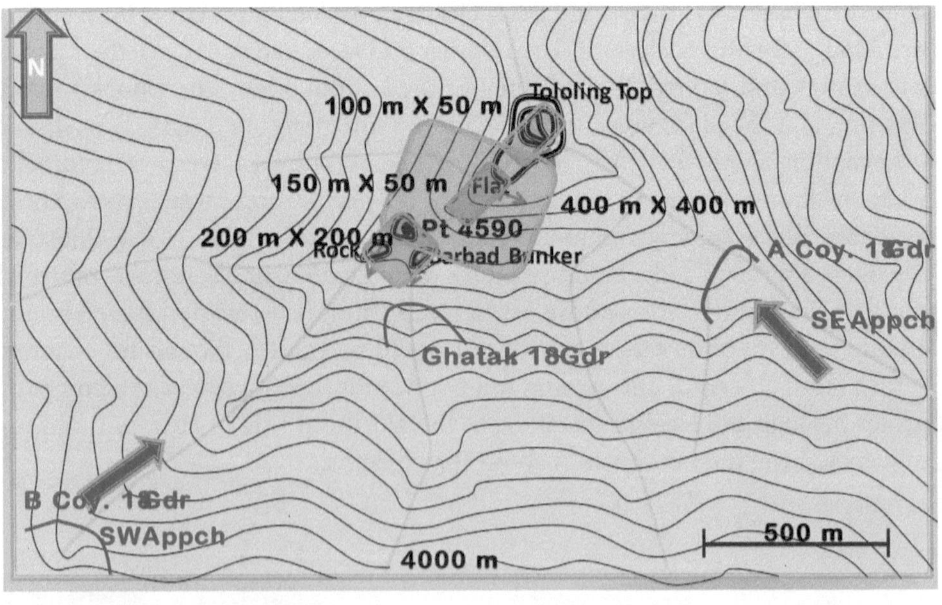

The information gathered helped me to start formalising my plan[22]. I mulled over the inputs, visualised the objective and made a tentative plan for attack. A huge quantity of ammunition had to be dumped at the firm bases before launching the attack. The fire bases had to be planned to support the attack along the approaches. Detailed coordination had to be carried out with the Firm Base battalion, 18 GRENADIERS, but at the same time, intermingling and interaction with these troops had to be minimal.

05 June 1999

The next day, in the morning I discussed the tentative plan to capture the objective with the Commander and indicated that I needed to recce from the South-Western direction before finalising the plan. It was absolutely essential for me to see the objective from all possible directions to get first-hand information about the enemy and the objective. Brigadier Aul generally agreed with my plan and ordered me to start the process of dumping ammunition as soon as possible. The GOC 8 Mountain Division was also to be briefed about the Brigade plan. Coordination was also required to be carried out with Artillery. I requested him for one more day to complete my recce, which he readily agreed to, though I am sure that there must have been tremendous pressure to launch the attacks and evict the enemy from the higher HQ. By then, numerous statements had been taken out in the Press about the likely time frame required by the Army to flush out the so-called Mujaheddin, which had already surpassed the deadlines.

Meanwhile, I instructed Major Bajaj to carry out a recce of **Tololing** from the Southwest direction. He also gave me valuable inputs that corroborated what Major Mohit and Major Acharya had told me. Major Bajaj had always rendered professional advice to me. Together we formulated a tentative attack plan, which was to be a bi-directional attack. Since the two approaches for the attack were widely apart, Major Bajaj and I would be in charge of each approach to control the battle. I also wanted all the men up to Section Commanders to

22 Harinder Baweja, *A Soldier's Diary: Kargil, The Inside Story*, Page 46.For two days, on June 5 and 6, the 2 Raj Rif CO and his company commanders conducted a detailed reconnaissance after which they come to the conclusion that the Tololing complex could broadly be divided into four major assault areas: (1) Tololing Top – which they decided is open to assault from the South Eastern approach; (2) Area Flat – also to be assaulted from the South Eastern approach; (3) Point 4590 – can be assaulted from the South Western approach; and (4) Barbad Bunker – can be attacked from the South Western side. The approaches had been identified but fire bases had to be stocked, arms and ammunition carried up. The bases were built at a distance of approximately 600 metres from the objective, on each axis. The last 600 metres are the most crucial, for once the troops start moving, the artillery guns have to stop firing in order to avoid shelling their own soldiers. Fire support is essential. Continuing fire, first by the artillery batteries, then using our own MMGs, Automatic Grenade Launchers (AGLs) and Rocket Launchers (RLs). This enables the troops to close in on the objective.

go and carry out recce from the firm base location and see the objective so they could be mentally prepared for the battle. The next day, I decided to go along the South Western direction to recce **Tololing** and **Point 4590** features.

06 June 1999 - Preparations Begin in Real Earnest

I had crystallised my attack plan and had decided that the attack would be led by Charlie (Vivek) and Delta (Mohit) Companies along the South Eastern and the South Western directions, respectively. After the recce from the South-Western direction, I called the Officers and JCOs and directed the company commanders to commence detailed planning and preparation for the attack. The feeling of an actual attack was required to sink in the troops and the Commanders. They now had to get into the nitty-gritty of planning a battle.

I instructed each company to prepare a sand model of their objective area with the maximum possible details to explain to their troops. A realistic attack plan was to be brainstormed amongst the commanders at different levels of the company. Time and distance had to be worked out to the objective. This could give some realistic understanding to the troops about the likely task at hand. The momentum for a bloody assault had to set in. Preparation of load tables, carriage of ammunition, water and rations, distribution of heavy loads, firing and checking of weapons, distribution of specialist detachments of the Support Company were some of the tasks that were undertaken by each company. The companies had to check radio sets, batteries, and night vision devices, distribute grenades to all the sections, mini flares to commanders, and carry extra ammunition and support weapons. They practiced assault on the objective by fire and movement method and rehearsed the bunker bursting drills. They had to devise realistic methods of taking cover and crawling amidst heavy enemy fire. The only difference in our practice and in actuals was that the location of the bunkers and the enemy were unknown, and there was no enemy fire. Practice in peacetime is always very different from actuals. Innovative methods had to be thought of to beat the enemy sitting on the dominating heights.

Major Rathore, the Quarter Master sent teams to check all the equipment and weapons with the companies. He also planned the emergency rations to be distributed to the troops. On his own initiative, he liaised with the Q Branch of the Division HQ to get extra cold climate (ECC) clothing released for the troops, which was a must for such high-altitude terrain. Major Rathore was known for his improvisation skills ('*Jugaad*' as we call it in Hindi). His administrative skills made it possible to pick up required items like automatic weapons, special rations, ECC clothing, water cans, etc. He had the knack of taking out some links or the other with the dealing agencies through which we always managed to get over and above the requirement of the battalion.

The Brigade Plan

At the Brigade HQ, I discussed the final attack plan with Brigadier Amar Aul. Meanwhile, 18 GARHWAL RIFLES had also formulated its plan. After carrying out detailed recce, fresh troops were being launched for this attack. After almost two hours of brainstorming in the Brigade HQ, the Brigade attack plan was formalised. The Commander was to brief the GOC on the final attack plan, which he approved. This plan had to succeed, as the three previous attempts to capture **Tololing** had failed. The GOC tasked Commander Artillery Brigade to formulate the Artillery fire plan in consonance with the brigade attack plan. The approved brigade attack plan was as follows:-

a) 2 RAJRIF was to launch the main two-directional attack along the South Western and South Eastern directions and capture **Tololing.**

b) 18 GARHRIF was to launch a diversionary attack on **Point 5140** from the North / North Eastern direction and capture it.[23]

c) 2 NAGA was to launch a feint attack on **Pathar** and **Rock** from the NW direction.

---

[23] Harinder Baweja, *A Soldier's Diary: Kargil, The Inside Story*, Page 48. 18 Garhwal had been asked to launch a diversionary attack on Point 5140 to engage the enemy on more than one point and divide their fighting capacity and resources. A feint attack has all the necessary backup; a sustained artillery barrage to give the impression of an impending assault. There is no actual ground movement by the troops, but it is hoped that the enemy will fall for the feint. The feint was important. After operations by the Grenadiers on Tololing and by the Nagas on Point 5140, it was clear that the intruders were well entrenched in these places. They were, in fact, holding coordinated defences with well - sited machine guns, backed by effective counter - attack plans. Therefore, a decision was taken to launch deliberate operations to capture Tololing and Point 5140 backed by adequate artillery fire support.

Attack Plan 56 Mountain Brigade

Major General Puri was briefed about the dumping plan, which involved dumping at least one first line, one second line and War Wastage Reserve (WWR) ammunition for automatic weapons at the firebases along each axis to support the battalion's attack after the artillery fire had lifted. Inter Battalion transfer of company support weapons had to be ordered and executed within the Division to ensure the availability of maximum fire support. All this would have entailed that the attack could only be launched after 10 June.

Major Mohit Saxena in a helicopter ready for aerial recce

Not a very happy situation for Major General Mohinder Puri as he was under tremendous pressure from HQ 15 Corps and Army HQs to launch attacks and bring success to the Indian Army. Despite the pressures, he instructed his Division Staff to provide the maximum possible assistance to the attacking battalions in preparation for the attack. Brigadier Amar Aul also did not want to take any chances, as his COs demanded extra time for foolproof preparation before launching a coordinated attack. All efforts were being made to ensure that the attack was a success. For the first time, the Artillery Brigade was introducing the concept of 100-gun fire in support of the 56 Brigade Plan.

Helicopters were made available to carry out aerial recce of the objective for the CO and the leading company commanders on 7 June in the early part of the day. Self, Major Vivek and Major Mohit went for the aerial recce. The objective area was shown to the company commanders from almost five km distance as the pilots had orders not to cross the Drass River. There had already been a Mi-8 Chopper that had been hit by an enemy Stinger missile a few days back and had supposedly fallen in the Tololing Nala. Not much could be appreciated about the objective area from that distance. Both the company commanders were overwhelmed by the helicopter ride, which was probably the first in their lifetime. I could see Mohit very excited after the ride, though I am sure he would not have understood much in that short flight span.

After approval of the plans for the brigade attack, the artillery Battery Commander party and the Forward Observation Officers joined the battalion in preparing the artillery fire plan to support the attack. Additional ATGM detachments with MILAN missiles were also provided to the battalion. These were to be employed in the bunker bursting role from the Fire Base locations. The Brigade Signal Coy had also attached its Bravo 1 detachment to ensure communication of the brigade with me. I gave my final orders on the 7th of June.

Aerial Recce - Major Vivek Gupta in a helicopter

07 June 1999 – My Attack Orders

I started my orders by telling my officers and JCOs that the enemy was holding the **Tololing Ridge** to include **Tololing Complex, Hump** and **Point 5140** with a company/company plus. **Tololing Complex** consists of **Point 4590, Barbad Bunker, Area Rock, Area Flat** and **Top**, which was likely to be held by a platoon plus. **Point 4590, Barbad Bunker** and **Top** were in mutual support, and attack on these positions was likely to be interfered with heavy resistance. The route from **Point 5140, Hump** and **Top**, was the route of reinforcement. There were likely to be several automatic weapons deployed in the **Tololing Complex**.

2 Rajputana Rifles, 18 Garhwal Rifles and 1 NAGA, along with attached troops as part of 56 Mountain Brigade, were to launch a three-directional attack

to capture **Tololing Complex** on the night of 10 /11 June duly supported by Artillery.

2 RAJ RIF Officers before the Tololing Attack. Col Ravindranath, the CO is seated third from right

Without further harping about the tasks of other battalions, I spelt out my battalion's mission: '2 *RAJRIF and attached troops will capture Tololing Complex by 0600 hours on 11 June*'. A bi-directional attack was to be launched to capture **Tololing Complex** with Delta Company (Mohit) tasked to capture **Point 4590** and **Barbad Bunker** by attacking along the South West approach with Alpha Company (Acharya) as its reserve. Charlie Company (Vivek) was to be launched 60 minutes later to capture **Area Flat** and **Tololing Top** along South East approach with Bravo Company as its reserve. A stagger of one hour was given to keep the enemy guessing about the timings of the attack. Since attacks by 18 GRENADIERS had been along South West direction, the aim was to make the enemy feel that the same failures were being reinforced much against the teaching in our training institutes.

The final attack plan was bi-directional along the South West and the South East approaches. In the South West direction, the valiant Rajput's attack spearheaded by Delta Company (Mohit) with Alpha Company (Acharya) as reserve was to annihilate the enemy at **Point 4590.** They were to capture **Point 4590** in Phase 1 by 0200 hours and **Barbad Bunker** in Phase 2 by 0500 hours on 12 June 99. Likewise, the Gallant Jats were to be launched 60 minutes later along the South East approach, led by Charlie Company (Vivek) to capture **Tololing Top**, followed close at heels by Bravo Company. The stagger of 60 minutes was given to mislead the enemy about the actual point of attack. They were to capture **Area Flat** by 0200 hours and **Area Top** by 0500 hours on 12 June 99.

Both the Companies were given an Assault Pioneer Detachment and a Mortar Fire Controller as additional resources.

Attack Plan: Tololing

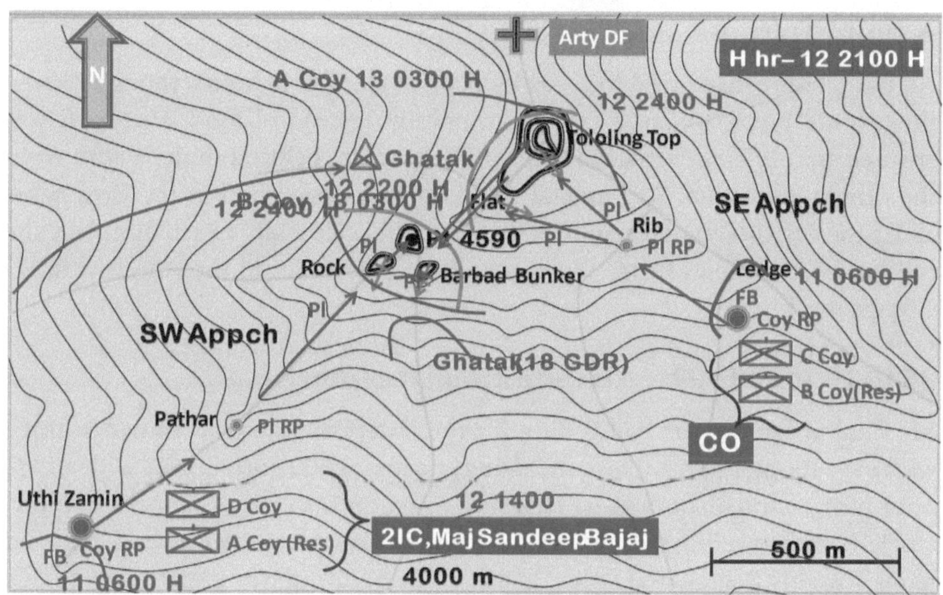

Fire Bases

Two fire bases were to be established, one along each axis, each having four Medium Machine Guns (MMGs), four Rocket Launchers, and two Automatic Grenade Launchers (AGLs), and one axis was to have a MILAN Missile Launcher. Two first-line scales of ammunition were to be dumped in each firebase. The fire support was to be provided for the first phase of the attack.

The Ghataks, under Lieutenant Neikezhakuo Kenguruse, were to establish a stop in **Hump** to prevent any enemy reinforcements from **Point 5140** and destroy the fleeing enemy from **Tololing Complex** towards **Point 5140.**

Artillery Support

Artillery was to carry out timed preparatory bombardment from 2100 to 2130 hours. They also had to provide covering fire on call on pre-registered targets for Delta and Alpha Companies. It was on call for impromptu targets for assaulting companies.

Lieutenant Saxena was the Forward Observation Officer (FOO), while Major Ashok, the Battery Commander, was with me in charge of the remainder of the artillery guns. There was one Bofors Gun in a direct firing role, too. Major

Sandeep Kala, who had just joined the battalion, was tasked to be at the direct firing location should the direct firing be required. The H hour was fixed at 2130 hours[24].

Administration

All troops were instructed to carry food and water for 48 hours, though I knew they would prefer to carry extra ammunition instead of food. Hot food was ensured by the Quartermaster, Major BS Rathore, before the departure from the camping location. Regimental Aid Post was established in the firm bases along the South West and South East directions. Casualty evacuation was the responsibility of the Mortar Platoon and the remainder of the Administrative Company.

08 to 10 June 1999 – Ammunition Dumping

My final orders set the ball rolling for the dumping plan to commence along each axis. It was a colossal task involving enormous 800 porter loads with an 11-hour turnaround on both axes. This task was coordinated by Major B S Rathore, single-handedly along with his administrative platoon, ponies he had gathered along with his Regimental Police section. The build-up was undertaken during the hours of darkness to avoid enemy shelling and detection. I was certain that Major Rathore would be able to complete the task by 10 June.[25]

---

24 Harinder Baweja, *A Soldier's Diary: Kargil, The Inside Story*, Page 49.As many as twenty gun batteries, including Bofors guns, had been put in place. A hundred and twenty artillery guns were pressed into service simultaneously to pound enemy positions and force them to keep their heads down

25 Harinder Baweja, *A Soldier's Diary: Kargil, The Inside Story*, Page 46.Mules are effective up to only one - third of the route. Loading and staging points too have to be set up. Considering that the turnaround of each fighting porter includes seven gruelling hours of climbing and another four hours of descent, one porter can undertake only one trip a day. Telephone lines have to be established and ration supplies dumped. With as many as sixty porters on each axis, it takes two days for this to be accomplished. Every single item has to be thought of, including water. It is available in the nallah at the first staging point on each axis but has to be ferried up for the troops and that involved a daily deployment of 20 men on each axis. Men from the Corps of Signals laid the communication lines – eight kilometres of line on the southwest axis and three kilometres on the southeast as the line laid by 18 Grenadiers is already functional. Kerosene too had to be carted up. The unit decided on 100 litres and it was ferried up on each axis by ten porters. Kerosene is important – it is needed to melt the snow and to heat up the precooked food. Medicines, life - saving drugs – they will surely be needed. And stretchers? That casualty evacuation is extremely difficult is a lesson Ravindranath has been taught before the battle commenced. Everyone knew what 18 Grenadiers had gone through and they decided to carry six stretchers up each axis. RAPs (Regimental Medical Aid Post) too were established – the closer, the better – just short of the firebases on each axis as directed by the Regimental Medical Officer. The unit had prepared for its share of casualties. Twelve stretchers were kept ready. There are other things to take care of: army mules and civil ponies

I am reminded of a carpenter of my battalion, Naik Uttam Singh, who was night blind and was to retire after two years. He volunteered to lug the MMG and AGL ammunition on his back. While climbing up at night, he tied himself with the person moving ahead of him with a rope to guide him upto the firebase.

The company commanders also planned their confirmatory recce of the objective along with their platoon commanders and section commanders. Detailed recce and monitoring of the objective area were carried out. The Fire Base party and the company support weapons were moved to the Firm Base along each axis. The company commanders also took the build-up phase as an opportunity to send all their troops to the firm base and see the objectives along both approaches. All the troops had seen the objective closely by 9 June and were now mentally ready for the attack.

However, the build-up of ammunition still needed to be completed, so I requested the Brigade Commander that I required another day to launch the attack. He did not take this very well, but reluctantly agreed and told me that he would request the GOC to postpone the attack by a day. The GOC finally agreed to the request, and the attack was postponed. The fighting companies were to induct up to the firm base on the night of 9 June 1999. The brigade attack would be launched on June 11/12 night, and the troops would be inducted on June 10/11 night to the firm base.

The GOC Talks to the Battalion

Major General Mohinder Puri, the GOC addressed the battalion on 09 June. In his address, he spoke about the rich history of the battalion, the various battles the unit had successfully taken part in and the traditions of the battalion. He also complimented the battalion for the smooth and fast induction and preparation for the battle. He emphasised that going into a battle is a rare opportunity that one gets in his entire service career. He fuelled the sentiments of the troops by reminding them of the sacrifices made by their forefathers. He emphasised the 'Izzat' of their platoon, company and the battalion. I distinctly remember him saying, '*Brave and bold actions would create a history that will be spoken about in times to come. You would be the talk of the town in your respective villages, and the parents of such gallant soldiers would be proud of their son's performance*.' This talk had really charged up my men. I could see a feeling of confidence building up in them to accomplish any given task.

---

were at work, so were the fighting porters. Loads of ammunition had to be dumped and the unit clerks and dhobis (washermen) were also pressed into action including the carpenter, Uttam Singh.

The General officer interacted informally with the troops for about 30 minutes after his talk. Jats love to talk when they find their commanders receptive and willing to talk. They also have all sorts of faiths and beliefs, which may not be practical, but they have a strong affinity towards them. One such belief was brought to the notice of the GOC during the interaction with troops. The attack was being launched on June 11/12 night. It happened to be a 'Friday or Jummah.' This day is considered the most important day for the Muslims (Pakistanis) in a week. Special prayers are conducted in Masjids, which is deemed an auspicious day for the Muslims. Even in the game of cricket, Pakistan always prefers to have matches against India on Friday. It gives them a psychological edge. Our troops did not want to take any chances. They did not want Pakistanis to have any advantage whatsoever. The fact that they were sitting on mountaintops was a very big advantage. In his typical Jat tone, one of the Jats spontaneously told the GOC, '*Sahab, hum to jumme wale din attack kar rahe hai, yo tho thik na hai. (We are attacking on the day of 'Jummah.' This is not fair)*'. I thought he did not understand what the Jat soldier was telling him as he did not reply to the jawan. Maybe he was not used to such a tone, being a Gorkha officer whose troops are docile and quiet. But I was wrong; the GOC, before leaving, quietly asked me if there was any problem with attacking on a Friday. Like a true soldier, I told him that while it was perfectly fine to attack on Friday as the battalion was fully prepared, the sentiments of the troops had to be honoured. Such sentiments do make an impact on a soldier's mind. The Division Commander must have pondered over it on his way back, and by evening, the orders for a change of attack date to 12/13 June had come.

This gave us some additional time to carry out preparation for the attack. It also gave me an opportunity to go and address the companies individually. Till now, we had been on the run carrying out recce, briefing, debriefing, planning for the attack, etc. I went to each company to motivate them, check their preparations and look into any issues that may have bothered the troops. It also gave me, in particular, some much-needed rest as we had been on the move every day for some tasks or other.

During one of the interactions in Charlie Company, I tried to speak a few sentences in Jat language to make the tense atmosphere light and cheer up the jawans. I asked them, '*Chai ka bandobast hai ke nahi, upar sardi ghadne hi hogi.' (Have you catered for tea arrangements? It will be very cold on Top)*. My aim was to make the troops speak in a light, jovial atmosphere; some laughter eased the tension in the troops' minds. But to my surprise and following true traditions of Charlie Company, Subedar Bhawar Lal stood up and said, '*Sahabji, subah ki chai hum aapko Tololing Top par hi pilayenge,' (Sir, we will serve you hot tea on*

Tololing Top tomorrow morning). I could see most of the men were charged up. There was a sense of self-belief. It gave me confidence that the men would do their best, whatever the result of the battle. Their josh was evident when I heard the war cry at the end of my address in all the companies.

The Fire Base is Established

The dumping of ammunition, which was running against time, was now completed. I was now satisfied that the complete preparation was done and the battalion was ready for the attack. The Fire Base party moved ahead on 10 June 99 along both the axes to set up well before the assault was to be carried out. I also wanted them to get used to the firing conditions, identification of likely bunkers, registration of targets by MMGs and AGLs, engagement during the night, and staying in the open throughout the day and night. Subedar Man Singh, along South West Approach, and Subedar Ram Kumar Lamba, along South East Approach, were the commanders of the Fire Bases. Each firebase had experienced firers behind the weapons. I wanted the Fire Base commanders to be well versed with the objectives and name different parts of the objective to bring down support fire when required in conjunction with the attacking companies. The dumped ammunition had to be properly camouflaged under the rocks to protect it from enemy air bursts. Both the JCOs did exceedingly well. When I reached the Fire Base on the South East Approach, Subedar Lamba briefed me in detail on the likely location of bunkers in **Area Flat** and **Top** and how he had gone about giving different names to the targets. He had coordinated these names with each section and platoon commander besides the company commander.

Fire Base Along SEAppch

Fire Base Along SEAppch

Some Divine Help

On 10th June, in the evening, the unit Panditji came to me and said that we must have a Mandir function before we go to war. I realised that this would also give me an opportunity to motivate my men just before the attack. I agreed and directed that the Mandir parade would be organised just before the induction of the companies on 11 June 99. I told Major Bajaj to organise the Mandir parade and that he must sit down with the Panditji and prepare his talk to the troops. Our troops have blind faith in God and the sermon from the Panditji of a battalion always has a positive effect on the troops.

It indeed paid rich dividends because the Panditji very beautifully and tactfully incited the issues of an individual's honour, parent's honour in villages, Paltan's izzat and said that the complete nation was looking to see the gallant feats that the Jats and Rajputs were known for. He also instilled the fear of God in them and encouraged them to take every possible action to defeat the Pakistanis. He reminded them of each soldier's pledge when he joined the Army.

The *'traditional Aarti'* that was performed drew out the josh of the battalion. It was loud, energetic, lively, and vibrant and gave me the real feel of my unit. While it was evident from the majority of the faces of the soldiers that they were all pepped up for the attack, there was also a feeling of fear, worry, anxiety and apprehension, amongst a few. This is bound to happen on the eve of a battle, as infantry combat is uncertain, unpredictable and involves a very high risk to life and limb. By the time the Mandir parade was over, it was nearing last light. The troops had already loaded their weapons and equipment on the vehicles. Immediately after the Mandir Parade, the troops took the blessings of Panditji and mounted the vehicles to depart for the debussing point with loud cheers of *'Bharat Mata Ki Jai.'*

The debussing point was the location to disembark the vehicles and commence the journey on foot towards the objective. I also met the Delta and Alpha Company Commanders, Major Mohit and Major Acharya and the 2iC, Major Bajaj. I wished them luck before departing behind the Charlie and Bravo Companies convoy. While I wished them luck, I had a heavy heart, not knowing whom I would meet again or whether I would be alive or not. It isn't easy to put up a brave front on such occasions.

FAITH AND PRAYER - MANDIR PARADE BEFORE THE ATTACK

CHAPTER EIGHT

TOLOLING: THE BATTLE

For a warrior these are the best of times; to stand on the mountain top victorious. "The objective given to my battalion has been achieved in full," Colonel Ravindranath radioed his brigade commander. "We have captured Tololing, sir." As he bestrode the crest of Tololing on June 13, breathing in the thin, crystal clean air at 4590 metres, he knew what the rest of India was soon to know: this was the first turning point of the war.

Harinder Baweja – India Today

12 June 1999 – The Climb Up

Alpha (Acharya) and Delta (Mohit) Companies moved to the Battalion Tactical HQ in Drass village from where they started their ascent from the South Western direction towards **Point 4590**. Bravo (Rautela) and Charlie (Vivek) Companies moved to the loading point near Thasgam to commence their move from South Eastern direction towards **Tololing Top**. The assaulting companies i.e., Delta and Charlie, were to be in the Firm Base on either approach well before first light.

I had specifically told the company commanders to ensure that the troops were well tucked in and camouflaged to avoid detection and to maintain surprise. The reserve companies were to be one bound (a prominent landmark in military terms) behind to avoid overcrowding in the Firm Base. Simultaneously the holding battalion (18 GRENADIERS) had to thin out from the Firm Base, less the troops already deployed for its protection.

By 0400 hours, I got a confirmation from Major Bajaj that the troops along the South Western direction had reached safely and had been camouflaged. Bravo and Charlie Companies had also reached the Firm Base by 0430 hours. Complete radio silence was observed. The existing telephone lines of 18 GRENADIERS were used to avoid any increase in radio traffic thereby maintaining surprise.

The complete day on 12 June was spent 'lying doggo' and observing the movement of the enemy. Till now, everything had moved as per plans with no major issues. The induction up to the Firm Base was critical, and I had my fingers crossed till such time I got confirmation from the Southwest approach. We had been able to maintain surprise. It was evident since there had been no artillery shelling during the induction phase. 18 GARHRIF and 1 NAGA were also inducting on the same night along different axes to launch diversionary and feint attacks on the **Tololing ridge line**.

Pre-battle Nerves

Spending the complete day for the troops with nothing to do made them restless. The men had been exposed to varying views all these past days, from the most despondent to somewhat grim, which was evidently playing on their minds. This was evident from their body language and exaggerated behaviour. While some displayed excessive bravado and took undue initiative, exposing themselves unnecessarily, others sank into self-created cocoons. Even more surprising was that those who were habitually talkative, went suddenly silent while the quiet ones suddenly became vociferous!

With an eye on troop morale just before a major battle, I could not help but eavesdrop to their conversation as we all lay tucked together in the rocky outcrops that day. There were some who were extremely tense, probably thinking about their near and dear ones. I even saw the officers sitting together discussing things and on occasion laughing and joking. I could sense the changes in a few of them at the Firm Base location.

A number of rumours were circulating about the enemy amongst the rank and file, which gave fantastic capabilities to the enemy - of very well fortified bunkers, **Tololing** encircled by a ring of only automatic weapons, their daily needs being supplied / bought from Unit Run Canteens of local units, women having been observed visiting enemy posts, etc. Such talk never does good for the morale of troops about to launch an attack and I was hopeful that they would not have infected my men; unchecked rumours can instil fear in the troops and therefore need to be nipped in the bud. But it was too late for me to dispel these rumours in my men. It was precisely for this very purpose I had kept my troops aloof and isolated from troops of various units who had been launched into battle and had not been successful.

Sitting alone at the top, thoughts of my wife, Anitha and my daughters, Prerna and Prarthana passed through my mind. I had refrained from telling them about our predicament and what it involved as I myself was dealing with the operation on a day-to-day basis, not knowing what the next day would bring. To be honest, the thought of not meeting my family again never crossed my mind.

Later I was told, that on the Southwest axis, the officers had even written letters home addressing their near and dear ones and had kept them in their respective pockets with an understanding that in case they were killed, their last letters home could be despatched by the survivors. It was moving, and inspiring, the letters that Major Acharya and Captain Vijayant Thapar had written.[26] The best way to keep such thoughts out of mind is to get involved with the men or with the planning of the operations.

08 JUN 99
9.55 AM.

My dear wife,

How are you. I am quite fine here and miss you and kaajal a lot. I hope you have recovered from the pain of Appa's demise and are now in good health. I hope you are in Hyd house now and taking proper rest. You must take care of your health and eat properly.

This place is really beautifully barren with clear streams and strong winds and rocks everywhere. I'll show you this place sometime later. You would love it. We'll take a tent on hire and go around the place.

I am having really good food here but not as good as what you make. when I get home you must make all the things that I like and I'll keep hogging & hogging. I do not require anything here. I am fully kitted out and have lots of chocolates which I bought before coming here.

Tell me what present you want from me. I'll get it along when I get back. What should I get for kaajal. Is she asking for anything? You must not neglect her. Try to support Ma and get Amma to stay with us in Hyd. Does kaajal want a brother or a sister. keep reading the Bhagwad Gita so that the child imbibes the same culture and good habits. No watching horror serials.

Major and Mrs Acharya as groom and bride (left) and the last letter written by Acharya to his wife

12 June 1999 – Daytime Preparations

The day was spent observing the activities of the enemy and intermittent firing. There was no enemy movement that we could spot. Even the pinpoint location

---

26 Vijayant at Kargil, Thapar & Dwivedi, Penguin e bury Press, 2020, Page 173. Robin's Last Letter. By the time you get this letter I'll be observing you all from the sky enjoying the hospitality of Apsaras. I have no regrets; in fact even if I become a human again I'll join the army again and fight for my nation. If you can, please come and see where the Indian army fought for your tomorrow. As far as the unit is concerned the new chaps should be told about this sacrifice. I hope my photo will be kept in the 'A' coy mandir with Karni Mata. Whatever organ can be take, should be done. Contribute some money to orphanage and keep on giving 50/ - Rs to Ruksana per month and meet Yogi Baba. Best of luck to Birdie, never forget this sacrifice of these men. Papa you should feel proud. Mama so should you, meet ____ [name distorted for privacy] (I loved her). Mamaji forgive me for everything wrong I did. Ok then its time for me to join my clan of the Dirty Dozen. My aslt [assault] party has 12 chaps.

from where the fire was coming could not be ascertained. The only thing we were sure were the types of weapons which the enemy was using to engage us. It included Heavy Machine Guns, PIKA (Russian PK is a belt-fed general-purpose machine gun), sniper rifles and Light Machine Guns (LMG). Own Fire Base was also intermittently firing to incite the enemy to engage us so that we could ascertain the exact location of their bunkers and weapon emplacements.

Dearest Papa Mama Birdie and Granny,

1. By the time you get this letter I'll be observing you all from the sky enjoying the hospitality of Apsaras.
2. I have no regrets; in fact even if I become a human again I'll join the army and fight for my nation.
3. If you can, please come and see where the Indian army fought for your tomorrow.
4. As far as the unit is concerned the new chaps should be told about this sacrifice. I hope my photo will be kept in the 'A' coy mandir with Karni Mata.
5. What-ever organ can be taken, should be done.
6. Contribute some money to orphanage and keep on giving 50/- Rs to Rukhsana per month, and meet Yogi Baba.
7. Best of luck to Birdie, never forget this sacrifice of these men. Papa you should feel proud. Mama so should you, meet [illegible] (I loved her). Mamaji forgive me for everything wrong I did.

Last letter written by Captain Vijayant Thapar

The day was also utilised to plot the route to be taken at night while advancing towards the objective. This helped my companies to exactly decide the path to be followed from the Fire Base to the objective. 'Bounds' or waypoints were earmarked during day assuming that the same would surely be visible at night. Alternate route for the platoons were also earmarked and shown to the section commanders. Code symbols were tied up with the Fire Base party to indicate the exact location of the leading platoon so as to assist them to shift their fire ahead on to the objective keeping safety of own troops in mind. Charlie Company had to move with two platoons up to attack **Top** and **Area Flat**, while Delta Company was to attack one up in echelons.

It was for the first time that I saw a sense of responsibility amongst the section and platoon commanders. The detailed planning and recce that was done by them showed their capability which we generally don't exploit. There were discussions, arguments, counter arguments, all these were healthy signs and reflected the will and desire to succeed. Often the JCOs of the Indian Army are considered as 'Black Sheep' who enjoy the maximum with least responsibility. Many officers do not exploit their potential and expertise which they are capable of. I for one was thoroughly impressed with their performance, grit, determination and the ability to motivate and lead. They are the ones who could select the right man for the right job because they understood the psyche of each and every man in their platoons. The outcome of the war is a testimony to what I say. Be it the distribution of ammunition, water, emergency ration, carriage of spare ammunition instead of food, making buddy pairs etc, all was done by these JCOs.

The Attack

The attack commenced with the artillery pounding the entire **Tololing ridge line** at 1730 hours. The Battery Commander (BC), Major Ashok Sharma along with the Forward Observation Officers (FOO) commenced the artillery gun battle with ranging procedure to register the different targets. By 1800 hours, the guns were firing tons and tons of TNT on the entire **Tololing** ridge including **Hump** and **Point 5140**. Bofors guns were also firing in direct firing role for the first time. The pounding of the guns on the objective was a sight to remember for every infantry soldier.

The heavy rounds shattered the rocks into a thousand pieces sending the debris flying high into the sky. The small pieces or the rock splinters which flew in the air sparkled against the fading sun light. It was a beautiful sight, although we were all aware of their deadly effect once struck by even the tiniest splinter. But, it gave us confidence and boosted the morale of my troops.

The guns in the direct firing role were more destructive and accurate than the ones firing in indirect role. The venom poured by these guns left little doubt

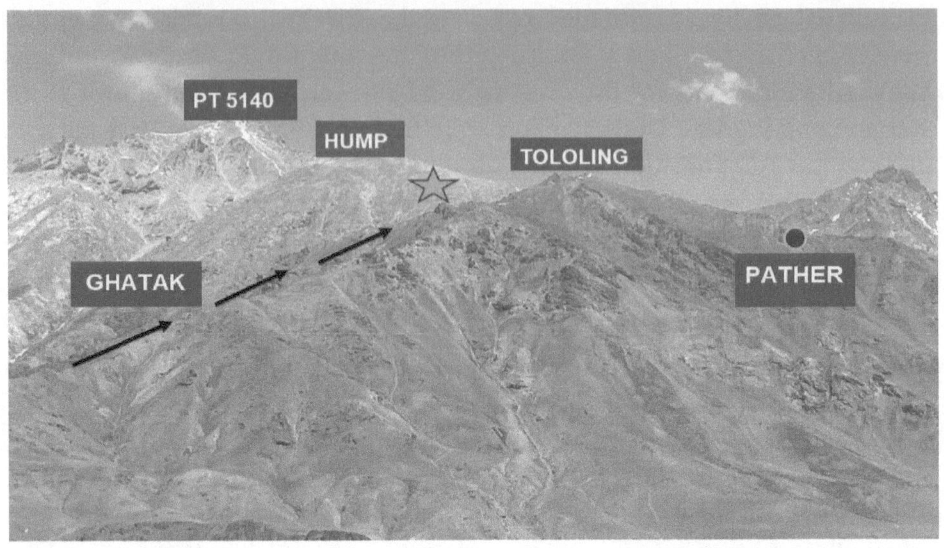

Route taken by Ghataks to establish a stop between Tololing and Hump

in our minds about the enemy presence on **Tololing Complex**. The accuracy at which they were firing gave us a feeling that almost each and every bunker must have been neutralised. The artillery engagement continued for the next two hours with short crunches intermittently thrown in. My troops were also delighted to see the effect of artillery. Most of them had never seen such destructive effects of artillery gun fire. The entire bowl was resonating with the sound of crashing artillery. Enemy counter bombardment was not very discernible. I was certain there would be many enemy casualties after this powerful artillery barrage on **Tololing Complex**. But surprisingly, after the battle was over, I did not see a single splinter injury on the dead bodies of Pakistani casualties that we came across on the objective.[27]

Unlike previous attacks that were launched on **Tololing**, the attack did not commence immediately after the artillery fire was lifted. Small crunches of fire with gaps kept the enemy guessing about the time of attack. The H Hour was 2130 hours for Delta Company and 2230 hours for Charlie Company.

---

27 From Kargil to the Coup, Nasim Zehara, Sand-e-Meet Publications, 2018. By 10 June, the Indian Artillery regiment had amassed a large number of fire units in extremely difficult terrain. On the military front, this Indian artillery fire turned the tables on Pakistan. The Indian Army lined up the Bofors guns on the NH-1, from where they directly and incessantly hit the Pakistani posts. They succeeded in reducing the posts to "powder" [A term used by Pakistani troops to describe the extent of damage inflicted through artillery fire) using short and long-range weapons. Op KP was facing sharp military reversals and singularly on account of accurate and timely delivery of TNT. The Gunners' fire assaults became the principal battle-winning factor. The intensity of artillery fire devastated both men and mountains. By June 10, India's infantry had the solid backing it had lacked during May and early June."

Before the attacks commenced, Lieutenant Kenguruse with his Ghatak platoon was to infiltrate behind **Tololing Top** and establish a stop at the **Saddle** which was in between **Hump** and **Tololing Top** with the aim to prevent any reinforcements of the enemy from **Point 5140** and also to neutralise the fleeing enemy towards **Point 5140**. Due to a steep cutting he could not reach the exact location, but he did establish a stop at a high ground from where he could monitor some of the movements of the enemy.

Actions of Delta Company (Mohit)

By about 2030 hours, Delta Coy (Mohit) had regrouped from various hiding places for the attack. They had gathered near the fire base and were to commence movement towards **Point 4590** at 2045 hours. The movement was perforce along the narrow ridge line initially and, therefore, was restricted to a single file. The distance from the Fire Base to **Point 4590** was nearly 600 to 700 metres. With the help of a Laser Range Finder, the distance to the base and top of **Point 4590** had been measured. The closest distance was 605 metres.

Delta Coy (Mohit) commenced moving towards **Point 4590** at 2045 hours sharp. 10 Platoon was leading under Subedar Karan Singh followed by Company HQ, 12 Platoon and 11 Platoon. The last artillery barrage was from 2015 to 2045 hours. Immediately thereafter, the Fire Base opened fire to maintain the momentum of fire on the objective. This continued till finally radio silence was broken and Major Mohit told Major Bajaj, who was controlling the fire at the Fire Base, to stop firing. It must have taken about 40 minutes for Delta Company to reach the base of **Point 4590** which was surely not as per the calculated time envisaged.

I was wondering why suddenly there was complete silence with no firing whatsoever. I asked Major Bajaj on the radio set who told me that he could see some movement of Delta Coy with the night vision devices and they appeared to be closing in towards **Point 4590**. There wasn't much that I could hear from my location as the two approaches were quite a distance apart. Initially I could see only the MMG tracers when **Point 4590** was being engaged and a few flashes of enemy fire.

Delta Company's leading platoon was advancing by fire and movement. They had deployed a light machine gun (LMG) at a raised ground while trying to negotiate **Point 4590** to give covering fire. Havildar Sultan Singh on the other hand, had slowly climbed on **Area Rock**, a hill top adjacent to **Point 4590** and had established a foot hold on it. Swiftly, he also deployed a LMG to bring down fire on the enemy. Though at a height, there was no cover available. He would fire on the enemy and withdraw into the reverse slope which was a defiladed position. In this way, his fire was effective but was also being continuously countered by enemy fire. The balance of the platoon tried to skirt **Point 4590** from the East (right) to launch the attack.

Suddenly there was an illumination round fired by the enemy which caught Major Mohit and the leading platoon by surprise in the open. During the illumination fire, which lasted for less than 10 seconds, a group of 10 - 12 men rose from their bunkers atop **Point 4590**, sprayed a volley of bullets on the leading platoon, which was in the open and just vanished. The platoon was totally flabbergasted by the enemy action. There was hardly any cover available except for a few boulders. There was almost nil retaliation by the platoon due to the shock and awe. The men did not follow the drill of dash, down, crawl, take cover and observe when illuminated, a basic drill taught to every soldier. This action by the enemy was also targeted towards Havildar Sultan Singh who had established a foot hold on **Point 4590**. This was the first encounter of Delta Company where they faced live bullets flying all around them. About three boys were injured in this action.

By the time the Company recovered from the shock created by the first illumination round, provide medical aid to the injured, the enemy struck again at around 2155 hours with another illumination round; this time with a greater intensity, more numbers and shouting slogans '*Allah Ho Akbar, Allah ho Akbar*'. Delta Company had barely got back to their feet from the first attack when the enemy fired another salvo. This time there were two overlapping illumination rounds fired which illuminated the area for about 18 - 20 seconds. But, learning from their initial mistake, showing presence of mind and probably recollecting the teachings in the Academies, Major Mohit Saxena shouted to drop down, take cover and freeze. This is the action taught whenever there is an illumination round fired. The platoon dived to the ground thereby suffering lesser injuries. Two to three soldiers however sustained bullet injuries again. The leading platoon had been jolted.

Mohit instructed this platoon to firm in, take cover and fire back at the enemy while he himself with his HQ moved back to explore the possibility of attacking **Point 4590** from the West of the location where the initial foothold had been established by Havildar Sultan Singh. He climbed to the spot where Havildar Sultan had deployed his LMG to get a better view of the area around to open another front for attacking **Point 4590.**

The enemy had probably reinforced **Point 4590** by thinning out on **Top** which was evident from the number of weapons which had opened fire on the company in the second attack. The enemy had seen the same tactics being employed by 18 GRENADIERS a few days earlier. Accordingly, the enemy had reinforced its strength on **Point 4590** from **Area Flat** to foil any chances of success to the Indian Army. **Area Flat** was in between **Tololing Top** and **Point 4590.** First field dressing (FFD) was applied to the injured persons while options to open a different front were being explored by the Company Commander.

Actions of Charlie Company (Vivek)

Meanwhile C Company under Major Vivek Gupta was eagerly waiting to be launched. He had divided his Company into three platoons but each platoon had two sections only. He had discussed this with me and I had agreed as I did not want to curb his initiative. His aim was to have the complete section strength of 10 men along with an officer and a JCO. The total effective bayonet strength was only about 60 - 70 men in a Company which were divided into three platoons of 20 each, weapons platoon and Company HQ.

Incidentally Major Vivek was an introvert who did not intermingle with the other company commanders and preferred to stay aloof. He had just come back from an Instructors' tenure in Infantry School, Mhow and therefore, had a number of ideas which he wanted to implement in his company. He also had Lieutenant Tomar as his Second in Command with barely six months of service. Lieutenant Tomar was also very quiet, an observant officer and a quick learner on attachment to my unit. He had led a number of patrols and ambushes in the Kashmir Valley with the men of this company. The troops had developed a liking for him in a short time because of his actions, attitude and calmness.

Seeing Delta Company halted by the wall of lead being thrown against them, Charlie Company under Major Vivek Gupta was launched from the SE direction with two platoons up towards **Area Flat** and **Tololing Top** lead by Subedar Dharamvir and Lieutenant Praveen Tomar respectively at 2130 hours as per the plan.

During the detailed recce of the objective, the only hurdle which they envisaged was a prominent patch of snow at **Tololing Top**. The company had accordingly made plans for the attack. It moved from its Firm Base which was at a distance of nearly 700 metres from **Top** at 2130 hours in a single file with 8 Platoon in the lead followed by 9 Platoon. 7 Platoon was in reserve. The company had decided to move in a single file up to the platoon release point from where they were to get in a two up formation and attack **Area Flat** and **Top** simultaneously. The platoon release point was 250 metres from the objective. It took them nearly 45 minutes to traverse 500 metres.

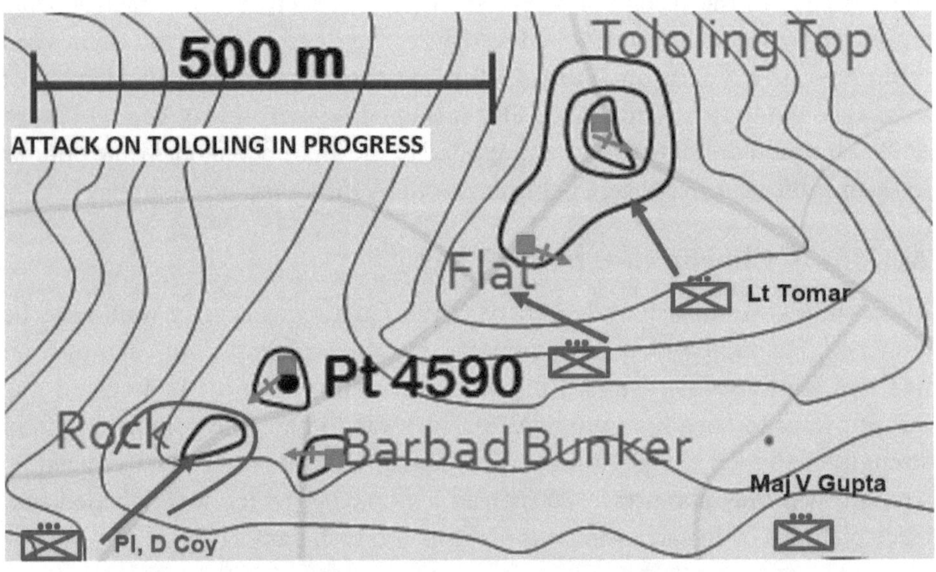

The intensity of exchange of fire between the Fire Base and **Tololing Top** had increased. Both the sides were engaging each other more vigorously than before for different reasons. While we were giving covering fire to our advancing columns, the enemy was retaliating and firing at us. The enemy always had the advantage of being static and firing from a height as it gave him a better view and clearer field of fire. However, the advantage for us was that we were a moving target for the enemy which is always difficult to engage and that too at night. The enemy fire was not very effective as it was a plunging fire. This allowed Charlie Company to close in with the enemy.

The two platoons commenced their advance by fire and movement ahead of the platoon release point. Subedar Dharamvir's platoon closed in with **Area Flat** at around 2230 hours. The LMG was deployed in the SE direction of **Area Flat** to provide flanking fire. It was envisaged by Subedar Dharamvir that the LMG could engage **Barbad Bunker** if it opened up, and could also provide flanking fire support on **Area Flat** to its attacking echelons. Luckily for the 9 Platoon, there was not much resistance on **Flat** and it was occupied without a fight. While there were three trenches on **Flat**, it appeared that the troops had recently been shifted towards **Point 4590** or **Barbad Bunker** to reinforce those locations to blunt the Delta Company (Mohit's) attack.

BUNKERS IN AREA FLAT AS SEEN FROM TOLOLING TOP

I was monitoring the radio set communication of Charlie Company when Subedar Dharamvir confirmed by 2230 hours that **Area Flat** had been completely occupied. Subedar Dharamvir also confirmed to his company commander that he had observed some movement towards **Barbad Bunker** which was barely 80 metres away. I later came to know that he had some verbal fight with the enemy as well. The enemy was trying to lure Subedar Dharamvir to come and get him but to his and my surprise, Subedar Dharamvir waited patiently, deployed a Light Machine Gun towards **Barbed Bunker** and started firing towards it. It was advantageous to Subedar Dharamvir as he was engaging the rear side of **Barbed Bunker.** I started to get a feel that the enemy had played into our plans exactly the way we wanted. He had readjusted his defences by moving troops from **Area Flat** to **Point 4590** thus providing an opportunity to capture **Flat** without much resistance. It was now envisaged that the attack on **Tololing Top** could be launched from **Area Flat** as the initial foothold had been established. However, the moment **Flat** was captured, there was a barrage of fire from **Tololing Top** on Subedar Dharamvir's Platoon. The HMG on **Tololing Top** now started creating a lot of trouble for Charlie Company and had to be neutralised at the earliest.

8 Platoon under Lieutenant Tomar had got stuck against the snow patch which had been appreciated during the recce. It was actually an ice wall which could not be negotiated without crampons, pick axe and other mountain climbing equipment. The ice wall was about 10 - 12 feet high and was extremely slippery. Till 2230 hours, the platoon had not made much headway.

Lieutenant Praveen Tomar decided to take a detour to attack **Top** from the South. He skirted the ice wall and tried to close in from the Southern direction. I could get an update on the Charlie Company radio net about the progress of the attack. Lieutenant Praveen had been talking to his Company Commander, Major Vivek who was closely behind 8 Platoon. Lieutenant Tomar decided to move his leading section through the gap between **Area Flat** and **Top** with Subedar Dharamvir's Platoon providing fire support.

Having skirted the ice wall, Subedar Bhawar Lal, his buddy, with two scouts moved up and closed in with the first bunker on **Tololing Top**. The Heavy Machine Gun bunker on **Tololing Top** had been continuously firing towards **Area Flat**, nearly the same direction from where 8 Platoon was now climbing. The enemy always had the advantage as they were inside a fortified bunker.

Taking cover of the ice wall and hugging it, both the scouts Rifleman Anand and Lance Naik Bachchan and Subedar Bhawar Lal along with his buddy moved up towards the bunker. When they reached nearly 30 metres from the nearest bunker, all four of them charged on to the bunker firing with all the personal weapons. The Pakistanis in the bunker, sensing danger to their lives, also opened up with all their weapons apart from the Heavy Machine Gun. There was a sudden volley of bullets from both sides. While the enemy, sitting and firing from a fortified bunker was protected, it was my troops who were at grave danger of being mowed down by the hail of bullets. The enemy bullets struck the charging brave soldiers of Charlie Company barely 10 metres from the bunker. Subedar Bhawar and Lance Naik Bachchan both died on the spot while Rifleman Anand was grievously wounded. One of the three Pakistanis present in the bunker was hit who later succumbed to his injury. We recovered his body after the capture of **Tololing**. These were probably the first fatal casualties for both the sides.

Charlie Company had attacked along the most likely approach which the enemy would have envisaged. Rifleman Anand and Subedar Bhawar were barely 10 metres from the **Tololing Top,** hiding behind one of the rocks close to the bunker. One of them had a serious bullet injury while the other was neither in a condition to attack nor could he withdraw. Rifleman Anand was crying in pain while his buddy was trying to console him to be quiet. Lieutenant Tomar with his buddy was barely 15 metres behind them. His aim was to somehow extricate both.

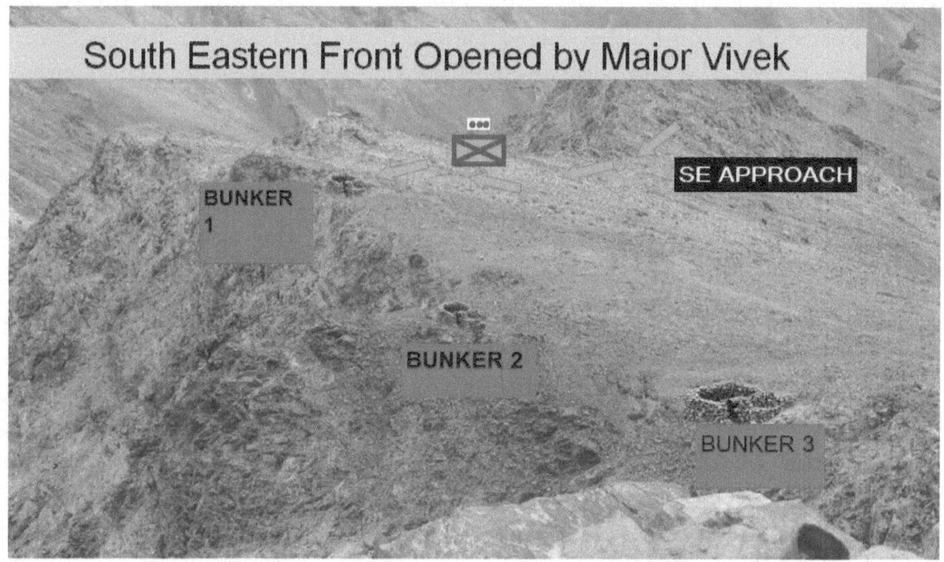

Lieutenant Tomar informed his Company Commander of the situation and soon Major Vivek and Havildar Digender rushed forward to take stock of the situation. It was essential to evacuate the injured. It was decided that Lieutenant

Tomar with the balance platoon would extricate the injured. Lieutenant Tomar with his platoon along with Subedar Dharamvir kept engaging the bunker to prevent it from firing at the injured persons who were trapped and were hiding behind the rock next to the bunker.

It was already 2330 hours and success still seemed elusive, except for the initial foothold at **Point 4590** by Delta Coy at **Area Rock** and capture of a vacated location at **Area Flat**. We had also suffered casualties till now on both the axes. I expected the fight to be gruesome but did not expect that there would be no success after three hours of battle. All odds seemed to be against us.

Seeing no headway in the attack, Major Gupta along with Havildar Digender decided to open another front by assaulting on **Tololing Top** from the Eastern direction with the aim to divert the enemy attention to extricate the men who were trapped. The enemy was firmly entrenched in a series of bunkers along the ridge. It was not known to Major Gupta that the enemy was actually observing his complete movement while he was changing his direction of attack from Southern to South Eastern and was accordingly prepared to engage them. But I must put on record the bravery of Major Gupta and Havildar Digender who took the leading section of the reserve 7 Platoon to attack the first bunker. The LMG group was deployed to a side while the leading section assaulted at the bunker. There was just no cover available; not even rocks or boulders. To rush and climb simultaneously while bullets are being aimed and fired from the opposite direction by the enemy takes a lot of guts and determination. It was a suicidal mission requiring an uphill ascent towards the entrenched enemy posts who had the advantage of height and a bird's eye view. Naik Virender and Rifleman Ashish, the leading scouts along with Major Vivek Gupta and Havildar Digender charged at the bunker.

The enemy was prepared and was awaiting the assault. The Heavy Machine Gun opened followed by a volley of bullets of AK-47 and LMGs from at least two enemy bunkers. Since all four persons were firing while charging towards the bunker, the accuracy of enemy fire had reduced. The enemy sitting inside the bunker were also scared to take an aimed shoot as bullets were also hitting their bunker. Naik Virender and Rifleman Ashish were the first to get hit. However, Major Vivek and Havildar Digender managed to charge inside the bunker and in an exchange of continuous fire neutralised the two Pakistanis inside it. It is difficult to imagine the chaos inside the dark bunker when they would have entered. This was the first bunker that was captured after a gruelling battle between the two sides. The fire fight had seen the battle swing on either direction. It was essential to hold on to this bunker as the enemy was known to launch a quick counter attack. Major Vivek knew this very well. He had just returned from Infantry School where he was an Instructor. He quickly ordered the LMG group which had provided the fire support, to rush to this bunker and deploy its LMG towards the likely direction from where the enemy could launch a counter attack. The capture of the first bunker bolstered the confidence of Charlie Company. The balance section got involved in evacuating Naik Virender and Rifleman Ashish who later succumbed to their bullet injuries.

There was an uneasy calm in the 7 Platoon. It had just lost two of its best jawans. A fear had set in but at the same time there was a strong feeling to avenge the death of their comrades. Major Vivek knew that the momentum gained had to be exploited in order to reach the **Top**. Otherwise, it could lead to more losses. Such decisions in battle are very difficult to take especially when you see your men dying. A balance has to be struck to look after the casualties or maintain the momentum of attack. Major Vivek quickly ordered Subedar Sumer Singh to push forward the next section for the attack on the next bunker from where the fire had started coming. However, the LMG would fire only intermittently, as its ammunition had been mostly expended. The magazines being carried by other riflemen had to fetch up. Who would get them or would someone go back and collect the magazines? Such questions always remain unanswered till such time the battles are won. The Company Havildar Major Yashvir Singh came to the rescue. He had been constantly pushing and motivating the company for the battle. He himself was only carrying grenades for the battle. No personal weapon was being carried by him. He collected all the magazines and brought them to enhance the fire of the LMG. He kept on throwing grenades towards the next bunker while the preparation for the next assault was on. The blasting of grenades was impacting the enemy. It was not allowing them to regroup for a counter attack. While lobbing one of the grenades, Company Havildar Major Yashvir Singh was hit by an enemy bullet and was killed in action.

Meanwhile Subedar Sumer Singh along with his second section moved up to launch the attack on the second bunker. It was once again Major Vivek, Havildar Digender along with the leading scouts Naik Chaman and Rifleman Jaivir who were part of the assault party to charge at the bunker. The bunker was barely 50 metres away but the route to it involved climbing with speed and momentum. The enemy had also reinforced the bunker. The sound of HMG fire coming from the bunker was deafening. There was no chance of survival in case of a hit. The enemy was now also engaging with his personal weapons as he was expecting the attack immediately.

We took some time to launch the attack as the ammunition for the LMG had to be fetched up. Another LMG of the second section was also deployed next to the bunker as there was little space and it too was in the open. Subedar

Sumer was made in charge of the makeshift Fire Base. The attack started with the Fire Base firing both the LMGs on the second bunker. Just before the assault by the two leading scouts along with the company commander and Havildar Digender commenced, a bullet struck Subedar Sumer Singh and he was martyred on the spot. The assault group rushed towards the bunker which was about 50 - 60 metres away. The three had barely moved 30 metres, when Rifleman Chaman received a bullet wound. Major Vivek, Havildar Digender and Rifleman Jaivir were now left with little option as the volume of fire had increased tremendously. They dashed forward and crawled towards the bunker. They could not have gone back and there was no way to extricate them either. They were gasping for breath too at nearly 15000 feet. The intensity and the sound of fire increased as they approached the bunker. Having regained some breath and in a '**do and die**' situation, they charged the bunker. '*It was now or never*' was the thought running through their minds. While they barged into the bunker with their weapons blazing, the fire base stopped firing and waited for the outcome. After some time, the fire inside the bunker stopped but it was not clear if the enemy had been killed, bunker captured or the worst possible thing had happened. No one was ready to accept or believe that the enemy had won.

There was a lull in the battle for some time. Everyone including me was glued to the radio set hoping to hear from Major Vivek that the second bunker had been successfully captured. There was some smoke that was now seen coming out of the bunker. The support group awaited orders to move forward. There was no radio communication from Major Vivek. Havildar Digender and

Rifleman Jaivir had been struck by bullets. Luckily, sense prevailed and the support group decided to rush forward to the bunker. As they reached there, they saw that Major Vivek was lying on the ground, Havildar Digender was bleeding profusely but still trying to put in a brave front. Rifleman Jaivir was also hit but had deployed the LMG towards the enemy. He was in deep pain but was also aware that the bunker had to be held at all cost till the arrival of reinforcements. Havildar Digender had told him to deploy the LMG immediately towards the enemy and to start engaging them. The support group tried to tie a first field dressing to Havildar Digender and evacuate him. Rifleman Jaivir continued to fire at the enemy bunker despite being hit. It was essential to evacuate both of them at the earliest. By then the third enemy bunker had also started engaging us. There was no commander - Major Vivek and Subedar Sumer were killed in the action; Havildar Digender was injured.

13 June 1999

The enemy meanwhile had also started preparing for the counter attack while 7 Platoon was still trying to evacuate the casualties and build up the strength to hold on to the bunker.

Lieutenant Tomar learnt of Major Vivek's martyrdom and rushed to that location to take control of the situation at hand. By the time he reached and understood the situation, the enemy launched a counter attack with about eight to 10 persons on the second bunker. At about 0200 hours on 13 June, the enemy section rushed the bunker and recaptured it. Rifleman Ashish kept on firing till the last moment before he was hit by a volley of bullets and was martyred. Later in this bunker gas masks were found. However, there was no evidence of any chemical weapons being used by the enemy. The body of Major Vivek did show signs of a chemical attack but the same was never corroborated. The back side of his body was absolutely black (like tanned leather) when it was finally evacuated.

I decided to move forward to take stock of the situation as Lieutenant Tomar was too young in service to handle and progress the attack. By the time I reached there, Lieutenant Tomar had the situation well under control. He had taken charge of the company and was my best bet as he was well aware of the success on **Area Flat**, the unsuccessful first attack on **Tololing Top** and now at this front, where Maj Vivek had just lost his life and the enemy had launched a successful counter attack.

I simultaneously tasked the first platoon of Bravo Company to move forward to further launch the attack for capture of **Tololing Top** from the direction of **Area Flat**. Lieutenant Tomar by then had taken control of the situation and was planning an attack on the second bunker to recapture it when I reached. I did not want to curb the initiative of the youngster but at the same time a coordinated bi-directional attack had to be launched.

The situation at around 0300 hours in the morning was far from satisfactory with barely two hours left for day light. Not much success had been achieved till now along either of the axes. D Company had established a foot hold on **Area Rock** while Subedar Dharamvir had captured **Area Flat**. Only one bunker had been captured at **Tololing Top** and consolidated. All odds seemed to be against us. Surely, after the first successful counter attack, the enemy must have been planning for attack on the first bunker too. But that had now been reinforced by Lieutenant Tomar.

Meanwhile on the South Western approach, where Delta Company was continuing its attack, Major Mohit, the Company Commander decided to launch a bi-directional attack on **Point 4590** and **Barbad Bunker** with one platoon each to increase the volume of attack against the enemy. The bayonet strength had to be increased to succeed or to make the enemy vacate and run away. The quantum of fire on all the bunkers also had to be increased. Accordingly, Mohit decided to press the attack on both the objectives. The MMG was deployed to provide the fire base along with the LMG. **Barbad Bunker** was also being engaged from **Area Flat** by Subedar Dharamvir's platoon. But, neither Delta Company nor Charlie Company Commander was aware of this. For them, **Barbad Bunker** was interfering with the attacks of both the companies. It is extremely difficult at night to identify the objectives and distances between them. Neither of the Company Commanders, Major Bajaj and even I was not aware how **Barbad Bunker** was interfering in the attacks of both the companies. It was difficult for Major Bajaj or for me to influence the battle from the Fire Bases. While both the platoons pressed the attack, the enemy held the defences strongly and put up a determined fight. Any progress by the sections of 10 and 12 Platoons met with a heavy resistance of automatic fire. Subedar Karan Singh did manage to reach up to the base of **Barbad Bunker** but could not make it to the top.

I was in constant touch with Major Bajaj to understand the progress of attack on the South Western front. It was evident that neither of the attacks had been successful. A and B Companies were still to get involved in battle. More than fifty percent of the troops had not got bloodied. I had to overwhelm the enemy with numbers, firepower and even psychologically. The only way was to launch a coordinated attack simultaneously and not allow the enemy the freedom to readjust his defences. The ferocity of the attack had to be increased exponentially. The volume of fire and the war cry of nearly 300 soldiers would surely impact the enemy. With barely two hours left for the first light, I decided to launch an all-out attack on all the features. Major Bajaj and I decided that one objective had to be given to each company. It was a double-edged decision as it would expose a large number of troops to enemy fire. I had to take a risk and hope like hell that we succeed as that was the only chance.

In the South Western direction, Alpha Company was tasked to take on **Point 4590** while Delta Company was to continue the attack on **Barbad Bunker**. Major Bajaj also moved up to control the battle on that axis.

In the South Eastern direction while Lieutenant Tomar was ready for the attack, Bravo Company was also launched from **Area Flat** to capture the **Top**. Thus, a bi-directional attack was launched on **Tololing Top** and **Point 4590**. While it took some time for Alpha Company under Major Acharya and Bravo Company under Lieutenant Rautela to move up, it was the attack by Charlie Company under Lieutenant Tomar which was the turning point of the battle. The attack was once again launched on the Second Bunker which had been recaptured by the enemy after deploying one MMG, two LMGs at the makeshift fire base to increase the volume of fire on it. Lieutenant Tomar with his section charged at the bunker. This time it was the entire section that was charging at the bunker and successfully captured it. In doing so they neutralised two enemy soldiers.

A near simultaneous attack was also launched by Bravo Company from **Area Flat**. The enemy now started vigorously engaging as it could see a lot of movement on either shoulder of **Tololing Top**. The last bunker on **Tololing Top** was also witnessing a similar build up. A major build up was also taking place along the South Western direction. Major Acharya and his Company were moving towards **Point 4590**. Since the company was fresh it had the josh to move at a faster pace to contact the enemy. It was probably the simultaneity of attack which resulted in the capture of **Tololing Top** and **Point 4590**. It was much later after we captured the entire objective that the sequence of enemy activities was understood by all of us. The inputs which I got from the Company Commanders, JCOs and soldiers after interaction with them helped me to put the jigsaw puzzle together to understand how we were able to capture the entire objective in the last two hours.

How the Battle Played Out

The mass scale movement of troops had instilled fear in the minds of the enemy sitting on top. While Delta Company was engaging **Barbad Bunker** with all its might, Alpha Company was charging towards **Point 4590**. The enemy resistance had started diminishing towards Delta Company. The quantum of fire had reduced. There were no illumination rounds that were being fired.

There was neither a group of men spraying bullets as was experienced by Major Mohit earlier. In the thick of battle, it is very difficult to read such a situation especially when you are under fire. I could not have expected young officers to do the same. But all this in hind sight are lessons learnt to be told to young officers who may face similar situations in future battles. The enemy had also not experienced such vehement attacks earlier which had been earlier beaten back by them successfully. But this was a battalion which was not ready to relent and kept pressing home the attacks one after the other despite casualties, despite a successful counter attack by the enemy.

The enemy had vacated **Barbad Bunker** and had moved towards **Tololing Top** by skirting around **Area Flat**. Some of the men from **Point 4590** had also vacated the post. All these Pakistani soldiers had probably regrouped to launch the counter attack to retake the bunker on **Tololing Top** which they had successfully accomplished. But, in doing so, the enemy had thinned out from **Barbad Bunker** and **Point 4590**. They felt that the most dominating height must be held at all cost else the defences will be turned. The enemy had been successful in taking **Tololing Top** but in the bargain had probably vacated **Barbad Bunker**. Not known to us, **Barbad Bunker** was constantly being engaged by firing from **Area Flat** and from the South Western side by Charlie Company and Delta Company respectively. Delta Company had to undertake a steep climb to reach **Barbad Bunker**. Even Subedar Dharamvir's platoon which was almost at the same height as **Barbad Bunker** was not aware that the post has been vacated as they were involved in guiding Bravo Company to launch the attack towards **Tololing Top**.

The battle procedure to clear the objective continued and it was by 0500 hours in the morning that Delta Company gave a report that **Barbad Bunker** had been captured. Meanwhile Alpha Company had closed in with the enemy at **Point 4590** by 0330 hours. Major Acharya had launched a bi-directional attack on **Point 4590**. There was not much resistance offered by **Point 4590.** The strength had depleted and the balance enemy were trying to hold on to the objective. The superiority in terms of manpower and volume of fire also suppressed them. The enemy on top had got trapped. They were neither able to escape nor were they giving a pitched battle. Probably Bravo Company was now moving towards **Tololing Top** on the same route which was the escape cum administrative route of the enemy towards **Tololing Top**. Alpha Company also continued to press home the attack and due to their momentum were able to capture two persons who were trying to escape. Two Pakistani dead bodies were also recovered. The emotions of the men are extremely difficult to control at such times. There was vengeance in the minds of the troops. The feeling of revenge, insult, hatred for Pakistanis was palpable. Major Acharya was also one such Company Commander who would motivate his men to the hilt, push them hard and be a part of them by leading from the front. Before he could act and pass orders to capture these Pakistanis, our men had shot them. At around 0515 hours **Point 4590** and **Barbad Bunker** had been captured by Alpha and Delta Companies respectively.

The battle in the other front along South Eastern direction was much tougher as the enemy was giving a pitched battle. Though the second bunker had been captured by Lieutenant Tomar and Bravo Company had also pressed in the attack along **Area Flat** towards **Tololing Top**; the Top still had one to two bunkers which were holding on. They were not only dominating the area but could see the movement of our troops and carry out adjustments. The freedom to move within the bunkers and carry out surveillance had to be curbed and the enemy had to be engaged constantly to achieve success. While Lieutenant Tomar was gathering the next section to attack the highest bunker, Bravo Company under Subedar Chandrabhan was tasked to attack the bunker closest to **Area Flat** where we had lost three jawans earlier. A makeshift fire base was prepared on either side. Ammunition was running low and it was essential to engage the enemy to allow movement and build-up of own troops. LMGs were augmented on the makeshift fire base as relatively higher quantity of ammunition was available.

I pushed both Bravo and Charlie boys to launch the attack as this was the critical moment in the battle. The top was visible, the tide appeared to be turning in our favour after nearly seven to eight hours of battle. The enemy was probably the most ill prepared now; they were running and the morale was dipping. No reinforcements had come to them the whole night. We needed to kill maximum number of enemy soldiers and capture the top. And, we needed to be extra careful not to lose any men now. The attack was launched by both the companies. **Top** had yet not fallen and was still holding on. I could not afford to be complacent nor overconfident. The attack started with Lieutenant Tomar engaging **Top** with maximum fire power from the second bunker which was the makeshift fire base. Simultaneously the attack was launched by Subedar Chandrabhan. At first light, we were closing in with the **Top** from two directions. The enemy was feeling the heat. The enemy could also see some of his men escaping towards **Hump**. From the enemy's point of view, it must have been a Catch 22 situation for the Commander seeing some of his men fighting while others having lost the battle were running. Lieutenant Tomar with his section was now charging on the Bunker at the **Top**. The exchange of fire was at its peak. The quantum of fire from the second bunker prevented the enemy from clear observation. Also, there was a steep climb and so the chances of aimed fire on Lieutenant Tomar's section were reduced. The enemy had started throwing mines and grenades from the top in the likely direction where the sections were attacking from. It was not known to us about scattering of the mines till such time we captured the **Top** and our men came under shelling. Tomar pressed on with the attack and so did Subedar Chandrabhan. The intensity of enemy retaliation started to reduce. It was becoming increasingly evident since I was at **Area Flat** monitoring the progress. Around 0445 hours, the enemy fire almost stopped.

At about 0430 hours, I got a call on the radio set from my Ghatak Platoon Commander, Lieutenant Kenguruse saying that he could observe a lot of movement towards **Hump** and further towards **Point 5140**. It was evident that the enemy was trying to escape. This is generally the enemy tactics that whenever they are surrounded, they try to escape rather than give a pitched battle. The call to engage them had to be taken. I did not know the exact location where the Ghataks were; were they in a position to engage, were they under cover, could they see the enemy approaching or could they see them running towards **Hump**? I took a call to engage the fleeing enemy. They would not have expected that someone will open fire from that location which in the minds of the enemy would have been a secure location. I immediately told him to start engaging the escaping enemy while taking due precautions. Both Tomar and Chandrabhan reported having captured the bunkers. Surprisingly, only one Pakistani body was recovered. There was a sizeable number of arms and ammunition. I immediately told both the attacking commanders to deploy their LMGs as the enemy was known for swift counter attacks though I also knew that they were now escaping. The enemy was escaping was not known to me alone, other Company Commanders would have also heard my conversation with Lieutenant Kenguruse. The fact that only one body was found made it evident that the Pakistanis had left everything and were running for their lives. By 0530 hours the entire ridge line had been captured with no further resistance offered by the Pakistanis.

I asked Major Bajaj about the progress of the attack from the South Western direction. He told me that Alpha and Delta Companies had captured their objectives and were carrying out consolidation of the area. At around 0530 hours I was sure that **Tololing Top** had been completely captured. I asked Major Bajaj to fetch up to the **Top** and meet me. After meeting him, I informed the Brigade Commander Brigadier Amar Aul and I told him, "**Sir, I am on Tololing Top. 2 Raj Rif has completed the task allotted to it.**" The entire Brigade HQs were monitoring the battle on the radio set throughout the night. Though he was aware that the task was over, he was awaiting a confirmation from me. He said, **"Well Done! Congratulations! Look after your casualties. Out."** [28]

As if waiting for this conversation and monitoring this frequency, the enemy's artillery bombardment started on **Tololing Ridge** as soon as the call was over. I could hear the shells flying left, right and centre. There was utter chaos. The men started running helter-skelter for cover behind the rock features. I immediately ordered on the radio set to disperse the companies. Those shells were accurate and the splinters were sharp, flying with very high velocity and were striking the rock features shattering them into smaller pieces which in turn were flying in the air. It was a horrific situation. The intensity of shelling was too high. I felt so helpless. I saw people running for cover. I saw dash, down, crawl and take cover what is taught in the training days in actual like never before. But the difficult part was yet to come. As people ran, I saw them stepping on the mines which the enemy has scattered before escaping. I can distinctly remember one soldier of Delta Company who stepped on the mine, blasting off the mine and thereafter only his shoe lace was hanging to his ankle. There was flesh all over, blood stains on the rock and the individual was crying in pain. We rushed towards him, shouting for the Nursing Assistant who promptly also ran with his medical satchel to give him first aid dressing and a morphine injection. At least three - four soldiers were hit by artillery splinters. Shell dressing and first field dressing were applied. But, the gush of blood was too heavy for even three to four shell dressings to stop the blood. Eventually the shirts of the individuals were torn and tightly tied to the wounds.

In order to de-clutter the area, I immediately ordered Delta Company and two platoons of Bravo Company to de-induct. They were told to carry the walking wounded with them. I immediately passed the message to the Brigade HQs for helicopters to evacuate the wounded as it would take seven to eight hours to carry the wounded to the road head if they were evacuated on foot. The chances of survival would be much more. The Brigade HQs also acted promptly and within half an hour we could hear the sound of a helicopter coming toward us. Meanwhile, we had identified and prepared a make shift helipad which could be constructed near **Area Flat**. Subedar Dharamvir was tasked to remove the big stones and boulders for the helicopter to land. The wounded were also shifted near the makeshift helipad. The intensity of the artillery shelling subsided after

---

[28] Harinder Baweja, A Soldier's Diary: Kargil, The Inside Story, 44. However, Ravindranath is not rejoicing. Neither is Thakur. Thakur has already lost men, including his beloved 2iC. Ravindranath is no better off. While standing on top of Tololing, he had seen eight of his men lying around him in just about a 10 - metre radius. He'd led his battalion to 'victory' but had gone back to his tent that night and wept. The loss of your men is always more overpowering than the pleasure of having performed your duty.

15 - 20 minutes. We were certain that the wounded would be air lifted soon. The sight of helicopters was a big relief. But as soon as the helicopter approached to land, the enemy shelling once again intensified. The enemy artillery was preventing the helicopter from landing at **Tololing**. The helicopter immediately turned back much to our dismay. Our hopes suddenly nosedived. We waited for another 30 minutes for the helicopters, but the moment they arrived the shelling started. I realised that we could not rely on helicopters and ordered the men to evacuate the critically wounded persons without further loss of time. A minimum of 8 - 10 persons were required to evacuate each casualty. There were only a few stretchers which were also in a bad state. Improvised stretchers were made by tying ground sheets, ropes, shirts, jackets on rifles. Some wounded were carried by the men on their back. It was very difficult to lug another soldier on your back but that was the only option. Six to eight men by rotation were carrying the wounded on their back. The pain and the agony suffered by the wounded cannot be imagined. Major Acharya was made in-charge of evacuation of all the casualties. Major Bajaj was sent down immediately to manage the casualties along with Major Rathore and Major Madan. Blankets and groundsheets were rushed to the top. Major Rathore played a major role in this exercise. Some of the men were critical and required immediate medical attention. Company Battle Field Nursing Assistants went along with the casualties and kept giving morphine injections enroute to reduce the pain. Lieutenant Rautela and Major Mohit were also ordered to move down and ensure fastest possible evacuation of casualties along with their companies. Ambulances were kept ready at the road head by Major Rathore. On reaching the road head, the casualties were rushed to the makeshift surgical centre and to 92 Base Hospital, if required in an ambulance or by a helicopter.

Having evacuated the casualties, it was time to evacuate the martyrs. We had lost one officer, two JCOs and seven other ranks. It was yet another difficult moment to see and supervise their evacuation. The stretchers and the blankets were being fetched up by the fighting porters under the supervision of Major B S Rathore. It was a solemn morning. Major Vivek Gupta, the Company Commander lay still in the stirring breeze. Adorned in the shroud of tricolour with his brazen wounds, the ornament of his martyrdom, a testimony to his vow "*I will get you Tololing Top*", he lay there with the other two JCOs and five brave hearts of my Battalion.

The emotions and sentiments amongst the troops were palpable. The troops call rang out to burn the enemy dead. While the officers were sitting on the rocky outcrop, one Alpha Company Havildar who had carried the image of Karni Mata spoke up. He stood bravely amongst all the smashed-up rock

V for Victory - at Tololing after its capture

and fallen enemy strewn around in the freezing cold and said, "*Nahi Sahab, yeh bhi Sainik hai. Hukum milne per ładne aye the. Dushman the jab tak laday. Ab yeh antkal ke liye so rahe hai. Apna Dharam bolta hai devangat ko samman dena chahiye. Inko inke riwaz ke anusar bidai detey hai. Nahi to hum mein aur dushman mein kya fark rah jayega.*" (No Sir, they were also soldiers. They fought for their country on orders from their superiors. Till the time they were enemies we fought with them. Now they are dead. According to our religion, the dead should be treated with respect. They should be buried as per their religion.) Major Acharya was the senior most officer present there. He nodded in acknowledgement to what his Havildar had said. The realisation of the statement slowly crept in with the morning chill. There was a true feeling of loss of our comrades while there was respect for the ones on the other side too who had sacrificed their lives for their nation. Grudgingly but in acknowledgement of our age-old ethics, we dug up graves on the cold lonely mountain top to lay to rest the fallen foe, who we respectfully as much as we could in the existing circumstances, bid a good after life. The paltan had maintained their izzat.[29]

---

[29] Zehra Nasim, From Kargil to the Coup, Events that Shook Pakistan, Pg 154. In fact, it took about 10 days for the FCNA headquarters to convey to the 10 Corps headquarters the news of the fall of the first post at Tololing. The Indians had completely evicted Pakistani troops from the post. Following the fall of this first post, the commander FCNA also decided to sack Lt Col Mansoor Ahmad Tariq CO of NLI 6. The CO, who had been all along been critical of Op KP, had decided to withdraw troops from the Tololing post after the Indians had launched an air, artillery, and land attack on the post. Lt. Col Saleem Mahmud Khan was appointed the new CO of NLI6.

CHAPTER NINE

A FORAY INTO MUSHKO VALLEY A NEW TASK IN THE OFFING

After the capture of **Tololing**, the battalion was pulled back for rest and refit. On 17 June, we were tasked to reconnoitre for an offensive in the Mushko valley aimed at reoccupying the heights dominating the administrative base established by the enemy. This was to be in conjunction with operations of 10 PARA SF which was to move in from the direction of Sando, supported by 3/3 GR. We were tasked to be reserve for this operation.

Accordingly, on 18 June, I went to HQ 79 Mountain Brigade, Mushko Valley, met the Brigade Staff and was instructed to be ready to progress operations through **Tingle Nala** with a view to secure **Point 4388**, North of which was the Pakistani Administrative Base that was supporting the Mushko intrusion. I gathered that 12 MAHAR and 28 RR were in contact with the enemy on either side of **Tingle Nala** and decided to go there to gather whatever information I could get to assist me in planning.

Battalion HQ of 12 MAHAR was located at the base of **Point 4895** and I met the CO, who told me that they were in touch with the enemy at **Point 4895**. They had scanty information about the valley leading to the area of the enemy administrative base. Their biggest challenge was administratively sustaining the troops in contact as everything had to be man-packed. As in the case of 18 GRENADIERS, it took one man to sustain another man in contact. The situation was tougher here because the track supported only one ton traffic. I had lunch with Lieutenant Colonel Ravi Swaminathan, my coursemate from NDA, the 2iC. Given the situation I realised that we need to reconnoitre before we can start planning any operation.

While going for recce in the morning, I asked the company commanders to practice their 51 mm mortar fire. We had to pull out 51 mm mortars from the fire support as we could not accurately place the fire. I had also tasked them to check out the fuse lot for the No 36 Hand grenades; we had observed that some lots were not as consistent as others. They did this in the Nala next to the Mughalpura unit location. Given the fluidity of the situation, we had not informed anyone, as was the case during rehearsals for the attack on **Tololing**. This caused a minor furore in the Divisional HQ that had just shifted in after being subjected to heavy artillery fire on their earlier location at Matayen. All was forgiven quickly by the time I reached Division HQ to report the outcome of my recce and my plan to send out probing patrols along **Tingle Nala** on the night of 20 June after having built up my O Group and recce parties at the junction of **Tingle Nala** and **Mushko Nala.**

Considering that the whole of Mushko Valley was serviced by a jeepable track, I asked Major Bajaj to start dumping one first-line scale of ammunition (approximately seven tons) near 12 MAHAR, which started on 19 June. Most of 19 June was spent selecting the recce parties and briefing them on the method I had planned to adopt. I guessed that the enemy, like in **Tololing Ridge**, would have occupied the ridge line with little ability to stop determined movement along the nala. Even on the ridge line, locations were far apart with substantial gaps in between; I reckoned small recce parties were safe from interference. So we planned to push in along the **Tingle Nala**, bound by bound, led by patrols and securing the flanks as we progressed along the nala as far as we could. I planned to maintain the troops ahead by fighting porters along the nala. I was expecting to meet an enemy position somewhere enroute eventually, and I left the planning to clear that for a later stage. I was not sure whether it would be my unit or someone else. Given this, I planned to induct the unit into Mushko Valley in small sub-units based on the progress along **Tingle Nala**.

On 20 June, with the broad plan finalised, I went to the Division HQ to brief, but I was asked to stand down. I learnt later that the 50 Parachute Brigade had been inducted into the Mushko Sector, which could be the reason.

The mood in the Division HQ was upbeat; 13 JAKRIF had captured **Point 5140**, and the enemy's domination on the track to **Bimbat Gali** was removed. Troops of 16 GRENADIERS at Bimbat Gali could breathe easy. Operations were being planned to capture the **'Thumbs Up' feature** on the Western slopes of **Point 5140**. Major General Mohinder Puri, GOC 8 Mountain Division expressed his desire to address my battalion.

I immediately returned to the battalion to organise a '*Sainik Sammelan*'. In his address, GOC praised the unit for its actions at the **Battle of Tololing** and said the battalion had shown the way for the rest of the Army. He informed us that he had placed us under 56 Mountain Brigade and expected us to perform as well in our future tasks. His provocative question of whether we could do it again met with thunderous and emphatic commitment. Once he departed, I ordered the ammunition to be brought back from Mushko.

In the evening, we had a pleasant surprise: Major Sandeep Kala, posted at Army HQ, joined us. Being posted in the Military Secretary's Branch, which controls officer cadre postings, he had managed his posting to the unit before it was due. This speaks volumes about the character of the officer. Some were trying to avoid this type of duty, and some were actively trying to get away by ruse, influence or feigning illness. I had not served with this officer; I had met him only once when he attended the Golden Jubilee of the Battle of Poonch at Gwalior. What I had gathered from my casual interaction with officers and troops during eight months of command was that of a 'hands-on' type, which troops so adore. His long service with troops, especially in active field operation assignments endowed him with a vast social capital I personally lacked. He was professionally accomplished and commanded instant respect from troops. He was to prove his worth in the ensuing operations. He took over as 2iC of the battalion from Major Bajaj, whom I retained as Adjutant, a job he was already performing. Personally, it was a great relief for me. Major Bajaj was under tremendous responsibility to ensure all the wartime paperwork of casualties and keep tabs on the moods and morale of the battalion, besides coordinating the build-up for operations. Now I had two competent senior officers to assist me, just as well as the next few days were going to be challenging.

The Press Conference

Around 2000 hours on 20 June, we were informed that there would be a press conference at Moghulpura (near the relocated HQ of 8 Mountain Division) the next day. I was expected to brief and field questions from the press on the capture of **Tololing**. I enquired about what I was to say from Colonel AS Chabbewal, Col GS, HQ 8 Mountain Division. He asked me to briefly cover the events leading to the capture chronologically. I made a brief covering the salient issues starting from the Firm Base provided by 18 GRENADIERS, the recce, preparation and subsequent fight by companies to wrest the feature from the enemy.

On 21 June morning, I was summoned to the HQs for briefing by Brigadier General Staff (BGS) 15 Corps, Brigadier Arun Chopra. I was handed over a written statement I was to make, and the line I was to take in responding to the questions. I went through the statement, and it was as bland as a military document can be, giving the chronology and units, ground features and dates. What caught my notice was that **Tololing** was not mentioned against my unit!! It was **Point 4590**. I immediately recognised that this **Point 4590** would soon be forgotten in a heap of Points that dot the mountains when history is written. **Tololing** had some character to it, something that would have better recall value. I pointed this out to the BGS. He was unrelenting in insisting I say **Point**

4590 without explaining why. I was highly upset, perturbed that my battalion was not being given the rightful honour to claim the capture of **Tololing**. I was frustrated and angry. In this mood, I met Colonel AS Chabbewal again, pleading my case and entreating him to influence the BGS. After listening to my emotional outpouring he asked a question. "*In whose hand is the mike?*" How absurd, I thought, he repeated it, and then I got it.

The party of press reporters had been flown in from Srinagar. After the initial remarks by Brigadier Chopra, the mike was handed over to me. I set aside the dictated note and briefed the press on the sequence of events, the preparations and hard fighting and ended with the statement that 2 RAJRIF had successfully captured **Tololing** by 0700 hours on 13 June. Questions followed, of which one was how tough the opposition was. I replied that the enemy was well-trained, motivated and fought bravely, but we were better than him and had carried the day. This was telecast and appeared in print. Though I had informed my wife of our losses and victory on 13 June itself, this was the first time the press had been officially briefed in the sector. After that, none of my family members moved away from the TV till the end of operations. After the press conference, the Brigadier was livid and hauled me over hot coals; why I mentioned **Tololing** and how I could speak so highly of the enemy. I stated that in exuberance, **Tololing** just slipped out and tried to reason with him regarding the rationale behind my praise for the enemy. How could I have told the press that the enemy was incompetent, cowardly and ill-prepared without giving rise to the question, I reasoned, why it took so long to remove such an incompetent enemy? I pointed out that we had out-fought the enemy and were thus professionally superior. I think Brigadier Chopra missed the point, he was more worried about **Tololing** having been mentioned. I did not understand why such an issue was being made until much later.

Looking back, this was a master stroke as far as the '*power of suggestion*' goes! 2 RAJRIF owes its **Battle Honour 'Tololing'** to Colonel A S Chabbewal.

I observed an interesting display of human nature during our interaction with the press. The location for the press briefing was about 100 metres from the prominent bridge on the National Highway. We had few staff officers from HQ 3 Mountain Division in attendance. As the press party started arriving, they were clicking away, capturing the terrain, the troops, etc. Suddenly, I found Col GS, 3 Mountain Division, spreading a map on the ground, looking through binoculars into the nearby hillside, animatedly telling something to his uninterested subordinate, gesticulating with his right hand. He was repeatedly pointing to different features and pointing to the map. Initially, I thought he was finding his own position through ground-to-map study! Being 100 metres from a well-marked bridge it should have been easy. We were miles behind the enemy and our troop deployment. His intent study of terrain did not make any sense to me. I was wondering what this man was up to. And then it clicked. He was giving an opportunity to the press to get good war photos!!! Unfortunately the press missed this shot.

Some press reporters visited the unit to interview officers and men who had taken part in the **Battle for Tololing**. Subsequently there was some excellent press about the Army's performance in general and that of the battalion in particular. They were seeking some photographs of live action. I confess that the thought of getting some photographs had only occurred to me once the Ministry of Defence photographer came along and was sent to **Tololing** along with Captain Tomar on 14 June. Major Acharya, Captain Vijayant Thapar, Captain Somnath Basu – the medic and some others had clicked photographs, they sent their films with the reporters. Unfortunately some of those interviewed would not live to see them in print, to the utter shock and disbelief of the reporters who interviewed them.

The press party happened to have a lone reporter from Karnataka, my home state. Mr Ravi Belagere, owner and chief editor of '**Hai Bangalore**' – a Kannada language tabloid, published an article on the capture of **Tololing**, in which I figured prominently. This made me an instant hit in my hometown. As someone from my village would put it '*You have become World Famous in our village!!*". In all the coverage, my father's interview was personally touching to me. He had said, '*Ravi is not my son; he is the son of the nation, and we are proud of him*'. That was such a relief, people back home not lamenting their fate or airing their fears: I am sure they were worried sick to the core and totally helpless. Such was the case of numerous families of troops of my unit who had written very encouraging letters. The running theme in these was asking us not to worry about their future and to concentrate on doing our duty to our motherland. Some even asked us to stay motivated, fight with all courage, and not turn our backs in defeat. One person had received a letter from his family that, to paraphrase, said, **'Should it come to receiving your dead body, we want to see the bullets in the chest and not at the back**'. It was an extremely charged atmosphere in the battalion; I believe it was so in the rest of the country.

Dark And Macabre Dialogues

Mood in the battalion was not all positive. It filtered to me, through my buddy, that Major Acharya had said that all of us would die and that the unit would put a garland on the Alpha Company group photo. He reported that the men had taken this statement very badly. Major Acharya always had a penchant for dramatic presentation; I asked him about this. While talking to his men in training, it transpired that he had chided them to get their act together. Or he had said '*We will have garlanded photos. With so many dead they might as well just garland the group photo of the Company*'. There was a lot of dark humour doing the round. Sometimes it did not evoke the mirth it was supposed to. It happens, especially when situations are uncertain and pregnant with danger. We tried to defuse this tension by asking officers to maintain close contact with the troops. There were all types of conversations reported.

In a particular instance, the topic turned to the benefits to those killed and wounded. The government had just announced an enhanced package of compensation and benefits to the families of those killed in action. Discussing this, someone laconically said, '*Murda Sipai Lakh Barabar, Zinda Sipai Khak Barabar*' (A Soldier 'Dead' is worth lakhs, A Soldier 'Alive' is worth nothing). Everyone around burst out laughing after that. It was jokingly used to nullify the fear of death, at least superficially. Macabre as it may sound by saying, "*Fikar mat kar, marne se tere family ko, tu jo de sakata hai, usse jiada paisa milega*" (Don't worry, if you die, your family will get more money than you can ever give them). This is how determined people in imminent danger of death rationalise to remain sane.

CHAPTER TEN

THE BATTLE OF THREE PIMPLES – THE ATTACK PLAN

21 June 1999 - The Orders Arrive

Events that eventually resulted in the battle of **Three Pimples** were set in motion on the evening of 21 June 99 when I was informed that the battalion was tasked to capture **Point 5100** and **Area Junction**. The preliminary planning was scheduled at 0900 hours on 22 June 1999 at HQ 56 Mountain Brigade.

22 June 1999 - The Brigade Plan

Major Sandeep Kala accompanied me to the meeting. He had arrived in the battalion on 20 June 1999 and had taken over the duties of the Battalion 2iC. His arrival had greatly boosted my morale and that of the troops who admired and liked him.

At HQ 56 Mountain Brigade, I was received by Major Patro, who had been recently posted as the Brigade Major in place of Major Mohanty, with whom we had coordinated the **Tololing Battle**. Major Patro was from 17 MADRAS (Cochin), the unit I was commissioned into where I spent my formative four and half years. I owe much to the officers and men of this great battalion with

JUNCTION - THREE PIMPLES RIDGE BETWEEN TIGER HILL - SANDO TO THE WEST AND TOLOLING TO THE EAST

a chequered history for teaching me a great deal about mountain warfare and handling troops in combat. I was happy to meet Major Patro but felt apprehensive as he had been catapulted directly into live action from the Staff Course at Wellington. The logic behind this change of principal staff amid a critical operation escaped me.

The Brigade Commander, Brigadier Amar Aul, Colonel Alok Deb, Direct Support Artillery Regiment Commander, Colonel Rana, CO 16 GRENADIERS, Colonel Patil, CO 1 NAGA and Major Jain, company commander of 16 GRENADIERS were already present. The situation was that 1 NAGA was attacking that night to capture a feature West of **Point 5140** that was still holding out. To maintain the momentum, 56 Mountain Brigade had been tasked to capture **Area Junction** and **Point 5100** - these landed on our laps.

The Terrain

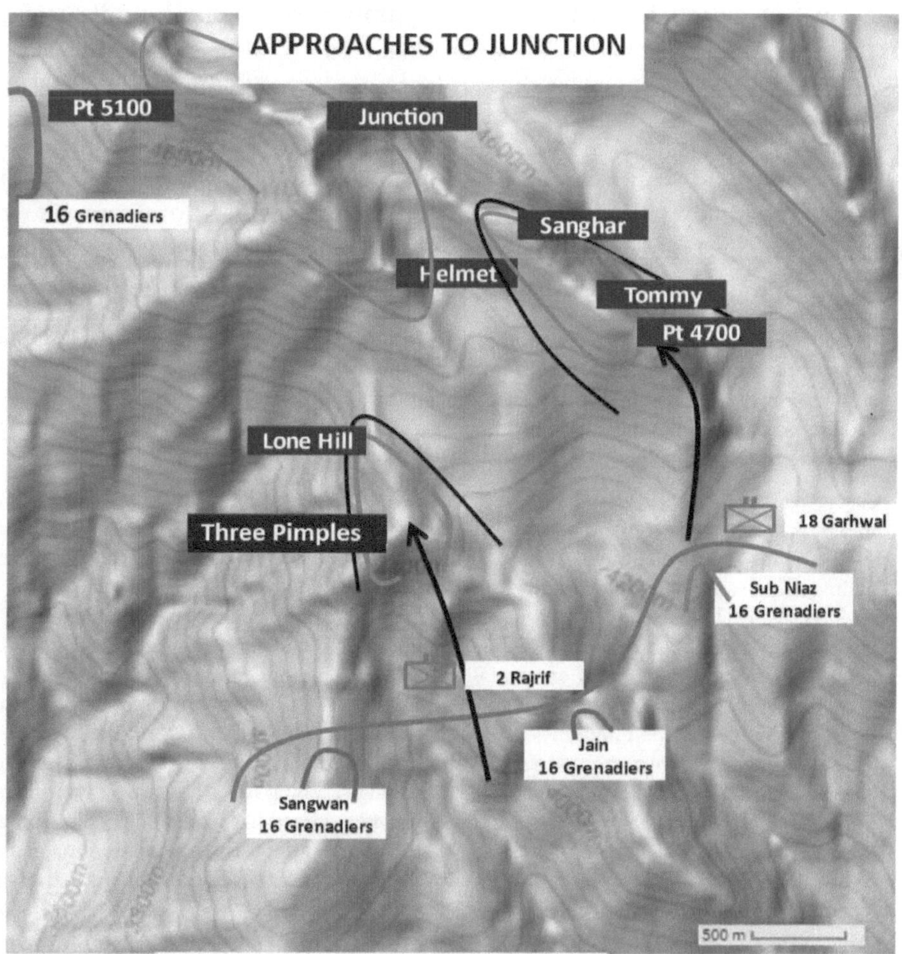

Area Junction is a dominating feature located approximately five km Southeast of Marpola. The LC runs along a ridgeline starting from the Eastern shoulder of Marpola, initially in the SE direction for about four km and then turns East, continuing to Bimbat Gali. A secondary ridge, however, continues in the South-Easterly direction on which lies **Point 5100** and **Area Junction**. Earlier attempts to clear **Point 5100** by troops of 1 NAGA, 8 SIKH and, subsequently, 16 GRENADIERS had resulted in a detachment of 16 GRENADIERS getting close to the enemy.

56 Mountain Brigade had been tasked to capture **Area Junction** along the ridge from Marpola towards Bimbat Gali. Possible approaches were from East along **Point 4700**, South from **Black Rock - Three Pimples** and West from **Point 5100.** Major Sangwan and Major Jain of 16 GRENADIERS held positions on the ridge lines emanating to the South and Southeast from **Three Pimples**, respectively. Both approaches were considered impossible for assault. Major Sangwan had reported a cliff face that was impossible to climb under enemy observation. Major Jain had said the terrain ahead was a sheer drop, hence not negotiable. My unit was tasked to recce to explore the possible approaches to **Area Junction.**[30]

From Area Junction emanate two ridgelines, one continuing along a South-Easterly direction up to **Point 4700**, which the enemy held. Another ridge forks South to a terrain feature named **Three Pimples**, also referred to as **Area Black Rock**, which was reported to be held by the enemy. From **Area Three Pimples**,[31] a

30 Harinder Baweja, A Soldier's Diary: Kargil, The Inside Story, Page 82.Three Pimples Ridge (so named because it consisted of three hillocks resembling pimples) emanates from Point 5100 on the Marpo La ridgeline to the west of Tololing nallah. Bifurcating into two ridgelines at another point called Junco, one ridge branches off towards Point 4700. The feature effectively dominates not just the national highway but Drass town and Sando Valley.

Capturing these points is vital. It will pave the way for attacks on Point 5100 and Point 5060, after which the area east of Sando nallah in the Drass sector will be free of enemy intrusion. Simultaneous attacks on Point 4700 and Three Pimple have been planned tonight, along with a feint attack from the South, towards Junco, by 16 Grenadiers

31 *Kargil Victory The Battle from Peak to Peak, Col SC Tyagi,* Speaking Tiger Publishing Pvt. Ltd., 2019,Page 100. Three Pimples Ridge would have to be captured in conjunction with Point 4700 in the first phase by one battalion each. In subsequent phases, it would be better to capture Point 5100 rather than Point 5060 to reach the LOC faster—the ultimate goal of all these attacks. The Three Pimple Ridge, which emanated from Point 5100 on the Marpo La Ridgeline, was to the west of Tololing Nala. It bifurcated into two ridgelines at Junction Point, one ridge going towards Point 4700 and the other ridge moving south towards Lone Hill and Three Pimples. Thus, any attempt to capture Point 4700 would have been interfered with by the enemy's presence at Three Pimples. Besides this, Three Pimples effectively dominated the National Highway, the Drass town and Sando valley. Capture of this area would pave the way for capturing Point 5100 and subsequently Point 5060, thus effectively isolating all intrusion east of Sando Nala in Drass. Three Pimples, alias Black Rock complex, itself consisted of Three

ridge continued South towards the Drass Valley. Along this ridge, approximately 1200 metres away, was the detachment of 16 GRENADIERS commanded by Major Sangwan, known as the **Sangwan Location**. Another ridge moved along the SE towards the Drass Valley, flanked to the East by Tololing Nala. Along this, about 1200 metres away, was a detachment of 16 GRENADIERS commanded by Major Jain known as the **Jain Location**. Between the features described above and Tololing Ridge was a massif roughly triangular with its apex at the junction of Tololing Nala and a nala flowing in from North of **Area Junction - Point 4700** ridgeline and based on the LC. This feature rose to a height of around 5200 metres and was reported to be held along the slopes leading to Tololing Nala. A 16 GRENADIERS detachment commanded by Subedar Khayani was in contact with this enemy position at approximately 1200 metres distance. The enemy at **Point 4700** dominated the Khayani location.

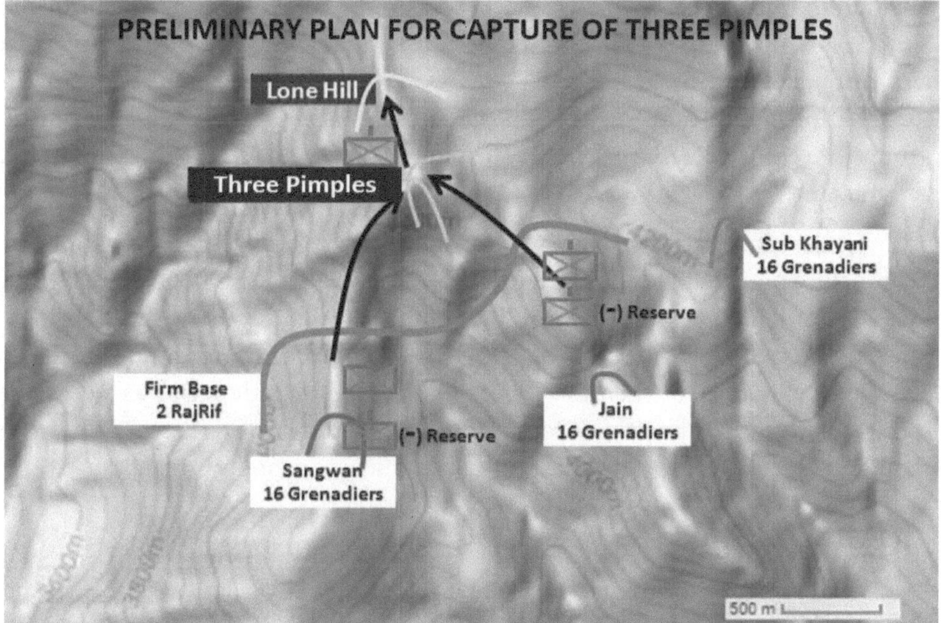

A Hard Nut

Enemy information was based on the scattered reports from forward troops clinging to their precarious perches. Helicopter recce had yielded only general terrain information. It was assessed that the enemy had shoulder-fired Surface

Pimples, Lone Hill, Knoll and Kajal and bifurcated into two spur lines along the southeast and southwest. Point 4700 Ridge consisted of Point 4700, Saddle, Tommy, Rocky, Sangar and Junction Point, which were a series of objectives to be recaptured from the enemy. The enemy had had the maximum amount of time to prepare a network of defences here, and had a well-coordinated set-up supported by effective artillery.

to Air Missiles (SAMs); hence, helicopters were prohibited from flying North of River Drass. We had already lost one MI 8 helicopter in this area, which had been shot down and crashed just East of the Jain Location. If there were any annotated air photos of the intended area of operation, they were not shared. Assessment of the enemy was depicted as red dots along the ridge lines on the Battle Map displayed in the Operations Room, with no specific strengths or weapon systems recorded anywhere.

Both approaches to **Three Pimples** along the Southern and South-Eastern directions were considered 'No Go' for assault. Along the Southern approach leading from the **Sangwan Location**, cliff faces were reported to be impossible to assault. On the SE approach, a steep fall North of the **Jain Location** had prevented further advance along this approach. It was assessed that though **Three Pimples** was weakly held, it was not easily assaultable, hence not suitable for building up troops for progressing operations on **Area Junction** from the South. At that juncture, it appeared that the quickest approach to **Area Junction** was through **Point 5100**, though I was wondering how we were to maintain surprise in the build-up for this assault. Major Patro tried to indicate on the ground **Area Three Pimples** (they called it Black Rock); I understood the general area.

Under these circumstances, I recommended that we carry out further recce before proceeding with a preliminary attack plan. Using 16 GRENADIERS locations of Jain, Sangwan and South of Point 5100 as recce bases was the best option. The next day, I tied up with CO 16 GRENADIERS for guides to these areas and left Drass for the unit. Before leaving the Brigade HQ, I asked Major Bajaj to set up the operations room and have a sketch of the area ready. The Battalion Orders Group was to assemble for my orders on my arrival.

The Ground Situation

By my assessment, troops had gone as far forward as cover was available, and it was possible to sustain them administratively. At both locations, contact with the enemy was not close; one could say the enemy was not fixed. The first task for us was to fix the enemy properly before attacking.

I tasked Major Mohit with Lieutenant Tomar to build up a platoon strength at the Sangwan location. At first light, they were to start closing in towards **Three Pimples** till they drew effective fire. Then they were to firm in at that location. A platoon moved at first light on 23 June to the **Jain location** to establish a firm base on the feature that Lieutenant Rautela had been tasked to secure and similarly evolve an attack plan along the South-Eastern approach.

Resolving the Terrain Friction

Based on a map study and information available at HQ 56 Mountain Brigade, we decided to explore the approaches from the South through **Three Pimples**. Since the shortest route to **Area Junction** was from **Point 5100**, and the fact that a platoon of 8 SIKH was in contact there, induced me to explore this option too. Accordingly, three patrols were planned to assess the feasibility of launching operations along three approaches.

Major Acharya was tasked to reconnoitre the assaultability of **Point 5100** from the firm base held by 8 SIKH. Major Mohit Saxena and Lieutenant Praveen Tomar were tasked to assess the approach leading from the **Sangwan Location** along the Southern approach to **Three Pimples**. With the information available, I was not sure of launching an attack along this approach; I needed a clearer view of the objective and more information about the going.

I decided to go with Lieutenant Rautela and Lieutenant Kenguruse to the **Jain Location**. This being the open flank, this would be the decisive flank; hence, I decided to invest in this approach. I discussed this broad plan with Brigadier Amar Aul. Since no artillery Battery Commander was available to accompany me, Colonel Alok Deb, CO of 192 Field Regiment, volunteered to accompany me to the **Jain Location** on 22 June. He was a fine professional and a senior, and I was very happy in anticipation of sound advice.

I decided to secure the feature to the North, which by all indications, appeared to be unoccupied. I tasked the Ghatak Team under the command of Lieutenant Rautela to secure it by first light on 23 June. I advised him to take the route along the cutting between the **Jain Location** and this feature and tied up with Major Jain for covering their movement with fire from his location.

I tasked Lieutenant Kenguruse to take out a recce patrol to **Area Green Patch** to assess the going and enemy enroute through the Tololing Nala at night; he was to take GPS equipment and mark his location every half an hour.

On the drive back to the battalion, I kept going over the situation that looked hopeless from all angles. I had no clue about the situation at **Point 5100**. Eventually, if we were to progress operations through this feature to **Area Junction**, it had to be by fresh troops badly wanting to prove their mettle. At that juncture, Alpha Company under Major Acharya fitted the bill perfectly. Hence, I decided to tentatively task A Company to capture **Point 5100**.

With the capture of Tololing Ridge, the Eastern flank was secured. I sensed a gap between the **Jain** and **Khayani locations** that could be exploited to inject troops to contact **Area Junction** and **Three Pimples** from the East. I

NAGA had been conducting its attack on the **'Thumbs Up'** feature, exploiting the ridge rising from the **Khayani Location** without any interference, which gave me hope that this could succeed. If we were to infiltrate to **Area Junction** eventually, it had to be done by Bravo Company. Since Major Madan, the Company Commander, had yet to return, I decided to recce from this approach myself from the **Jain Location**.

If **Three Pimples** was assessed to be lightly held, it was difficult to comprehend why we could not close on to the **Ledge** that rose to **Three Pimples**. I was determined to give it a hard try by pushing as close as possible to **Three Pimples** from **the Sangwan Location**; I considered Major Mohit Saxena, the man for the job. By the time I reached the unit, a recce plan had started taking shape in my mind.

The Recce Plan

The recce would aim to assess the enemy opposition on **Point 5100** and **Three Pimples** and assess the assaultability of these features from as close as possible, closing in with the enemy defences till their effective fire prevented the patrols from drawing any closer. Also, if there were any intervening features along the approaches leading from own positions of **Jain, Sangwan** and location South of **Point 5100** and not held by the enemy, they had to be secured through physical occupation. I had supreme confidence in my troops' ability to assess enemy fire's effectiveness. In preparation for counter-insurgency operations, we had invested much time in acquiring this skill. Many in the unit could guess accurately the distance and direction by the sound of the firing and sharp report of a bullet.

The composition of the three recce patrols was as follows: -

Patrol 1. Led by Major Acharya, it was tasked to evolve a company plan of attack on **Point 5100** from the existing Firm Base to the South.

Patrol 2. Under Major Mohit Saxena to evolve a company plan for establishing a firm base and the subsequent attack on **Three Pimples** from the South.

Patrol 3. I decided to lead this patrol myself. I intended to select a suitable firm base for the attack on **Three Pimples** from SE, evolve an attack plan along this approach and assess the feasibility of infiltrating troops to **Area Junction** from East.

I shared my recce plan with the Brigade Commander, who approved it. I needed an artillery battery commander for fire support advice; Colonel Alok Deb, CO 192 Field Regiment, would accompany me for the recce. In practice, the artillery advisor's role is more comprehensive than advice on the use of artillery fire or the execution of a fire plan. He is also a close confidant of the infantry commander, his sounding board with whom you can share your doubts and one who not only assists in evolving the fire plan but also takes up the responsibility for its execution. It was a great morale booster for me that Colonel Deb would be available to us.

23 June 1999 – The Recce

At around 0600 hours on 23 June 1999, we picked up our guides from the Brigade HQ location and started our trek to **Jain Location**. We moved along a nala that originated from the South side of **Three Pimples** and emptied into Drass Valley. It was probably under enemy observation. By about 0900 hours, we reached a point where one started climbing to **Jain Location**. The valley, which was very narrow with steep sides, opened up a bit, and the sides eased into stiff, climbable slopes.

Just as we started our climb, we heard whistling from the area ahead along the nala and some rustling in the grass ahead. We could also make out some swift movement amongst bushes about 150 to 200 metres ahead along the valley on the slightly raised ground. We could see nothing beyond it.

Having heard of patrols being ambushed by the intruders, I was extremely edgy. Taking position behind some cover, I looked back to see the rest of my party within my visible range following suit. Our guide from 16 GRENADIERS, who was in the lead, had his head down and trudging along, oblivious to the world except his labours. I was frantically trying to gain his attention. Seeing us all deployed in tactical positions, he turned and started walking towards us, refusing to take cover as I was frantically signalling him to do! In the meantime, the movement on the high ground ahead ceased. I was waiting for the sharp report of gunfire anytime now. Nothing happened, and this NCO reached me and asked me, '*Kya Hogaya Saab*?' (What happened, Sir?) I told him there was movement on the high ground, which could be an ambush. With a quizzical, he replied, "*Saab who tho yahan ki gilheri hai*" (They are squirrels of this place).

This was my first introduction to the furtive Himalayan Marmots, and it was a great relief! It left me not a little shaken and somewhat embarrassed. I thought I could have made a better impression on the battle-hardened GRENADIERS NCO. Under threat, a human being is highly alert to the slightest whiff of danger.

I reached the **Jain Location** by about 0900 hours. Major Jain quickly orientated us to the ground and showed us the enemy's location. Only an

MMG and section worth was deployed facing the enemy; the rest of the platoon minus was tactically located on the reverse slope. The enemy's presence with some automatic fire was reported in the **Three Pimples** area. So far, the GRENADIERS had not suffered any casualties due to enemy fire in this location. **Three Pimples** location was partially screened by another dominating feature, approximately 500 - 600 metres to the North- Northwest of the Jain location. Major Jain informed us that they could not secure it because the North face of **Jain Location** was a steep rock fall. However, no enemy movement was reported from that feature.

Above this feature, the **Point 4700** ridge line ran to the left towards **Area Junction**. It had four distinct features, including **Point 4700.** Through our binoculars, we could outline the wall-like sangars on these features; however, no movement could be seen. Colonel Alok Deb and I quickly named them **Tommy**, **Rocky** and **Sanghar**. I accept the responsibility for these unimaginative names for features to be involved in a major battle later. No match to Tiger Hill in name!!

The Southern side of the **Point 4700 – Tommy - Rocky – Sanghar** ridgeline had what appeared to be a gradual, dry and open slope leading up to the crest. There was a **Green Patch** on this slope to the West of Sanghar, more in line with the **Area Junction** that was visible. Even after detailed viewing through binoculars, one could not assess the firmness of the ground, a factor that affects the speed of movement.

Binocular study of **Area Junction** also revealed more sangars but on a larger scale. I did not nurse great hope from Major Acharya's patrol. Colonel Alok Deb agreed that the enemy held **Point 4700** ridge in at least four places and could interfere with any operations towards **Three Pimples**, especially if we were called upon to infiltrate.

Three Pimples was made of jagged rock faces, though I could not see any route to the top; that was intimidating. I kept asking myself, *'How am I to capture this'*. With the information available, I was not sure of launching an attack along this approach; I needed a clearer view of the **Three Pimples** than what the Jain location could offer. I also needed more information about the going in areas leading up to **Green Patch** to assess our infiltration ability. One could observe **Three Pimples** easing into a longish ledge of approximately 200 metres towards the **Sangwan Location**, suddenly dropping by about 100 metres and an open ridge line running from its base to the **Sangwan location**, barring a few clusters of rocks halfway. Here, I was hoping that **Ledge** was not held and that Mohit would figure out how to get on to the **Ledge**.

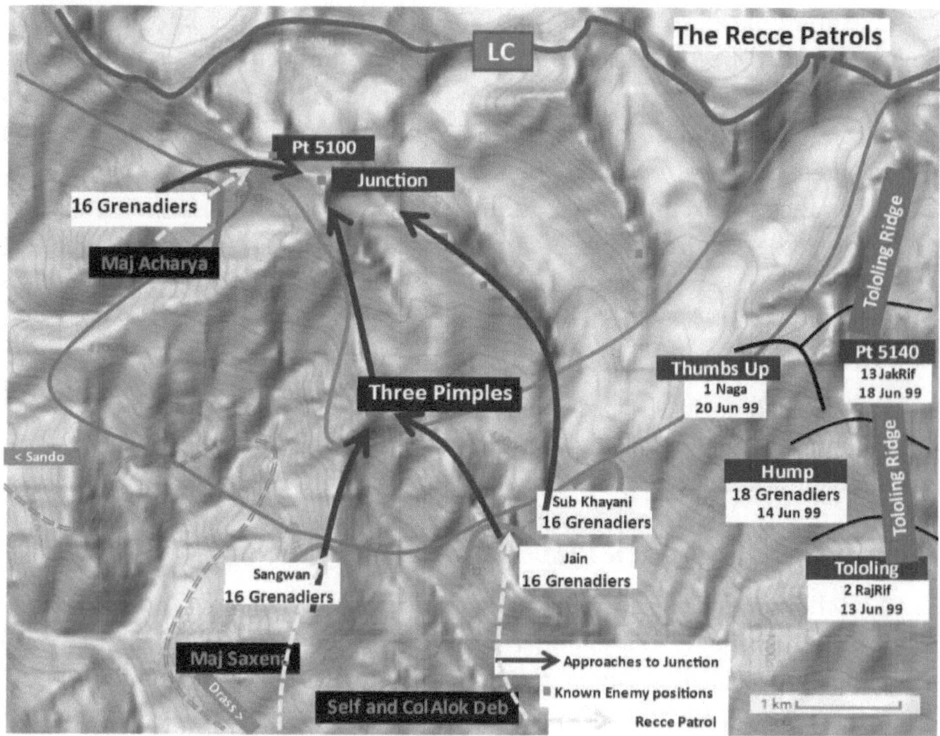

The **Green Patch** indicated to me the presence of moisture and firm ground. The soil texture gave me hope that the going between **Point 4700** ridge and **Three Pimples** was easy; I was hopeful that attacking **Three Pimples** from the North could be easier. I needed a patrol to infiltrate the **Area Green Patch** to assess the going up to that place and to bring back information on the assaultability of **Three Pimples** from North. Hence, all patrols had to be planned for this night.

Major Jain had consistently and forcefully argued that getting down from the North face of **Jain Location** was impossible. I could not induce him to occupy the dominating feature about 500 - 600 metres to the North and apparently unoccupied. So, we had to occupy the feature ourselves. I could see that the dominating feature in front had a broken rock surface facing us, which became a single rock face as it moved West and down the slope. The North face of Jain and the South face of that feature formed a gorge about 100 to 150 metres wide, the bottom of which was just North of the place the marmots had ambushed me in the morning. It was possible to climb this gorge and reach the feature in front. This move would be unobserved by **Three Pimples** if done at night, and the **Jain location** could cover their movement with fire should the enemy interfere from the apparently unoccupied feature.

Mohit's patrol to the **Sangwan Location** had gathered information that enemy fire had been observed from **Three Pimples**, but only a little enemy movement had been reported. Nobody in the **Sangwan Location** had been fatally injured by this fire though, putting a question mark on the location of the enemy and his strength. A massive rock face about 1000 metres to the North on the approach to **Three Pimples** was reported, and to assault, its closer recce would be required. This, I surmised, was the end of the **Ledge** I could see from **Jain**. I checked with Mohit for progress along the Southern Approach; he reported they had closed in towards a rock face on top of which they could see some sangars. I prodded him to try to figure out a route to the top.

I decided to task Lieutenant Rautela, Bravo Company and Lieutenant Kenguruse of the Ghatak Platoon to lead small recce parties to provide this additional information.

Firming up the Attack Plan

By 1300 hours on 23 June 1999, I was back in the Brigade HQ to discuss my plan with the Brigade Commander. I proposed that we establish a closer Firm Base for **Three Pimples**, which in military parlance is called 'Fixing the Axis', to deny the enemy the luxury of readjusting his defences at will. Having been thus collared from many directions, the enemy has to wait for the attack to manifest before he can readjust. It is like putting him on notice and allowing him to cook in the pressure of imminent attack. We planned to move as forward as possible towards enemy locations along both approaches to achieve this. I also shared my assessment of the difficulty in the assault on **Three Pimples** and my apprehension that it may degenerate into a series of long drawn-out minor actions capturing a rock face at a time. This type of operation is painstakingly slow and heavy in casualties; hence, it should be avoided wherever possible.

Such opinions, however, when aired, carry an inherent risk of one's superiors misreading it as trying to wriggle out of tough situations. No superior likes to be told that the task he has given cannot be executed; he is only interested in how it will be completed, and the objective achieved.

I also discussed my observations about the terrain to the North of **Three Pimples**. I shared my hope that the Northern direction may be an easier approach than the currently selected approaches, therefore, the need for more recce. I also highlighted the difficulty in building up for the attack on **Point 5100** and the problem of movement around **Area Junction**. I suggested that the patrol of Major Acharya be withdrawn to enable me to concentrate on the capture of **Three Pimples**.

Brigadier Amar Aul pondered for some time and then asked me to show the features on the ground. We came out of the Operations Room bunker. We could see the **Three Pimples** complex, **Ledge** and a portion of the ridge line leading to **Sangwan Location**, laid out like a real-life terrain model! The top of **Area Junction**, barely distinguishable as a separate feature, looked more like an extension of **Three Pimples**; **Jain** and **Point 4700** ridge lines were not visible. He then gave the go-ahead for establishing a closer Firm Base for the attack on **Three Pimples** along the Southern and SE approach and permitted me to pull back Major Acharya.

Certain concurrent actions could not wait. So, I instructed Major Bajaj to pull back Major Acharya's party to the battalion location at Drass and start dumping ammunition for the Fire Bases likely to come up at the **Sangwan** and **Jain locations.** Once these locations were secured, the Fire Base parties were to be ready to occupy them the next day, 24 June 1999.

The fear of my battalion coming under artillery fire in its current location had constantly troubled me. I ordered some buildings requisitioned in Drass to get the men out of the canvas. Meanwhile, Lieutenant Kenguruse and Lieutenant Rautela had fetched up at the Brigade HQ, and I drove with them to their drop-off point, from where we trekked up to **Jain Location**, arriving there by 1700 hours.

Lieutenant Rautela was tasked to recce **Kajal,** and in case the enemy did not hold it, he was to secure it by 0900 hours on 24 June 1999. The GRENADIERS were to cover his movement with fire from **the Jain Location**. Lieutenant Kenguruse was to establish the distance and time to **Area Green Patch** from the **Jain Location** and to assess if the enemy held any feature on this route. He aimed to skirt around **Kajal** along Tololing Nala and move West to **Area Green Patch**. He had GPS equipment on which I tasked him to record a reading every 30 minutes.

Having tied up the loose ends, I returned to the battalion HQ by 2000 hours, which had shifted to Drass. It was a pleasant surprise that Major Bajaj had commandeered Hotel Hill View and its Reception Area was converted into a makeshift Battalion Operations Room, duly sandbagged against artillery rounds. All the troops and ad hoc cookhouse were inside the building, safe from splinters. Even a direct hit would have little effect as the hotel was a double-storey building, and we were leaving the first floor unoccupied. The telephone exchange had also been set up, and we were connected to the command chain.

Major Acharya and Major Mohit Saxena too had returned. On debriefing them, it became clear that an attack on **Point 5100** from 8 Sikh Firm Base was highly risky. The complete bowl leading up to 8 Sikh Firm Base was under observation from multiple enemy locations of **Point 5353**, **Point 5280** and **Tiger Hill**. We swiftly ruled out this option.

24 June 1999

The next day, 25th June, was an important day for me - Anitha's birthday! I was keenly aware that a worried Anitha would be anxiously awaiting a call. With the situation so dynamic, I was unsure where I would be tomorrow and whether I would have access to a satellite phone on the 25th. So, I rang her up a day in advance to wish her. Before her quizzing could commence, I explained to her that I may not have access to a satellite phone on the morrow. I am not sure if she had grasped that we were on the verge of going on an operation, but I bid her bye on the pretext that there were others in the queue for making calls.

For a moment, I mused how difficult it would be for the families and how anxious they would be. The national news channels were now abuzz with news from the war front, reporters from across the country were milling around all along the Leh Highway, and Kargil was incessantly being played out on all TV channels. The Highway at Drass was open to civil traffic, and most activities were being carried on despite enemy firing to cut off the movement through sheer guts of the drivers of these vehicles, both military and civil.

I briefed Major Acharya and Major Mohit, who had returned after their ground recce, on the broad skeleton of the plan taking shape in my mind, which would crystallise only once I had inputs from Rautela and Kenguruse. The essentials were as follows: -

a) Capture **Area Three Pimples** by first light of 27 June 1999 (72 hours from now).

b) **Firm Bases** to be secured along the Southern and SE approaches by 1000 hours today, 24 June 1999, by a platoon each from Charlie and Bravo companies, respectively.

c) **Fire Bases** to be established by first light on 26 June 1999.

d) Alpha Company (Acharya) to attack along the SE approach with Bravo Company as Reserve.

e) Delta Company (Mohit) to attack along the Southern approach with Charlie Company as reserve.

f) Orders for the capture of other objectives to be given later as per the operation's progress.

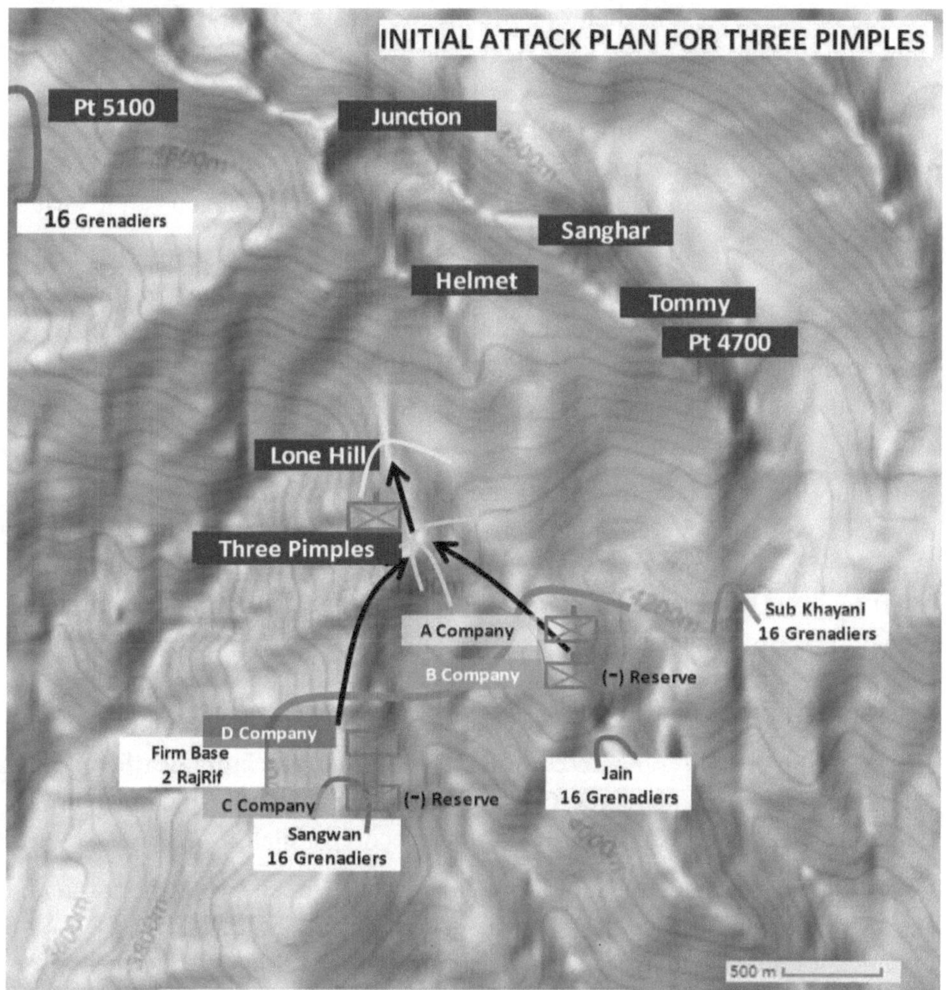

I was forced to incorporate some changes into my plan. Originally, Bravo Company under Major Madan was to lead the attack along the SE approach, but since its company commander had yet to report back from his trip to the hospital, I was compelled to task Alpha Company. Like in Tololing, the SE approach was going to be the decisive flank. I kept both the unbloodied Alpha and Bravo Companies along this approach. Besides being relatively fresh, they desired to prove themselves after the stellar performance of Charlie and Delta companies in the Tololing Battle.

From what I had seen of the Southern approach from the **Jain Location**, I did not have much hope along that approach; I reckoned it would be a stalemate. Yet it is not correct to share your apprehensions or feelings so freely with the men entrusted with the task for three reasons. If troops apprehend that you see no hope of success in their operations, they will not give it their best. Two, who knows what can happen when troops give their best: Delta and Charlie Companies, which had seen fierce action at Tololing, were highly motivated; anything was possible. Third, without actually capturing any feature, a fierce attack can tie down the enemy and ease the task of others attacking elsewhere. It is, therefore, best to keep these thoughts to oneself and do all you can to ensure the troops' success.

Therefore, I tasked Major Mohit to coordinate securing the Firm Base along the Southern approach and entrusted him with the responsibility of developing a plan for an attack on this approach. Charlie Company was down to one officer and 36 Other Ranks, so I expected this would, at best, be a holding attack.

I decided to place myself on the SE approach because I expected it to be a decisive flank where results were a possibility and, second because Bravo Company had no Company Commander. Should it come to employing them as reserves, I was most suited to command them. I decided to relocate myself to the **Jain Location** the next day.

The Confirmatory Recce

After briefing the two company commanders, I left for the **Jain Location**, asking Major Bajaj to push a platoon of Bravo Company in our trail which I would use to establish the Firm Base once Rautela had secured **Kajal.**

When I reached the **Jain Location**, it was already 0900 hours, and I expected Lieutenant Rautela to have secured **Kajal**. To my dismay, I found Lieutenant Rautela had just started the climb along the ridge line. I tasked Major Acharya to coordinate the fire support and cover the movement of Rautela's patrol to **Kajal.** We all waited anxiously as Rautela and his party moved from rock to rock, teams covering each other, hitting a dead end here, finding a route there. It was agonising; I kept scanning the feature for any sign of the enemy; one did not detect any, but the apprehension of the danger these men were facing was gnawing away at me. Finally, Rautela secured the feature by about 1100 hours. It was a great relief.

Lieutenant Kenguruse was waiting for me with his report. His patrol, having started after last light, had, with difficulty, climbed down to Tololing Nala and moved up along the Nala. He reported a wide-open area spreading to the West. Making use of moonlight, they had gone upto **Area Green Patch**, which was reached with the help of handheld GPS. The distance they had traversed was about 1600 metres on the way out and about 1400 metres on the

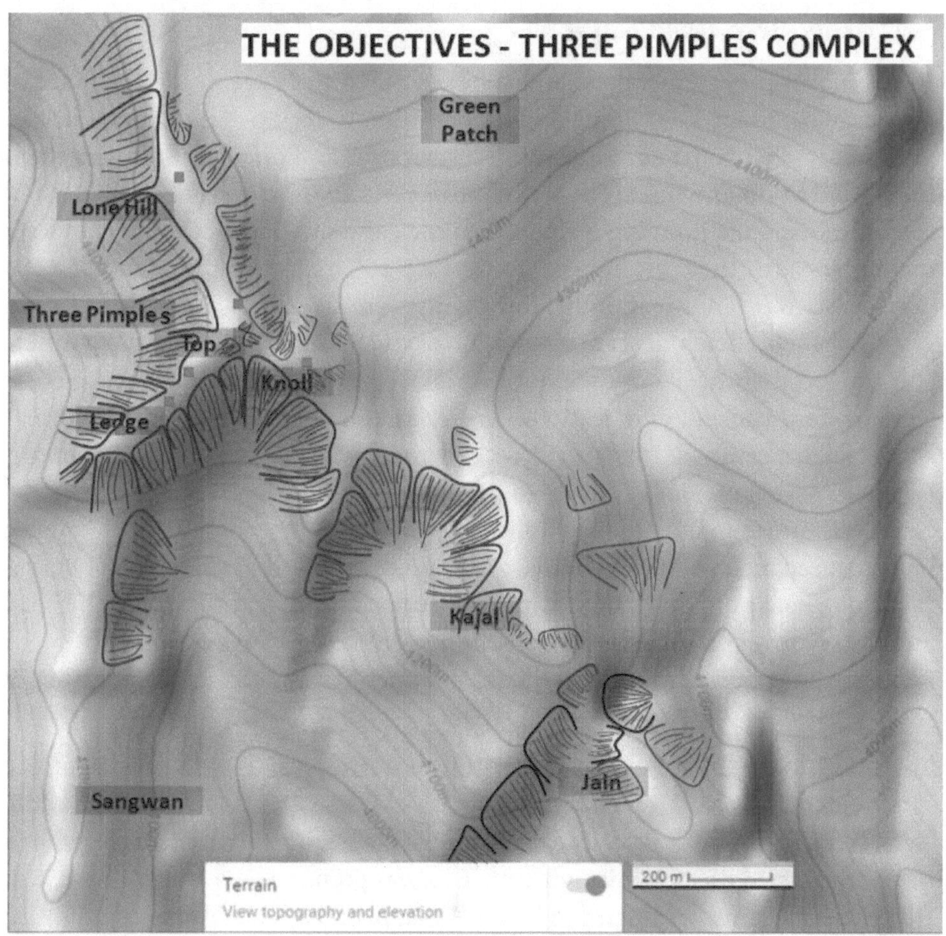

route in. The ground was reportedly hard and easy to walk on; the nala had a narrow stream of flowing water. No enemy was encountered anywhere along the route. The ridgeline of **Point 4700** was visible to the North at approximately 500 metres, as per the Laser Range Finder. There was another ridge line to the South at an approximate distance of 500 metres with gradual slopes leading to the ridgeline. The patrol had to move slowly to avoid being detected.

I was excited to gather that slopes North of **Three Pimples** were gradual; I was anticipating far easier approaches than the ones we were currently exploring. We heard firing at a distance to our West. We soon received information that Major Mohit had moved up along the ridgeline to occupy an area of rocky outcrops approximately halfway to the base of **Ledge**. He had immediately drawn enemy fire from the **Ledge**, which confirmed that the enemy was already there. I asked him to hold on to the feature and study the **Ledge** feature to see how it could be assaulted.

Securing Firm Base Kajal

In the meantime, Lieutenant Rautela had reached the edge of the rock face of the gorge by about 1200 hours and was now about to move into open, broken ground between **Kajal** and **Jain**. We were nervous and on edge expecting them to be fired upon any time. The patrol broke into three groups of two each and started moving up, jumping from rock to rock and moving tactically. They kept inching towards the crest line, approximately 400 metres from the saddle area. Our hearts were in our mouths, our palms were sweating, and our eyes were glued to the binoculars, scanning **Kajal** for movement. The machine gunners had trained their sight on the crest line ahead, and 84 mm Rocket Launchers were loaded, cocked, and ready to fire at a moment's notice. Hope and fear soared alternatively as the patrol inched their way up. Around 1400 hours, Lieutenant Rautela moved slowly to the crest line and soon sent a message that **Kajal** was unoccupied. A sigh of relief and elation ran through us as though we had captured an objective; two hours had just passed and had been most nerve-racking. A sense of hope that the feature be unoccupied, fear that it may be held, and the enemy is holding his fire and helplessness with the possibility of being unable to help the patrol should the enemy open up was all coming together. It was a tense day.

With Lieutenant Rautela successfully securing **Kajal**, we had to reinforce him quickly. I tasked Lieutenant Kenguruse to find a quick route to the **Saddle Area** through the rock face. The feature we have been referring to as **Kajal** had just been named as such this moment. This was going to be our Firm Base, and we needed to name it. I turned to Major Acharya and asked, "*Archy, what is your bitch's name?*" Major Acharya had a Bull Dog that looked mean but was entirely harmless. Acharya had the habit of taking it for a walk without a leash. It would rush towards all and sundry on the road in a friendly manner. But most of those who were approached were petrified and either ran for their lives or let out a cry. In our peace station at Gwalior, there had been many complaints against Major Acharya and his bulldog. My efforts to encourage him to leash it had met with partial success. Anyway, both Archy and his bitch were infamous in the station. "**Kajal**" replied Major Acharya. I named the feature **Kajal**. Would **Kajal** help us solve the challenges we were facing? We were about to find out.

Lieutenant Kenguruse, an Angami Naga, a man of the mountains, had spied out a route to reach the **Saddle Area**. He led us, and we followed. Jumping here, moving along a narrow rock ledge and sliding down a rock face at places, we reached the Saddle Area. Major Jain's reaction was one of disbelief; he commented that he never thought one could get down the steep rock face. We made our way as quickly as possible to Lieutenant Rautela, who was perched up on a rock face about 10 to 12 feet high. He quickly briefed me there was no enemy on this feature. Major Acharya and I slowly moved up the rocks to a vantage point with some assistance from others. I did not want my party - five officers and six other ranks including my radio operator humping the set with antennae - to be spotted by the enemy. We would present a plum target for a single mortar round!

I checked with Major Mohit for progress along the Southern Approach. He reported they had closed in towards a rock face on top of which they could see some sangars; I prodded him to figure out a route to the top.

As I peeped over the rocks, the area came into view for the first time. What struck me was the gentleness of ground features to the North of **Three Pimples**, which was easy to traverse. Kenguruse, too, had reported firm ground, mainly following the stream bed and around up to **Area Green Patch**. This contrasted with Lieutenant Rautela's torrid time in reaching **Kajal** and the tough-going Major Mohit was facing as he approached **Three Pimples** from the South.

The View from Kajal

North-Northwest of **Three Pimples** ran a ridgeline towards **Junction**. South of Area **Junction** was a prominent rock head, which we named **Helmet**. Further East of **Junction** was **Sanghar**, **Rocky**, **Tommy**, **Point 4700** ridge line approximately 1500-2000 metres North of **Kajal**. The area hemmed in by **Kajal**, **Three Pimples, Helmet, Sangar,** and **Point 4700** was shaped like a rectangular bowl with gentle slopes easing into the Nala emanating from near **Lone Hill**.

Approaches from North to **Lone Hill** and **Three Pimples** looked very inviting but dangerous because of the presence of the enemy on the **Point 4700** ridge line to the North. I was toying with the idea of going directly to the **Junction Area** as there appeared to be no enemy in between. This looked more promising than **Three Pimples**, which was rocky and broken and required a painstaking daytime operation.

Three Pimples Complex

Let me describe the **Three Pimples** feature as seen from **Kajal.** Geographically, **Three Pimples** is a feature on the ridgeline located west of **Tololing Ridge** and East of **Sando Nala**. The feature was also referred to as **Black Rock** as it appeared to be a mass of black stony features when viewed from Drass. Only a close look revealed three distinct and closely clustered features. Therefore, the name **Three Pimples**, being more descriptive, stuck.

The highest feature was **Top,** which was about 1000 metres from **Kajal.** Along the ridge line leading to **Kajal**, approximately 700 - 800 metres, was a distinct **Knoll** whose Northern side sloped towards the dry nala about 300 metres away. **Knoll** sloped towards **Kajal** for about 300 metres and eased into a narrow ridge of approximately 20 metres wide for about 150 - 200 metres. From there till where we were located, was a sheer rock escarpment about 10 to 15 metres high with ridge width varying from one to five metres, behind which the enemy could not observe.

From the **Top** along the ridge towards **Sangwan** was a **Ledge.** At the edge of **Ledge** was a sheer vertical drop of about 300 feet, and it continued with a few rocky outcrops to the **Sangwan location**. I reckoned that was where Mohit was stuck.

The enemy had occupied **Knoll**; we could make out about four Sangars facing our direction, with none facing North, as far as we could see. Though there were some sharp rock faces, there was plenty of broken ground along the Northern slopes of **Knoll.** The spur line towards **Kajal** sloped sharply for about 300 metres before easing into a narrow, flat ridgeline. This ridgeline, about 200 metres long, connected **Kajal** with the forward slopes of **Knoll** and provided another possible direction of attack. The Southern side dropped into the valley below sharply and was not assaultable. **Knoll** had to be captured for progressing operations towards **Three Pimples.** I tasked Major Acharya to plan for its capture and turned my attention towards **Three Pimples.**

It looked as formidable from **Kajal** as it was from **Jain.** The Northern face appeared steep, and the slopes leading to it could not be judged as **Knoll** masked them. One could make out two to three sangars at the **Top.** It wasn't easy to pick the features or Sangars clearly as the sun cast a shadow on the Eastern face. What was visible made me cringe at the thought of having to assault it. I could hardly detect any approach to this citadel-like feature. The **Ledge** was now clearly visible, and one could make out two to three sangars facing **Jain.**

There should be a route / track along the ridge line from **Junction - Helmet** to **Three Pimples** for administration and movement of enemy troops. The approach to **Saddle** on this ridge from **Kajal** was gentle and appeared uncontested. Was there an enemy at **Lone Hill**? If the enemy were low on strength, then **Lone Hill** would not be held. I was excited by the possibility of surprising the enemy from this direction, isolating him from **Area Junction,** and cutting off his supplies.

Further, it gave me two directions of attack and the possibility of using Bravo Company as a pooled reserve for both directions of attack. Compared to this, the task I had envisaged for Delta Company along the Southern approach could, at best, hold down **Ledge** for some time and the enemy would soon realise the impotence of the attack and readjust his troops to face our assault from the direction of **Kajal**. A day earlier, what appeared to be a viable task for applying maximum forces onto the enemy started appearing to be a waste of troops.

Fire Base

Now I started looking for a suitable **Fire Base**. The escarpment we were on was around 100 - 125 metres by 5 metres, which was ideal for a firebase. However, the number of weapons one could deploy was limited. With an inter-se distance of 10 metres, we could deploy about ten weapons sufficient to support one company assault. We could cover the enemy at **Knoll**, **Three Pimples Top** and **Ledge. Knoll** was masking **Lone Hill** for most weapons. From here, it was possible to support an attack on **Knoll** by flanking or overhead fire support, depending upon the direction of the attack.

FIRE BASE AT KAJAL

Lone Hill was about 1000 - 1200 metres from **Kajal**. The firebase supporting this attack had to be offset to North and West to be effective. The northern slopes of **Kajal** dropped gently into a flattish area of 100 metres by 200 metres hemmed in by the nala into which it sharply dropped. It had a few rocky patches that could give some protection against flat trajectory weapons. It was not the best of positions for a Fire Base, but my choice was an awfully located Fire Base or attack without fire support. I chose the former. In life, they say you cannot have it all your way. For an attack to have a reasonable chance of success in the mountains, one has to shoot the infantry into proximity of the enemy; after that, the benefits of superior numbers kick in.

I checked with Major Mohit on the progress of the Southern Approach. He had not been able to figure out any route to reach **Ledge**. The only option was cliff assault using ropes. We were not trained in cliff assault; outside help would be required to establish the ropes for the assault troops. This approach was increasingly appearing impossible.

Change of Plan

This called for a radical change from the preliminary plan, requiring approval from my Brigade Commander. Though I had come prepared to stay put in the firm base till the execution of the attack, I decided to return and reorganise my operations. Lieutenant Rautela was tasked to hold on to **Kajal** while Naib Subedar Dharmpal of his company would fetch up to reinforce him. Major Acharya was tasked to prepare a detailed plan for the capture of **Area Knoll** with his Alpha Company. Leaving Lieutenant Rautela behind, the rest of the party descended through the gorge.

As we got out of the cover into the valley, we heard a machine gun firing, but it was nowhere near us. Soon, artillery shells started landing around us, and we all ran to take cover behind a massive rock more than 200 to 300 feet tall, located about 100 - 150 metres away, and all made it safely. We thought we had been detected and were the target, but later, Lieutenant Rautela revealed that he had tried to push forward to the area earmarked for the Fire Base to secure it and was fired upon. I had not explicitly told him that he was at the highest part of **Kajal** and hence it was to be secured, and that once more troops become available, he was to spread out. With barely three months of service, Rautela was already performing tasks far beyond his training or pay grade. He always compensated his shortfall in training with dash and courage!

This rock we had taken cover behind, though located barely 1000 metres from **Three Pimples** and Northern Face under direct observation, provided cover from observation and fire. Since it was narrow and steep, it was safe from enemy artillery fire, for it was in a dead zone of about 200 - 250 metres where no shell could land. Since the evening was setting in, we waited for the artillery fire to ease. The stream that was draining this valley passed around it.

While biding our time, I was arranging and rearranging my arguments to support the change of plan and the consequent delay it would cause.

Bringing Administration Closer to Fighting Troops

My thoughts turned to logistic arrangements for the upcoming operations.

In the mountains, providing food and water to troops engaged in attack is a challenge, which needs to be factored in by the operations staff. At Tololing, we faced a significant challenge in maintaining two companies that had resulted in an angry outburst from Major Acharya; it had taken Major Sandeep Bajaj's persuasive skills to control the situation and have some food and water sent to them. Troops can last on packed / pre-prepared food for two days at most. Considering that assaulting troops are involved in strenuous activities, the effect of the altitude becomes more pronounced, dehydration being the primary concern. Any attempt to supply freshly cooked food from the safety of rear areas calls for enormous logistics overhead in terms of manpower.

My observation of troops whose operations were stalled indicated that after the second day, every man up required another man to supply freshly cooked food, not hot meals. Given our strength and the demand for dumping ammunition needed for infantry support weapons, it was challenging to spare manpower. Cooked food weighs more than the dry rations that go into it, mainly because of the water added.

I wondered if I could establish a cookhouse behind this rock face. I started checking the factors for choosing the location of the cook house, water and proximity to forward troops - yes; safe from enemy fire - yes; adequate space – yes; smoke not detectable – no; easy to supply dry rations – no; protection from enemy raids – no.

We could arrange a single dumping of rations to ensure food for about 100 people for three days: about 300 kgs @ 1 kg per person per day and about 200 kg of utensils. The enemy would be able to pick it up sooner or later. The only threat was the possibility of a physical raid; there were no troops between the enemy located 1000 metres away at **Three Pimples** and this location. To do this, the enemy had to get down sheer rock faces. His chances of doing so while being engaged from the **Kajal** and **Sangwan Location**s were lesser, so we decided to go ahead with this. I ordered Naib Subedar Balwan to establish his company cookhouse at this location.

Establishing a small administrative base this far forward helped us somewhat mitigate our logistic challenges. Troops from **Kajal** could come down by turns to have a hot meal and carry water back for others twice a day. It also acted as a staging point for troops dumping ammunition, a place to rest, catch a breath and consume an energy boosting hot sweet tea. Though the distance to **Kajal** was a mere 600 to 700 metres, it was a steep 1000-foot climb on a loose and sliding surface of small stones and pebbles. It took about an hour without load and about two with moderate loads of 10 to 15 kgs.

Once the visibility reduced, I instructed Major Acharya to get the platoon of Bravo Company up quickly and locate himself at **Kajal** to hold **Kajal** at all costs. My team consisted of a Radio Operator, a Buddy and an Intelligence NCO. The first team ferrying ammunition was, in fact, behind Naib Subedar Balwan's platoon that had been moved up to secure the Firm Base.

Major Sandeep Kala, the 2iC, Major Bajaj, Adjutant and Major Bhanwar, Quarter Master, had done a fantastic job organising ammunition dumping. All hands in the unit had been mobilised. I found the line was being pushed up, and the clerical staff had established a dumping control point at the road head. I found Havildar Jagjeet with complete details of what had moved up. For a CO, nothing is more reassuring than seeing his battalion performing the tasks, divining his thoughts without proper orders, even in his absence.

I reached the Brigade HQ around 1900 hours and made a report to Brigadier Amar Aul of the day's events and my current assessment. After a lot of quizzing and playing the Devil's Advocate, he concurred with the broad plan. I told Brigadier Aul I would finalise and coordinate the battalion attack plan from a tactical HQ at **Kajal** the next day. 29 June 1999 would be the earliest I would be ready with my assessment.

It was late when I reached Hotel Hill View after a long and strenuous day. I ordered the immediate stopping of ammunition dumping in the **Sangwan Location**. I called for the cook house to be moved to the base of **Kajal** and diverted all ammunition dumping to **Kajal**.

25 June 1999

On 25 June morning, we reviewed the situation and found we needed greater details of the enemy and terrain, especially the layout of his defences. We initiated a demand for Air Photos of the objective area and 1:25,000 maps. It was of great help that Major Bajaj was Staff Course qualified, and he got out the Air Photo demands in a jiffy. We hoped that the arrival of these photos and maps would help us develop an attack plan in greater detail than what we had collected from our ground recce.

A review of the progress of ammunition dumping indicated that we would miss our target of dumping two second - line weapons scales at the Fire Base. We had a shortage of manpower. Major Bajaj was tasked to procure some fighting porters effort from other units. Major Bhanwar commented that local porters were already employed with battalions that had arrived earlier.

This review occurred outside the hotel as I was preparing to leave for **Kajal**. While looking around, one could see a lot of ponies grazing peacefully near the hotel and slopes leading to Tololing Nala, so I asked, "*Why don't we use the local ponies*?" Major Bhanwar replied that the owners had been evacuated with civilians of the area to safer zones. "*Why don't we commandeer them ourselves*?" I asked. While I was asking this, my eyes rested on Havildar Binja Ram, a gangling Jat from Rajasthan with an impressive moustache. He was the Regimental Police Havildar, a minder of discipline in the battalion, a ceremonial baton bearer and the official interface with visiting dignitaries. His unstated duties are to keep a tab on the mood of the battalion, especially the bad hats, a sort of big brother and secret service rolled into one, who reported to the Subedar Major, the senior most JCO. Since the requirement for such services was low, I asked Binja Ram, "*Why don't you get hold of all the ponies?*"

Just then, Major Bajaj informed me I was required at the Brigade HQ.

A Curved Ball is Thrown

Major General Mohinder Puri, GOC 8 Mountain Division, was already at the Brigade HQ, and I was ushered into the office of the Brigade Commander. General Mohinder Puri and Brigadier Amar Aul were sitting on easy chairs side-by-side with Colonel Chabbewal, Col GS 8 Mountain Division and Major Patro, Brigade Major 56 Mountain Brigade, and Colonel Kushal Thakur, CO 18 GRENADIERS standing. I gave a status report highlighting the efforts to secure the firm base, establish the firebase, and do ammunition dumping, preparing the battalion for attack and finalising the attack plan. I informed them I was heading to **Kajal** to coordinate the attack plan.

"*When will the attack go in*?" asked the GOC. "*We require three to four days to be ready*," I said. The GOC got agitated and said, "*Ten odd riffraff cannot hold up a battalion for so long; we have to keep the momentum going; you have had adequate time to prepare; why don't you attack tomorrow?*" That was a shocker; it was the first time I had heard anyone put a number on the enemy one faced at **Three Pimples**, and that number appeared to be a gross underestimation, to me at least. I was looking at my Brigade Commander, whom I had briefed thoroughly and got his approval for changing the initial plan of attack to bail me out. Brigadier Aul did not say a word; evidently, both had already discussed it before my arrival and arrived at a decision.

I was feeling cornered; I was absolutely sure it was impossible to launch an attack the next day. Everyone was silent, and I was tense; it appeared the GOC was about to issue orders for the attack to be launched the next day. Colonel Alok Deb's words flashed in my mind, "*Do not accept a task you cannot execute.*" I blurted out, "*Sir, I, myself, have seen the objective only last evening. I could personally count at least sixteen 'sangars' on* ***Knoll*** *and* ***Three Pimples*** *facing* ***Kajal****; I have no idea of those facing elsewhere. Even if we consider two persons to a 'Sangar' we have 32, there must be others also holding defences. My company commanders have yet to see their objectives. They have just been withdrawn from different axes of attack. We have just started getting the Fire Base ready, and it will take time.*"

"*What were you doing so long? You should have done all this by now,*" said the GOC. He had seen my point of view in the previous attack on Tololing and given us adequate time for preparation, in the bargain taking on a great stress on himself. We were aware then that he was under tremendous pressure to launch his offensive early. I wondered what the issue was now; he was probably unaware of the series of task and formation switches we had done in the last ten days.

"*If you had given me the task earlier, our preparations would have been ready; our task was allotted only two days ago; we need time,*" I persisted. I expected that GOC would see my point, but unexpectedly, he said, "*If you cannot do it, we may have to give this task to someone.*" It was like a punch landing on the solar plexus; I did not know what to say - I had just been issued a warning. Should I accept the order now? I saw no chance of success in it. I just shrugged my shoulders to indicate it was a 'pass' from my side, and it was now for others to decide. GOC said, "*You can go*". While I was leaving, Brigadier Aul said, "*Just wait outside.*"

I came out feeling miserable; what a fall from the glory of Tololing! I was wondering whether my actions were right. GOC had never been blind to the logic of a situation; the desire to maintain momentum is absolutely logical, but such insistence on attacking the next day, I could not fathom.

Over the years, I have tried to find a reason that could be a plausible reason — the next day happened to be 'Saturday'. A successful attack on Point 5140 had been launched on 19 June 1999, a 'Saturday'. My battalion had launched a successful attack on Tololing on 12 June 1999, again a 'Saturday'. It is amazing how we in the Army, like many others in professions with tough and uncertain situations, develop an eye for recognising successful patterns and trying to replicate them. This is my speculation!![32]

---

32 Vikram Jit Singh / TNN / Jul 2, 2019, http://timesofindia.indiatimes.com/articleshow/70035960.cms?utm_source=contentofinterest&utm_medium=text&utm_campaign=cppst. Lt Gen Amar Aul, speaking to Vikramjit Singh, said, "All my assaults were planned for Saturdays,

I waited outside gloomily; many thoughts were going around in my mind. How would history judge me a coward, a fastidious one taking his own time to complete his task or someone to whom success had gone into the head? No one was talking to me; humans instinctively know when one must be avoided, an essential survival instinct. Irreverent as it may seem, "*You are writing Military History,*" remark of Lieutenant General Khanna, Army Commander, flashed in my mind. I could visualise a question in the future Military History paper: "*What were the mistakes committed by CO, 2 RAJRIF in battle? How would you have handled the situation?*" A wry smile passed my lips, somewhat lifting my spirits a bit.

Colonel Chabbewal came out and called me in. I went in with trepidation of someone about to be sacked. "*When can you attack?*" GOC asked. "*By Tuesday (29 Jun)*" I replied. "*Make it on Monday (28th)*" he ordered. By then, loads of emotions were going through my mind, each creating its unique signature of chemicals in the mouth, now this exhilaration of being reinstated, this apprehension of delivering, and this fear of a chance of redemption disappearing. Anyway, I was exhausted by the episode and accepted the attack day. Then, turning to Colonel Kushal Thakur, the GOC said, "*You start preparing for Tiger Hill*". The results were seen when the battalion captured Tiger Hill on 5 July 1999. Troops given time to recce, plan and prepare will invariably succeed. Here was a GOC who was a quick learner. It showed me he had quickly seen that my unit operation was delayed due to inadequate time for recce, planning and preparation. That gave me a lot of confidence and renewed hope that if the tactical logic is correct and efforts sincere, this GOC would back me up.

Once GOC left, I discussed my options with Brigadier Amar Aul. Though I had come back from **Kajal** with an ambitious plan to attack in depth, I decided to settle for a more conservative three –phase attack along the ridge line. Alpha, Delta, Bravo companies respectively capturing **Knoll**, **Three Pimples** and **Lone Hill** in a phase each. Assaulting troops of subsequent phases were earmarked as reserves, and Charlie Company was a reserve for Phase 3. Given the compressed time frame, I requested help in dumping ammunition. Brigadier Aul thought

---

and they all succeeded against an entrenched enemy. I carried this legacy from the counter-insurgency operations in the Valley. For the assault on Three Pimples, I had again picked a Saturday (26 June), and the GOC (Maj Gen Mohinder Puri) had also accepted the date as a good augury.However, the commanding officer of 2 RAJRIF, Lieutenant Colonel MB Ravindranath, said he would not be able to go for the assault on the planned day as there was a chasm that his troop could not cross to keep the deadline. The GOC was very upset at the delay. We finally went two nights later on 28th June and captured the feature, but it was a bloody battle where 2 RAJRIF lost three officers in one night (Major P Acharya, Captain N Kengruze and Captain Vijayant Thapar)."

that the ammunition being planned was very high. My reasoning was based on the premise *'It is better to err on the plus side'*.

With this, I took leave and returned to my Tactical HQ around 1500 hours, where I briefed my Orders Group that 28 June would be the D Day. Working backwards, we fixed the night of 27/28 June as the day assaulting troops would be inducted.

I ordered Major Mohit to abandon the Firm Base and fall back to Drass, leaving the ammunition already dumped behind. We had to finish our ammunition dumping for the two firebases up to **Kajal** in three days, i.e., by first light on 28 June. You could trust Major Bhanwar to try and carry out what his commander desires. He, with CHM Binja Ram, had rounded up around 30 local ponies. They had improvised carrying harnesses with camouflage nets. 2 RAJRIF had improvised its own Animal Transport Platoon! This battalion has a history of finding practical solutions to its problems. These ponies carried the ammunition forward along the Nala. Given the time frame, more was needed. Major Sandeep Kala had mobilised everyone to dump ammunition at Moghulpura. Unlike the Tololing operation, we did not have the luxury of time and dumping had to continue day and night. We were also allotted MILAN - anti-tank guided missile detachment; carrying the awkward load of missile launchers and missile tubes was extremely taxing in terms of manpower and time-consuming. We started preparing for our second attack in fifteen days, a feat not done by any other battalion till now. We were also allotted a Rope team of HAWS (High Altitude Warfare School).

I wanted to get the Delta Company Order Group under Major Mohit up so they could get maximum time to recce, plan their attack, and coordinate with their firebase; the earliest they could leave was early on 26 June 99.

Major Madan Refuses Combat

Around 1700 hours, Major Sandeep Kala reported the arrival of Major Madan at Moghulpura. I asked to rush him up as part of Bravo Company was already up; I wanted him to move up and get to know the area as I planned to use Bravo Company as a reserve. After some time, Major Kala called to inform me that Major Madan was refusing to move up, stating that his knee had still not recovered. I felt gutted. I had sent this officer with the mortal remains of Major Vivek Gupta to Dehradun, hoping that the kind of response his heroism was evincing would rouse Major Madan. I had also granted him two days' leave to meet his family at Meerut. On his own, he had gotten additional leave sanctioned; knowing the situation, I wondered how anybody could have done that. There were so many men who had terminated their leave and rejoined.

After all this, I had failed to motivate him. I informed Major Kala that I would meet him at Moghulpura the next day.

Maj Mohit arrived around 2200 hours, and I briefed him on the sketch about his task, the capture of **Lone Hill.** I asked him to recce and prepare a plan for my approval by 27 June at **Kajal.** What if Major Mohit raised the issue that he had already been through an attack while Bravo Company had not? Throughout the night, I wondered about the possible repercussions of his actions on the operations and drifted off to sleep.

26 June 1999 - Leadership Lessons

On 26 June 1999, Major Bajaj and Major Bhanwar were extremely busy getting the weapons and ammunition pushed up to **Kajal**. I went to the battalion's main location to talk to the men. Many men in the battalion were unhappy that we had been tasked again. They felt it was unfair to the battalion.

Most troops need help understanding the bigger picture; for them, the battalion had attacked and done its bit. It is now, they felt, time for others to chip in. As an argument, it looks infallible. Dangerous situations heighten our instinct for self-preservation. As a CO, they felt it was my failure to put this across. They did not say it, but you could see it in their body language. Hush –hush discussions that broke upon seeing me and evasive answers to questions are some indicators. Having served with various troops for a long time, one can make out when troops avoid eye contact and know that all kinds of theories are floating around. My 'driving ambition', my 'total lack of guts' to say 'No', and my 'lack of concern' for troops being an 'outsider in the battalion' would all be aired.

'Loneliness of Command' had been flagged as one of the biggest challenges in combat by Field Marshal Slim in his book '*Defeat into Victory*;' I was experiencing it first-hand. I practised a studied indifference and detachment to the current situation, always focusing on the task at hand. I had a prop in a book I read during our attack on Tololing; now, I had no prop, and things were moving fast.

Some of the 'stalwarts' without responsibility had the most innovative strategies to evict the enemy. Exaggerations and rumours were floating freely. Add to this, the media, with its battery of cub reporters who had scant knowledge of military operations, were on the lookout for any information they could quote and attribute to the spokesman of the Army. They depended on the Army units along the road for their food and administrative needs; the Army never failed them. Many of them have gone on to become iconic figures in media. Gaurav Sawant's "*Dateline Kargil*" book has a good collection if one wishes to sample the kind of rumours floating around. Of all such trash being aired as a strategic solution, the most outrageous was the one that suggested "*we do nothing, and the enemy would be forced to withdraw in winter*"; this was attributed to our very own Major Madan!

Explaining the Larger Picture

Indian Army had been mobilised, and there was a general alert on all borders, with each unit tasked to perform a specific role. There was no way any fresh troops would be allotted to 8 Mountain Division for the ongoing operations. It would be a slugfest to evict the enemy intruders, feature by feature and ridge by ridge. My assessment was it would go up to or beyond September. We were in it for a long haul, much like the unit operations during 1947.

I had tried to convey this by ensuring continuous training and repeatedly letting it be known that we would be soon tasked. Frankly, given the situation, the military hierarchy had no option but to commit us into attack again. The Tololing Battle had mauled Charlie Company; Alpha and Bravo companies were relatively unscathed and had their command elements intact. Delta Company had suffered some casualties but still was potent. I addressed the men in a Sainik Sammelan, informing them of our impending task and our great challenge in moving the ammunition.

"*We have done great, but war is not a one-battle affair*", I started, "*We have to go on till the enemy is finally subdued. It is not for personal glory that we fight, it is not even the glory of the battalion we fight, and it is for fulfilling a pledge we took when we donned the uniform that we will go wherever we are asked to, by land, by sea or by air. We will do what our superior asks us to do*," I reminded them. "*It is on this promise that when the nation is in peril that we will not hesitate or flinch; it is on this promise that when the need arises, we too will rise to the occasion and deliver our part of the bargain that the nation has fed us, clothed us and heaped love and respect on us*," I continued. "*Now is the time to redeem our promise, now is the time to repay the nation its dues, now is the time to apply all our skill, knowledge and courage to complete the task given to us, and now is time we must make up in blood for what we lack to complete the task, '**Why me?**' is not a question a soldier is entitled to ask. No soldier is entitled to an answer to this question: '**If not we, then who?**' A nation whose soldiers fail is doomed to be enslaved,*" I said. "*This is not a time to say I chose wrong or I am not ready. You broke through the defence at Tololing; the nation is celebrating your victory. You opened the gates of success, and other units are exploiting it; you have made yourselves famous. We are soldiers, and I hold you to your oath*," I challenged. "*Only cowards ask this question because they seek a face-saving escape from their fear. We are soldiers* *of 2 RAJRIF with a long history of bravery; so many before us have fought and died to establish a name for the Battalion. We cannot be the ones to let down all those who have sacrificed themselves upholding the oath they took on the 'Nishan and Namak'. We do what we are asked, not question, '**Why me**?' It is not for us to decide what we should do; that is the task of every soldier's superior. We can only decide if the task allotted to us is within our capability. I am convinced it is within our capability; we have two fresh companies, one partially used and one at half strength. I am convinced about your capabilities; we are not finished, not yet. I will be there with you, I will reach you when in trouble, I will safeguard you when in danger, I will expose you to danger no more than necessary*" I promised. "*But I cannot do your job. You do your job, and I will do mine. When we do that, I have no doubt that we will succeed. Are you all ready to show the world what 2 RAJRIF is made of? A Battalion that has not lost a single battle in its entire history! Are you ready to win this battle?*" I questioned." **Yes**" was the thunderous reply.

I told them I would leave for the firm base tonight to prepare a plan worthy of their courage. I asked them to practice their drills and prepare their weapons and ammunition, and those not involved in fighting to carry ammunition and food forward. With this, I concluded the Sainik Sammelan. I was satisfied that the veil of gloom and defiance had lifted and troops were in the right mood.

I then briefed the Officers and JCOs on the outline and induction plans to the Firm Base at the Battalion Operations Room. After summing up the recce results thus far, I outlined the preliminary plan of attack with Alpha and Delta Companies leading and Bravo Company reserve in Phase I and Phase II attack was to be led by Bravo Company with Charlie Company as a reserve.

Major Madan, Yet Again!

I asked Major Madan to accompany me to **Kajal** to take over command of his company, part of which was already up. I called him out and asked him why he had returned so late from his temporary duty to Dehradun; he said there was some problem at his house, so he got leave sanctioned by the Regimental Centre. I had sent him with the hope that the respect he would receive for being part of 2 RAJRIF would make him feel guilty, and he would return a changed person. I was wrong; he had used the goodwill to secure himself leave while fully aware of the situation of the battalion. Contrast this with Major Acharya, who had refused to go on leave to attend the funeral of his father–in–law a few days earlier. "*My father–in–law is not going to come alive if I go; the battalion requires me more than anyone else now.*" "*Why did you refuse to come upto Drass yesterday?*" I asked. He replied, "*My leg is still not OK; I cannot climb?*" "*Drass is on the road; no climbing was involved. Why did you refuse?*" I continued; there was no reply. I informed him he was in fit shape, at least on paper; hence, I could not excuse him from his duty until he was medically certified. I ordered him to get himself checked by the RMO and went to the Mandir, where the battalion had congregated to seek blessings.

While I coordinated various issues for the impending attack, I asked Major Kala to talk to Major Madan and put some sense in to his head. Given the psychologically delicate moment, any action by an officer to avoid combat would impact adversely, making the execution of our task that much more difficult. Major Kala was well aware of the situation and had already tried to talk Madan to relent through the previous evening and night. Kala knew Madan closely; they had worked together in the battalion previously. Madan had been his company officer, and Kala, his mentor. Major Kala tried again and reported that Madan was adamant, on which we conferred on what needed to be done. If ever a perception were formed that officers are allowed to duck duty while ranks are being sacrificed, we would have a serious situation on our hands. At its mildest, it would result in resentment and dragging out of actions, resulting in a failure without it being attributable to anyone. Groups would soon coagulate in fear, and mistrust amongst them would spread. At its worst, there may be an open rebellion. We concurred we needed to act decisively. We decided that the time for informal communications was past, and we needed to go formal in our actions. I asked Kala to bring Major Madan to my office tent for formal counselling. I called Captain Basu, the Regimental Medical Officer (RMO), and enquired from him about the status of Madan's knee. Superficially, it appeared normal, he reported.

Around 1400 hours, Major Madan accompanied Major Kala to my room, which doubled up as my office. Having formally confirmed from Major Madan that he was not moving up because of his bad knee, I asked him when he had this problem. He said he has had it for a long time, and it aggravated after falling in the bathroom on 05 June. I pointed out that it was 20 days since the fall, and the medical records do not mention any history of the knee problem. Moreover, all his actions to date indicate that he was not immobilised due to the knee; why did he not go with his company? He said he could not climb. I explained to him in detail the repercussions of his action and how the officer community in the battalion would forever stand discredited. Even if we come out victorious, the ranks at critical times of confrontation with an officer on any issue will say, "*We know officers ducked duty in the Kargil War; why are you acting so righteous?*" Seeing no effect, I asked him to command the firebase and firm base, a static duty, a task I was undertaking, seriously impeding my freedom of movement, thus restricting my ability to influence the battle decisively. I offered to have him moved on mule and men's shoulders if required; all he had to do was make up his mind.

With still no response, I placed the course of action he had forced me to take in front of him. I read out the letter I had drafted to CO, 308 Field Ambulance, which categorically requested that Major Madan's knee be examined and an opinion rendered. Should the opinion be adverse, I threatened to pursue the 'Malingering and Cowardice in the Face of Enemy' case to its logical conclusion. Still, there was no reaction; I asked him, "*Tell me, Madan, I can see the knee is not your problem, then what is your problem?*" He replied, "*You don't understand*". I understood that here was a man whose instinct of self-preservation had tripped him into a path where all threats appeared minor compared to the danger perceived in obeying orders. I called for the Head Clerk and asked him to produce this letter for my signature. While he was away, I tried again. I told him of Naik Nawal Kishore, who with a similar problem, went into attack with his section against medical advice. And how that section adores their commander who chose to share their dangers and how his company will worship him if he too moves up.

The emotional approach had no effect on Major Madan, who had clearly made up his mind. Major Kala, who had been a patient listener, butted in and said, "*He is not going to go. Sir, you have more important work waiting for you; let's go,*" I called Captain Basu, handed him the sealed letter addressed to CO 308 Field Ambulance, and tasked him to accompany Major Madan for the medical examination. I asked Major Kala to ensure they left immediately.

Seeking Divine Help

Subedar (RT) Bisht was in his element, quoting copiously from the Bhagvad Gita. "*Karma and Dharma are the two paths to human salvation; death and life are phases in our journey to salvation. When we do our duty with a single concentration on it rather than what follows it, we move towards salvation (Mukti). But when we do our duty with always thought on what follows death or award, we tie our Atma to the cycle of 'Life and Death' (Bandhan). Only when you understand that Life and Death are not real can you overcome love (Moha) for your physical self and be courageous. You will be enroute to Moksha only when you choose an ideal, something bigger than self-preservation. Go, brave soldiers of 2 RAJRIF, and do your duty to your country, battalion and family. God is With You.*" He concluded by blowing the conch and singing of Aarti.

It is amazing how much a good sermon does to ease and calm the heart and see life and duty in a bigger and broader context. Under uncertain, dangerous and conflicting times, different things motivate different people. Most useful are those who are self-motivated; they are the prime drivers of any organisation. The reason for motivation may differ, but they are willing to drive themselves towards the goal in the face of constant danger. Of these, there are two genres, one cautious and another daredevil. **Cautious** types plan, prepare and act - they make good leaders because they are concerned with goal accomplishment and not risking themselves or their subordinates. They are mostly self-confident, concerned for people and socially well-adjusted.

On the other hand, **Dare Devils** are a bit of a show-off and unnecessary risk-takers. They mostly verbalise their bravery and are always daring others; if intelligent, they can be valuable assets in tight situations; if foolish, they can be misguided missiles. Most people fall into what can be classified as 'passenger class'. They form the ballast, the working force, the mass. They are amenable to orders and capable of great fortitude when led well, but they are also susceptible to swinging moods and vulnerable to rumours. Here too, we have two broad classes: one set is **loyalists** and the other **floaters**. Loyalists stick to the assigned tasks, execute them diligently and believe in their commanders. In any organisation, cautious leaders and loyalists execute most of the work; they persevere, exert and mostly reach the goal.

This leader material and their loyalists must permeate the organisation for organisational success. It is essential to catch the '**floaters**' and harness them to achieve the organisational goal. 'Floaters' are naturally observant with a keen situational and contextual sense. They have views and ideas but need more confidence to take responsibility; they forever suggest how a thing should be done and who should do it. They tend to gravitate towards powerful personalities and be influenced by others, especially those who are empathetic to them. A smart leader can spot them, try to assure them, and monitor them during tough times. When handled well, they provide the dash in a tight situation.

Major Kala wanted to come with me to **Kajal**. I could understand his enthusiasm; he had not volunteered to rejoin the battalion to be left behind. Given the situation, I shared with him that it was prudent that he stayed back and controlled the fighting echelons. He pointed out that he would be better positioned to support me if he knew the situation first hand. That is a hallmark of a good commander; he always tries to gain first-hand knowledge of the situation under which he is required to execute the task. I conceded and started for **Kajal** with Major Kala.

Enroute, I went to the Brigade HQ and briefed the Brigade Commander on the broad outline plan and the progress of preparations. I also informed him that I was leaving for **Kajal** and would be there till the operations were completed. I then apprised him of the Major Madan episode and shared my views and determination to bring the officer to book should the medical authorities find no serious handicap in him. I requested that Brigadier Aul take action if I were not to return for any reason. We resumed our journey to **Kajal** by about 2200 hours.

27 June 1999

The route was busy with troops carrying ammunition. We kept encouraging them as we trudged behind them in single file along the steep, narrow mountain trail. We reached the Administrative Base area around 0100 hours and were greeted with a very welcome steaming cup of tea and some rest before resuming our journey. The climb was tougher than I had envisaged; the slope up to **Kajal** was almost 60 to 70 degrees or more. The ground was gravelly and slippery; the feet would constantly disappear under the slipping gravel; it was like walking on fresh snow but worse. The snow becomes solid once stepped on, it then is easier for those following. While patrolling snow-bound areas in my younger days, we would lead by turn to conserve energy. Here, it was like everyone was walking on fresh snow. The previous day, I had been disappointed with Lieutenant Rautela taking almost six hours to reach **Kajal**, which I had felt should not take more than two. By the time we reached Kajal, it was around 0600 hours, and we were utterly exhausted. My admiration for the troops involved in ammunition dumping went up a few notches, and I wondered whether we could dump adequate ammunition to support our attack.

CARRYING AMMUNITION TO THE FIRE BASE

Fine Tuning the Attack Plan

Major Mohit had already fetched up. Major Acharya had done his planning, and we also met the 'Rope' (a mountaineering term to describe a group of mountaineers who are climbing together, called as a 'rope team') from HAWS led by a JCO of 15 RAJRIF, who had also reached. They had put ropes to help the Fire Base to move up the weapons and some ammunition. The remaining ammunition was being dumped at the Firm Base due to lack of space at the weapon emplacement. Subedar Ram Kumar Lamba and Subedar Ranbir Singh had created weapon emplacements and started preparing the task and target data sheets.

I asked Major Acharya to brief us. He felt a maximum of one platoon strength occupied **Knoll**. He had planned to attack **Knoll** from two directions - North and SE. The Northern face appeared daunting on the face of it, but he assured me it was possible. He had discussed it with the HAWS team and had been assured of roping up in difficult areas if required. I talked to the JCO of the HAWS team, who confirmed it was a very moderate grade of slope, a route to the top could easily be found, and a fixed rope put in place.

I asked Major Mohit for his plan. He reported that it appeared possible to reach **Lone Hill** as there appeared to be no opposition, but he was apprehensive that the route through the nala leading to it moved very close to **Knoll**, barely 150 metres away. He assessed that the movement would be easily detected, possibly intercepted. He was unsure what type of domination the **Three Pimples** and **Lone Hill** area had on the nala, which ran parallel to the ridge line at approximately 200 to 300 metres.

I asked Lieutenant Rautela for his assessment of how to reach **Helmet**. The **Helmet** was part of the **Junction Complex** of defences on the ridge line to **Lone Hill**. On 24 June 99, it had appeared unprotected and very inviting; it was not part of my task. It could, at best, be an exploitation objective. Lieutenant Rautela said he had not seen enemy troops on the route leading up to **Helmet**; the ground appeared firm and going easy. He felt it was possible to follow a route between the ridges of **Three Pimples** and **Point 4700** ridge line at a distance of 500 metres from both and reach **Helmet** undetected.

Though **Helmet** kept attracting my attention as an objective in depth that could be attacked, I ignored it for the time being. At this time, the plan for an attack on **Knoll** looked settled, barring a few coordination issues. **Lone Hill** was looking inviting but dangerous. Right from the beginning, I had an aversion to **Three Pimples**; it looked even more menacing. I had only two companies with company commanders, Alpha and Delta. Would Major Madan change his mind when he saw the writing on the wall on what would happen to him? I hoped he would. I could then position myself with Bravo Company and have Major Bajaj moved up, once the coordination tasks of the Adjutant were done, to lead Charlie Coy. I could not decide between the conventional **Knoll - Three Pimples – Lone Hill** and the slightly more ambitious **Knoll** and **Lone Hill – Three Pimples** sequence.

Either way, the fire support requirements were the same. We could cover the Eastern and South-Eastern faces of the objective with our firebase. The only way to bring effective direct fire on the Southern side of **Knoll** and **Three Pimples** was by directly firing Bofors Guns and weapons. But coordinating close support fire from the **Sangwan Location** would take a lot of work; we needed to visit each other's locations to mutually identify and agree upon targets. The time available did not permit it. The Grenadiers at **Sangwan** could contribute by launching a feint on **Ledge**. We had already dumped ammunition at the abandoned firm base that could be used to keep **Ledge** engaged. Major Kala had seen the target and knew the possible plans; he would be able to coordinate the fire of Bofors guns.

Major Kala offered to command Bravo Company or be at the Fire Base. Under a different set of circumstances, it would have been a great relief. Right then, I was worried about other things, and I needed his contribution somewhere else where it would play a more critical role.

Keeping the Men Pepped Up

The behaviour of troops in combat is mercurial; it can change rapidly. My experience in counter-insurgency has taught me that they are most enthusiastic and positively nervous in their first operations. Much like a rookie paratrooper on his first jump, the second one is the scariest one. In operations, too, it is the second one that is unnerving. You have experienced first-hand the dangers, and you know you are alive because of the great role chance has played. You have enough experience to be scared but not enough to prepare to counter the imminent danger. It is the same in defence; the first shelling is a surprise, the second one scary, and it is only after the third one that one starts to recognise the patterns and know what safe and dangerous behaviour is.

At this juncture, my battalion was in that delicate phase, a twilight zone between a bunch of still rookies and budding veterans. The body language reflected the pride of winning the first battle and the hesitation to commit fully to the second operation. It is the time when troops need encouragement, cajoling and plain pushing. My command element was up with me; Major Bajaj and Major Rathore were exerting themselves to the fullest to push the ammunition up at Drass. But all were youngsters at Moghulpura, where the bulk of the battalion was.

Even with their enthusiasm and commitment, their influence on troops would be minimal. Troops would rather have a more authoritative figure in whose judgment and ability they have confidence to push them. Before leaving Moghulpura, I had shared my apprehension with Subedar Major Madan Singh and Subedar Adjutant Kuldeep; I had asked them to keep a lookout for any self-defeating talk by JCOs that would demoralise the troops and nip it in the bud.

I was worried the troops may come ill-prepared for the attack. I needed someone strong, senior and committed to be there and bring up the rear - literally. Major Kala was the man for the job. Of all of us, he had the highest social capital with the troops. He had been commissioned into the battalion and had long tenures with the men. During the previous field tenure, he was with the men in the posts along the LC. He had handled them under some tough and delicate conditions in terrorist infested areas where the rear areas were under the greatest threat. Men knew him and were comfortable with him.

As a matter of principle, the CO and 2iC must be on the same wavelength but not necessarily in the same place. They need to be so positioned that the whole outfit is jointly under their combined supervision. Having briefed Major Kala, I tasked him to coordinate the direct firing of Bofors during the attack. He was to return to Moghulpura and ensure that the morale of the battalion held steady and that they were inducted in small groups - Alpha, Delta, Bravo, Ghatak Platoon and Charlie Companies being the order of induction.

Many Doubting Thomas's were given a well-deserved rap by Major Kala. He also put his considerable organising skills into effect to push, encourage and enthuse the troops to move into battle positions. Some highly intelligent and capable people use their abilities to beat the system. The simpler ones try to duck unpleasant and dangerous duties by resorting to a variety of methods, volunteering for some other crucial role to keep themselves safe. The more sophisticated ones subtly, sometimes not so subtly, try to rope in others to scuttle the plans. Such sabotage results in catastrophic failure for the organisation, ruining the commander's reputation and many others. Even if such efforts are found out, the mastermind usually remains safe; it is the minor players in the sabotage effort that get rapped. To my dismay, I realised that an officer of mine, Major Madan, was capable of such intrigue. With him behind with the main body, I was always worried. I could not take him out of the system without creating a huge morale effect, as my Subedar Major had warned me, nor could I leave him in the system without running the risk of a meltdown. It is far easier to organise recce, plan an attack, man and command a firebase and even be with troops in operations than to shepherd troops earmarked for the attack who are vulnerable in mind.

Major Kala later shared with me the direct and indirect efforts used to influence him by Major Madan and some other '*pseudo well-wishers*' of the battalion. He confided that, at times, he was petrified that the whole battalion would collapse around him and that he would be blamed for such a dramatic and disastrous turn of events after the blazing performance at Tololing. It is entirely to the credit of Major Kala that he kept his nerve, wit and natural common sense to gather those who believed and, through them, rally the rest successfully. It was his greatest behind-the-scene contribution to the battle, albeit with little glory to claim later once victory had been won.

Mentally Wargaming the Plan

The prospect of attacking **Three Pimples** from the direction of **Knoll** was looking bleak. We could not distinguish the lay of the ground between **Knoll** and **Three Pimples** from **Kajal**. The map was useless as it did not reveal the finer details, especially the dead ground. The air photos and the 1:25,000 maps we had requisitioned had yet to arrive. The fire support from **Kajal** had to be overhead, and **Knoll** shielded the lower portion of **Three Pimples**, which would force us to shift the firebase to **Knoll,** in turn implying delay during the execution.

In contrast, the approach from **Lone Hill**, clearly visible, was a smooth open ridge. We could easily support the attack with much-desired flanking fire from **Kajal** itself, which meant the attack on **Three Pimples** could start as soon as **Lone Hill** was captured. I got down to examine the option of attacking **Lone Hill** in Phase I and the challenges it posed with Major Mohit, the man who would execute it.

The shortest route to **Lone Hill** was along the nala leading to the **Saddle** on the ridge line between **Lone Hill** and **Helmet**. It passed close to **Knoll** defences at approximately 200 metres from the top on which we could spot sangars. We had yet to spot any movement on the slopes to the Northern face of **Knoll**. It had some stiff rock faces, the top of which overlooked the nala, but were they held? We were not sure. Any attempt to go through the nala could easily be interfered with from these locations.

Then, we examined possible routes further North. It was possible to get to **Green Patch** from **Kajal** and, from there, turn West to hit the **Saddle** area. It was longer by about 400 to 500 metres and was around 400 to 500 metres from the **Knoll** - **Three Pimples** ridge. Earlier patrol by Lieutenant Kenguruse had already been to **Green Patch**, and we knew the going was good and there was no enemy enroute. Yet we lacked any information about **Lone Hill** terrain or enemy disposition except what we could observe from 1000 to 1200 metres. There needed to be more than this information to commit a company to the task. So, we decided that Major Mohit must lead a patrol that night (27/ 28 June) to gather the required information. Major Mohit left with his patrol around 2100 hours. He was being continuously tracked by the fire base with weapons. Major Acharya was tasked to launch and retrieve the patrol in case it ran into trouble.

I tried to analyse the possible interference to my plan from the enemy. If the enemy were to reinforce or counterattack, it would most likely come from the **Helmet – Junction Feature**. One sure way of stopping it was to attack it. **Helmet** was about 500 to 600 metres from **Green Patch,** and it would take about the same time as reaching the **Saddle** area, why not attack **Helmet** instead of **Lone Hill**? This was the thought that was emerging in my mind. The more one studied the feature, the more I was convinced that if we succeeded in the capture of the **Helmet**, we should have the ability to assault **Junction** in the next phase, which implied a requirement of at least three companies, including reserves. Otherwise, a strong counterattack from **Junction** could retake **Helmet**.

Point 4700 Ridge and **Three Pimples** Ridge were around 500 metres from the approach to the **Helmet** and could easily interfere. The distance was even lesser at places. Even if we succeeded in capturing the **Helmet** and holding it, maintaining it logistically would be difficult with the **Point 4700** Ridge Line dominating it from the North, it too needed to be secured.

Securing **Point 4700** Ridge Line offered great tactical advantage; it opened the secured Eastern Approach to **Area Junction**, our Brigade objective; it gave observation into the enemy deployment to the North up to the LC thereby reducing his flexibility, and finally, it would make the capture of **Three Pimples** redundant. **Three Pimples** would become isolated as soon as the assault was launched on **Junction** from the East. I looked closely at the **Point 4700** Ridge Line; it was at a distance ranging from 1200 metres to 1500 metres. It was located about 500 metres higher than **Kajal** with a uniform Southern slope leading to the crest line, culminating in the four features **Point 4700**, **Tommy**, **Rocky** and **Sanghar** all held by the enemy. From **Kajal**, we could launch a two-company-up attack on **Rocky** and **Sanghar**, and to my assessment, the capture of **Point 4700** Ridge Line appeared more assured and having greater tactical impact than the possibility of capture of **Three Pimples**.

Welcome News

I came down from my vantage point to where the landline was terminated to report my assessment to the Brigade Commander and seek a change of objective. At that moment, we saw some movement in the Tololing Nala around 300 metres East of **Kajal**. I checked it out and learned it was a recce patrol of 18 GARHRIF. I went down to shouting distance and asked the patrol officer about his task. I learnt that 18 GARHRIF had been tasked to capture **Point 4700** Ridge Line, and they, too, were attacking the next night.

It was strange; I had been to Brigade HQ last evening, and no one had informed me. I wondered if this could have been a recent development. This was the first time I became aware of the plan for an attack on my right flank, and I was elated. I could see the chances of my operation succeeding going up manifold. In any offensive operation, the more points of contact you can bring to bear on the enemy, the greater the chances of each point of contact succeeding. The reason is simple - the enemy is physically and psychologically stretched, and weaknesses show up. Success after that depends on how well one is prepared and poised to exploit them. I abandoned my proposed request for a change of objective and decided to keep all my operations South of Line, joining **Kajal – Green Patch – Helmet,** a sort of inter-battalion boundary of my own.

Enemy Artillery Zeroes onto Us

A stream of people was moving to and from the roadhead to **Kajal** and back. The enemy constantly targeted these columns with artillery fire. By skilful use of ground cover, these columns had secured themselves against enemy artillery; however, in one such shelling, we lost Naik Satbeer Singh of Alpha Company in the gorge area. The Fire Base, too, started being targeted; each time the enemy opened fire, we would retreat into every crevice we could find or stay close to the rock faces.

We lost Rifleman Vikram Singh when he took food for his comrades in Fire Base 2 on the Northern Face. The route to this Fire Base 2 was via a crack in the rock face through which one had to pass through almost crouched, one at a time. The Southern face was relatively safe, consisting of numerous cascading rock faces with terraces 10 to 15 metres wide. The angle of fall of shells had become steeper; I suspected the enemy had moved up the mortars or howitzers were being used. As a precaution, we built sangars to protect us from splinters that could land on these terraces.

The men relentlessly soldiered on in the face of all the enemy interference to complete the ammunition dumping on time. Major Kala, Major Bajaj and

Major Bhanwar had mobilised every available soul towards dumping, including rations to the Administrative Base. Drivers, Mortar Platoon, clerks and tradesmen were all pressed into service. These, along with assistance from 100 men of 18 GRENADIERS, 50 men from 2 NAGA, and 30 men from Pioneers Corps, made a herculean effort to dump the ammunition. The Fire Base parties were busy preparing the weapon emplacements and ranging their weapons by live fire whenever they got a respite from the enemy's harassing fire. All the officers later agreed that the battalion had this unique quality to somehow retrieve a hopeless situation by coming together in the nick of time.

Artillery Support

Unlike conventional operations under more stable conditions, the artillery support plan would have emerged concurrently with my battalion plan. But here I was, planning in isolation with no clue what big guns were being kept on standby in my support. I was pleased when I received Major Ashok Sharma, Battery Commander of Heavy Mortars, who arrived at **Kajal** accompanied by Captain Saxena as the Forward Observation Officer (FOO). Having tucked them in next to my location at **Kajal**, I informed him of the situation and the tentative plan of attack.

Major Ashok Sharma apprised me of the artillery support allotted for our attack. We had been allotted Fire units consisting of Field, Medium, Heavy Mortar and Light Mortars. Captain Saxena was part of the battalion attack as the FOO with Delta Coy, a task he was to repeat.

In Tololing, we had learnt that artillery had a restriction of a minimum target size of 400 metres by 400 metres. **Three Pimples**, **Knoll** and **Lone Hill** had a maximum spread of 400 metres and depth of 300 metres; hence, it would be a single target for artillery. All I had to decide was when to bring down and when to lift the fire; this posed a challenge. According to the emerging plan, the attack on **Knoll** would go earlier than **Lone Hill**. Therefore, the final part of the approach to **Lone Hill** would be without fire support.

I shared this with Major Ashok and asked him if he could somehow ensure close support for our attack on **Lone Hill**. He assured me that he would get the three targets **Knoll**, **Three Pimples**, and **Lone Hill** addressed, and the fire on each target would be independently controlled. I was pleasantly surprised and asked him to reconfirm he was actually going to give us independent control over artillery fire on the three objectives. The answer was emphatic: 'Yes' and I was very happy. I pointed out **Helmet**, **Junction** and **Sanghar** on the **Point 4700** ridge line as targets that could interfere with my assault.

I asked him to ensure at least one Bofors gun in a Direct Firing Role; we had found it very effective during the Tololing attack and decided to have it for this attack too. I asked him to go through the registration and informed him that I would confirm my tactical plan by 1000 hours on 28 June 1999, the next day. With this, the preparations for artillery fire support started.

Tying up the Loose Ends

For close coordination and control of the firebase supporting the assaulting troops, it was decided to have line communication backed by radio communication. Accordingly, the battalion signallers laid telephone lines (WD cable) from the command post to each Fire Base commander. Fire Base commanders were also put on the company radio networks of the company they were supporting. Command posts fortified with sandbags and all the weapon emplacements were made ready that night. Around last light, I went around to pep up the troops and check progress.

To my utter shock, I found out that some of the troops had been in this location for three days, and they had nothing substantial to eat other than 'Churma' (dried gram flour mixed with jaggery and made into balls) and water, both of which were scarce. We had taken a risk in establishing an Administrative Base right under the nose of the enemy, yet we were not able to provide nourishment and water.

I got in touch with Naib Subedar Balwan and asked him the reason. It seemed we lacked containers to ferry water and no dedicated manpower to carry food or water to the men in forward positions. In our obsession with ammunition dumping, routine administration had been totally neglected. This oversight needed immediate corrective action. Resourceful as ever, Major Rathore had procured five 20 Litre plastic cans and they were already on their way to the Administrative Base. I asked Naib Subedar Balwan to commandeer the next ammunition party that arrived and to use them to ferry water and food. This task was finally entrusted to the Mortar Platoon, some of the toughest boys who were not being used in their traditional fire support role for the battle as there was no space to deploy the battalion's six mortar tubes within range of enemy targets.

I received reports from Major Kala that the Fighting Group of assaulting troops had left Moghulpura, and he would move to Drass after tying up some last-minute details. I enquired about the OC Forward Surgical Section (FSC) report on Major Madan's alleged knee injury that had been keeping him away from all the action. Kala said that the report was with the Regimental Medical Officer (RMO) and that Major Madan was not accompanying the Fighting

Group. With my last hope of having a company commander for Bravo Company fading, I ordered Major Bajaj to command Bravo Company in the attack.

We had pre-marked locations for the companies as they arrived to minimise confusion. Alpha Company was to be in the Firm Base next to my location. Delta Company was to be around 100 metres to the rear on the first terrace. Part of Bravo Company, which had come up on 24 June, was withdrawn to a broken rocky area just North of the Saddle between **Jain Location** and **Kajal** along with Lieutenant Rautela, where they would regroup with the rest of their company elements now arriving. Charlie Company was to locate itself in the **Saddle Area** along with the Regimental Aid Post (RAP).

The whole battalion was on the move. I had asked the Fire Base commanders to ensure that the detachments rested well after preparing their weapon emplacements, as they would have a long night ahead of them the next day. I, too, went to sleep, expecting the troops to start arriving by 0400 hours.

Around midnight, there was a big commotion outside my pup tent. Water and fresh food had arrived, and the troops, desperate for fresh food, were attempting to grab maximum portions. The NCO in charge of the party was resisting, and rightly so. Troops hungry and thirsty can lose composure at the sight of food and water. If they feel or suspect that it will be scarce, then they would want to horde. I stepped in and brought food and water to my tent. Seeing the CO, the level of agitation went down; having taken stock of the situation, we distributed packed food and some water.

There were around 100 people in the Fire Base area. We had five cans of 20 Litres each, i.e., about 100 litres of water. We were all to get about one litre per person, just about enough to fill every soldier's army-issued plastic water bottle. Considering that the assault companies would be arriving soon, the strength in the firm base area was about to go up to 320. Even at a frugal scale of two-litre / per person / per day, the requirement of water alone would be 640 litres. With our current capacity, it required at least 6 to 7 trips.

I told the NCO in charge that the water-carrying party was to make as many trips as possible; the same was conveyed to Naib Subedar Balwan Singh at the Administrative Base. Luckily for me, the troops were more resourceful; they had managed a large number of 5-litre cans, and each section was carrying one can. This and the personal water bottle ensured they had water for 24 hours when they arrived. Without the independent initiative at the junior level of command, I would have faced a situation where troops would be launched into operations thirsty and, worse, with empty water bottles.

Alpha Company started arriving around 0330 hours; it was still dark, and they were quietly guided to the area just behind the Fire Base. The Administrative Base reported that Charlie Company and Ghatak Platoon detachments had crossed them around 0400 hours, the time the visibility starts to improve at this time of the year. I was satisfied that all the assault troops were in the safety of the gorge area before daylight.

In the meantime, Major Mohit's patrol had reeled into the safety of the Firm Base. Major Mohit had done his recce almost up to the base of **Lone Hill**; he confirmed that the approach had no obstacle or enemy. Reporting on the enemy's presence, while he was sure that **Knoll Top** appeared to be held, he had not seen any defences facing the North. The **Three Pimples** area was about 300 metres away, but he had heard no movement, but we knew the enemy was there. He was not sure if **Lone Hill** was held, but the most disturbing piece of information was that there was a reasonably high feature to the North of **Three Pimples**; he was not sure if that was held. The map did not show any such feature; we had not been able to spot it on the ground, and it had not at all figured in the planning. Could he be wrong?

We went back to the command post and carefully studied the **Lone Hill** feature. When we looked hard, we could make out a feature whose silhouette was blanked by **Lone Hill**. This feature was about 200 - 300 metres short of **Lone Hill** and appeared unheld. It was unclear what its connection was with **Lone Hill**, **Three Pimples**, or **Knoll**. This complicated the plan to infiltrate and attack a feature in depth. The questions were whether the infiltrating force should attack **Lone Hill** or this newly discovered feature and what kind of impact this feature would have on the attack on **Lone Hill**. Since Major Mohit had reported that he could not detect any enemy positions on the Northern slopes of **Knoll**, I concluded there would not be any enemy on this new feature; therefore, if one managed to achieve surprise, it may not have any impact on the attack on **Lone Hill**. Would it be advantageous to capture it first and progress operations from it? We were unsure how it was interconnected to **Lone Hill** or **Three Pimples**. Would it meet our original intent of attacking in depth to isolate the objective - one was not sure as it appeared a bit off-set from the ridge line **Lone Hill - Three Pimples**.

Considering all these things, we decided to go on with our original plan of attacking **Lone Hill**. I tasked Delta Company with the task and allotted it the only artillery FOO available. Delta Company had just arrived. They got right in earnest to work. I was apprehensive that there would be resentment in the company, but these brave Rajputs embraced this task without a murmur.

Major Bajaj arrived with Bravo Company and brought a cake baked by his wife, Tina, sent all the way from Chandigarh. Soft and spongy, the cake tasted divine, lifting the sombre mood that had descended, making it lighter with the arrival of Major Bajaj. To date, I have yet to figure out if the cake or the personality of Major Bajaj did the trick. I could sense joviality amongst the officers in the face of adversity that we were facing, and it was a welcome sign. This joviality rubbed in on those of us who had been in the Firm Base longer. Suddenly, enthusiastic activity was all around; arriving troops appeared cheerful and well-motivated, credit for which must go to the complete team under Major Sandeep Kala.

Artillery Fire Coordination

Having tasked Delta Company, I got down to coordinating the fire support requirements with Major Ashok Sharma, our 'In Direct Support' Battery Commander. We decided there would be preparatory bombardment that was 'Timed' and subsequent covering fire would be 'On Call'. Heavy Mortars and Light Mortars were 'In Direct' support. He and his team busied themselves in registering **Three Pimples, Lone Hill** and **Knoll**. Heavy Mortars did this; it was highly accurate, and Major Sharma could adjust the fire down to 25 metres. He assured me that **Three Pimples** would be kept under fire while fighting was on at **Knoll** and **Lone Hill**; that was very reassuring. He then tried to adjust the Light Mortar fire to the registered targets, but the fire proved inaccurate. Then attempts were made to give corrections, which proved a challenge.

I assessed that the weight of the shell mattered. Heavy Mortars and Bofors Medium Guns were accurate, and their fire was highly predictable, making them easy to control. Light Mortars and Field Guns were more difficult to control; the lighter weight of the shell was possibly more impacted by the altitude and the high prevailing winds. After several attempts at fire correction with the Light Mortars proving unsuccessful, I asked it to be stopped as we drew retaliatory enemy artillery fire on the Firm Base. Major Sharma immediately got on the D5 Net requesting counter-bombardment (CB) fire. I could overhear over the static the heavy volume of radio traffic on the D5 Net; clearly, everyone under enemy fire was demanding CB! I told Major Sharma to refrain from persisting as the enemy would realise his fire was effective. I was worried that if the enemy only monitored the D-5 Net, he would get more than a fair picture of how his artillery fire was panning out behind the ridges. He only had to correlate our panicked reactions to the timings of his artillery shoots!

The enemy was intermittently shelling the Fire Base. As soon as we heard a passing shot, we would hit the ground as close to the rock faces as possible behind the shallow stone walls we had created. Charlie Company was deployed in the Saddle area between the **Jain Location** and **Kajal**, which happened to be the lowest and widest area in the Firm Base. I was looking down at them. I spotted Lieutenant Praveen Tomar talking to some men when suddenly, an artillery shell landed not more than 10 metres behind him, engulfing him in a cloud of dust and debris. Fearing the worst, I watched as the dust dissipated - expecting to see a bloody welter of mangled arms and legs. To our amazement and immense joy, young Praveen walked out unscathed, coughing and swishing away the dust from his face! A lucky man indeed. Despite the fairly accurate enemy artillery fire, we were very lucky to have survived without any casualties in the Fire Base.

My plan was firming up in my mind, but I still had to confer with a most critical player in my plan, Major Sandeep Bajaj, the newly crowned Bravo Company commander. What I had in mind for his company was a slew of contingency tasks that needed some tactical maturity. Many of these tasks required on-the-spot decisions based on the situation. It was to act as a reserve for the assaulting companies; they were the only proper reserves I could employ independently, and I wanted them to capture **Three Pimples** if we had to. I wanted them to be ready to rush forward to exploit any fleeting opportunity to capture **Helmet** and push to capture **Area Junction** should we succeed in isolating **Three Pimples**. I was banking on **Three Pimples** surrendering once they had been isolated with no hope of help from **Helmet** or **Area Junction**.

Major Sandeep Bajaj was the ideal choice for this kind of task - tactically sharp, recently empowered with the prestigious year-long course at Defence Services Staff College under his belt. More importantly, he had enough service to dominate his command and the will to do so. He quickly grasped what was required of his company and asked for Subedar Ram Kumar Lamba back as one of his platoon commanders. Subedar Ram Kumar Lamba was the Fire Base commander, a critical responsibility. I agreed to release him as I reasoned that by the time Lamba's platoon moved out of the Firm Base, the role of the Fire Base would have become redundant.

CHAPTER ELEVEN

THE ATTACK ON THREE PIMPLES

28 June 1999 - The Day of Reckoning

At around 0100 hours, I was woken up to attend an 'urgent' call from Brigadier Amar Aul. The Brigade Commander was short, almost curt, when he uttered, "*Chief wants to speak to you.*" I was still wondering whom he meant when a deep voice on the other side said, "*Is this Ravinder speaking?*" Still confused as it did not sound like General Puri, I responded, "*Yes.*" The voice on the other side said, "*This is General Malik, your Chief!*"[33]

My Attack Orders

I gave my final orders to my Orders Group at about 1400 hours. Following the traditional format for such formal orders, I tried to keep them as crisp and to the point as possible. In any case, strung out as we were under effective artillery fire, we did not have the luxury to indulge in a great deal of discussions.

a) **Enemy.** He is expected to be holding **Three Pimples Complex**, **Point 4700 Ridge Line** and **Helmet - Area Junction** with platoon or platoon plus each. He may reinforce **Three Pimples Area** from Area **Junction / Helmet.** The enemy appears to lack mutual support and hence we can attack each without being interfered.

b) **Own Forces.** 18 GARHRIF was attacking **Point 4700 Ridge Line** tonight. (This was my guess; no one had shared this information with me)

c) **Mission.** 2 RAJRIF and attached troops will capture **Three Pimples Complex** by 1800 hours on 29 June.

[33] Vikram Jit Singh / TNN / Jul 2, 2019, http://timesofindia.indiatimes.com/articleshow/70035960.cms?utm_source=contentofinterest&utm_medium=text&utm_campaign=cppst "On the night of the assault on Three Pimples, I was at Drass and with Major General Puri. I asked him to get me on the radio with the 2 RAJRIF Commanding Officer, Lt Col Ravindranath, "Ravi". He was well forward with assaulting troops. He came onto the line and was pleasantly surprised that it was the COAS. I wished Ravi all the best for his battle. He was speaking over the radio set in whispers to me because he was very close to the enemy lines. And he and his troops did India very proud that night," General Malik told Times of India.

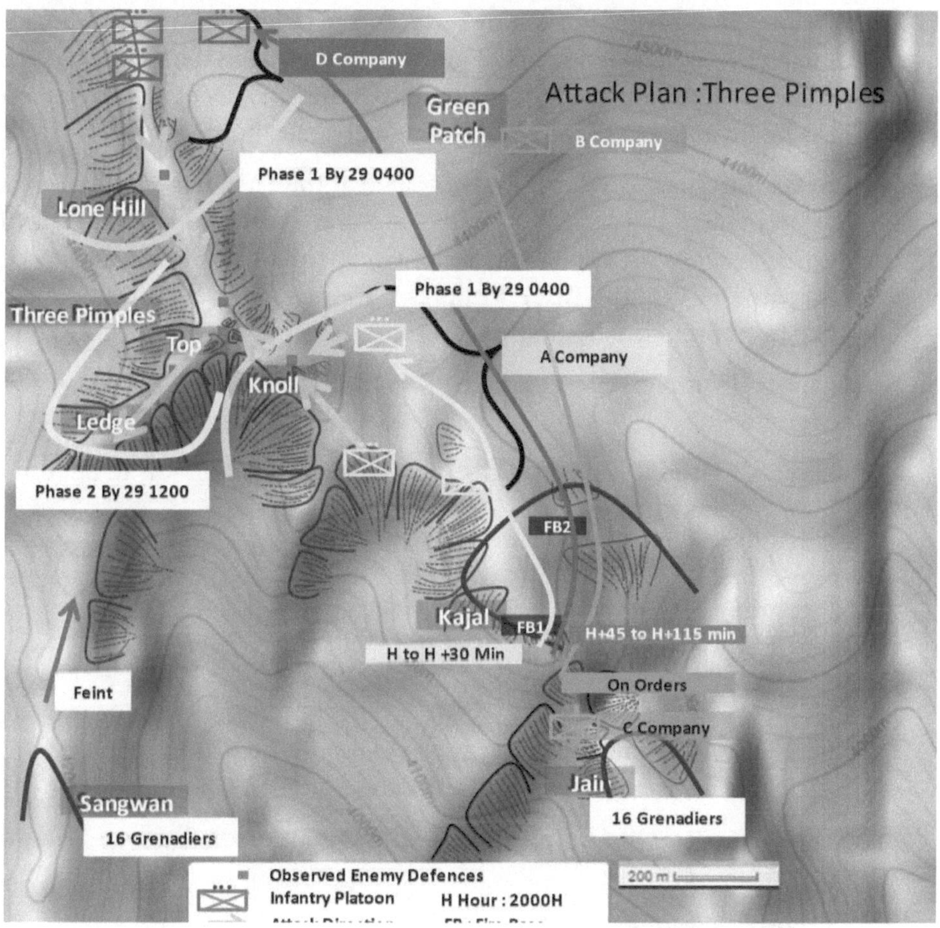

d) **Method.** Three Pimples will be captured in two phases.

Phase 1: Alpha Company will capture **Knoll** by attacking along the SE Approach by 0001 hours on 29 June. Delta Company will infiltrate and capture **Lone Hill** by attacking along the NW Approach by 0600 hours on 29 June.

Phase 2: Bravo Company to capture Area **Three Pimples** by 1800 hours on 29 June.

e) **Alpha Company** (Major Acharya). The task will be to protect the Southern Flank of D Coy during infiltration and capture **Area Knoll** by 0001 hours on 29 June. The additional resources allotted are a Rope Team of HAWS, a Ghatak Det, Mortar Fire Controller (MFC) and fire support will be from Fire Base 1.

f) **Delta Company** (Major Mohit Saxena). The task will be to capture Area **Lone Hill** by 0600 hours on 29 June by infiltrating in the wake of Alpha Coy. The additional resources allotted are an FOO, Det Ghatak Platoon (1 Officer and 2 OR) and fire support will be from Fire Base 2.

g) **Bravo Company** (Major Bajaj). Located at the Firm Base, the task was to be prepared to move to Green Patch on orders; to be prepared to act as reserves for Alpha and Delta Companies for Phase 1 and to be prepared to capture **Three Pimples / Helmet** on orders. Det Ghatak had been provided as additional resources.

h) **Charlie Company**. Located at the Firm base, the task would be assigned later.

j) **Ghatak Platoon**. Located at the Firm base, the platoon was to be ready to move on orders.

k) **Artillery Fire Support.**

Preparatory Bombardment – 1900 - 1930 hours timed.

Covering Fire. On Call on Pre-Registered Targets for Alpha Company, On Call for impromptu targets for Delta Company.

Fire Control. Lieutenant Saxena – FOO with Delta Company, Major Ashok Sharma, remainder artillery from Battalion Command Post.

Direct Firing. One Barrel at Bimbat School, Major Sandeep Kala to control.

l) **Infantry Weapons Fire Support**

Fire Base 1. Subedar Ram Kumar Lamba as the commander, with Alpha and Bravo Company weapons (MMG – 4, RL – 4, AGL – 2) and a MILAN Missile Launcher. The fire base was to support Alpha Company in Phase 1 and hold two first line scales of ammunition.

Fire Base 2. Subedar Ranbir Singh as the commander, with Delta and Charlie company weapons (MMG – 4, RL – 4, AGL – 2). The fire base was to support Delta Company in Phase 1 and hold two first line scales of ammunition.

m) **Coordination**. With H Hour at 2000 hours 28 June, the Order of Exit from the Firm Base was Alpha Company, followed by Delta Company. Bravo Company and Charlie Company were to stage forward to locations vacated by Alpha and Delta Companies, respectively.

n) **Administration.**

Food. Hot food before departure. Self-contained up to 48 hours.

Water. One Water Bottle for 24 hours.

Regimental Aid Post. Location Gorge.

Casualty Evacuation. Mortar Platoon and remainder of Administration Company.

A Flexible Plan

From the aforesaid, it would be obvious to any seasoned military campaigner that my plan was tentative, primarily because I had not firmed up the tasks for half of my command as yet. All actions and discussions up to this point had been exploratory in nature, but I was aware that subordinate commanders require firm orders to make their plans for execution and, more importantly, time to prepare, issue orders, and coordinate the finer details. I desisted from going for the conventional sequential phases (1, 2, 3, etc) by following the ridgeline. There were many compelling reasons.

Ground recce had revealed that we could contact the depth objective of **Lone Hill** and probably capture it if we could surprise the enemy. With this movement, we could cut off the enemy from his main defences and the possibility of external reinforcement. Attacking **Lone Hill** with **Knoll** allowed us to apply double the force in attack, forcing the enemy to divide his resources and attention. This would result in his inability to internally reinforce either of the features under attack by denuding **Three Pimples**, thus enhancing the chances of success of both attacks. Attacking thus would give us two independent routes to **Three Pimples**, and compel the enemy to defend both approaches to **Three Pimples** with available troops. Concentration on one approach while holding the enemy down on the other would speed up the capture of **Three Pimples**. Area **Green Patch**, North of **Three Pimples**, was located centrally to both Alpha and Delta Company attacks, thus a suitable location for reserves. But it was not possible to occupy it before the launch of the attack; we planned to relocate reserves to this location by midnight, the time frame I envisaged they would come into play. Accordingly Bravo Company, tasked as a reserve, was to be prepared to move on orders from the Firm Base.

More interestingly, if we could contact **Helmet**, the ground and enemy disposition permitted it, and carry the battle to **Area Junction**, then the enemy's attention would definitely shift to defend this key to all his defences.

Consequently, the enemy would either order **Three Pimples** to be abandoned to strengthen **Area Junction** or allow it to fend for itself as best as possible. Defenders thus isolated, without any hope of external assistance, are ideal candidates for surrender, especially if they face grave administrative challenges. My aversion to the physical assault of **Three Pimples** and the possibility of capturing it without a fight strongly motivated me to carry the battle to **Helmet** somehow. I had the required troops in Charlie Company, at reduced strength though, that could attack **Helmet** and give me the option of taking it with Bravo Company and Ghataks. But, I needed a commander capable of executing this crucial task. For all his courage and enthusiasm, Lieutenant Praveen Tomar, the Company Commander, was only in the sixth month of service; this task was far beyond his training. Major Bajaj had the requisite training, understanding and standing with troops to execute this task. But despatching him thus would leave a vacuum in Bravo Company for the capture of **Three Pimples** or to reinforce / exploit either of the Phase 1 attacks, a task of far greater importance. I had the option of taking command of Bravo Company myself and relieving Major Bajaj to command Charlie Company, but Bravo Company was to be relocated to **Area Green Patch** early in the battle to be poised to take advantage of the battle opportunities early. I did not have anyone to whom I could entrust the Fire Bases, which were to play a critical role in the attack. The troops at the Fire Base had been braving the enemy fire from 25 June onwards, despite taking casualties, and had stoically gone about the task of establishing the Fire Base. They needed a firm hand to guide them through the attack, so I decided to be with them as long as the attacks were rammed home. This resulted in Major Bajaj being loaded with an additional contingent task of being ready to capture **Helmet**. I missed the presence of Major Madan very badly. Had he agreed to man the Fire Base, I would have had the required freedom to move to the place where I thought I could contribute to achieving our objective, and he would have covered himself in glory.

Alpha Company (Major Acharya). Major Acharya had planned to assault **Knoll** along the Eastern face using the HAWS Rope team to assist if they came up against an unassailable rock face. This assault would get flanking fire support from Fire Base 1. Fire Base 1 was to suppress enemy fire on **Knoll** and **Three Pimples** that hindered movement and subsequently to shift to **Three Pimples** while fighting through the objective was in progress at **Knoll**. This attack was to be led by Lieutenant Vijayant Thapar. This attack incidentally acted as a screen for Delta Company to infiltrate along the Nala. Major Acharya had decided to position himself with Naib Subedar Shivnayak's Platoon at the base of **Knoll** along the SE approach as a reserve to Thapar's platoon. Acharya had decided to attack along the SE approach should Thapar get held up; if successful, link up quickly. Subedar Bhupinder Singh's platoon was to be echeloned 500 metres towards **Kajal**, awaiting orders. I was satisfied with the plan.

Delta Company (Major Mohit Saxena). Major Mohit had planned to follow Alpha Company out of the Firm Base and follow the route taken by Lieutenant Thapar's platoon between the two fire bases to reach the Nala and infiltrate along its course. His company was to be preceded by a Ghatak Patrol led by

Lieutenant Kenguruse to provide protection and act as guides. He had planned to lead with Subedar Karan Singh's platoon, followed by his party, and Subedar Shayar Singh's platoon brought the rear. On reaching the Saddle between **Lone Hill** and **Helmet**, he had planned to establish a Company Firebase and assault **Lone Hill** from the North. I told him to properly coordinate targets with Fire Base 2, as the weapons would be firing at their extreme ranges.

Bravo Company (Major Bajaj). Major Bajaj had nominated Lieutenant Rautela to be his lead platoon. Allotting him the Ghatak detachment, he had tasked him to be ready to contact **Helmet** on orders. He had tasked Subedar Chandrabhan to be prepared to go to **Lone Hill** and Subedar Maheshwar Dayal's platoon to be ready to go to **Knoll**. Given his tasking, there is nothing more he could have done.

My Expectations

In my mind, I was sure Alpha Company (Acharya) would capture **Knoll** given Acharya's plan and preparation, proximity to the firebase and preponderance of force. Delta Company's (Mohit) operation was a gamble. Information about the enemy was not complete, not even sufficient. The additional feature near **Lone Hill**, not on the map, was a question mark. Though the infiltration route was reconnoitred and free of unexpected obstacles or enemy positions, infiltration is always risky.

Additionally, **Lone Hill** was at extreme ranges of 800 to 1000 metres of infantry support weapons at the Fire Base. Close fire support for the actual attack would be challenging to control, especially at night. In Major Mohit, I had a commander who planned meticulously, understood the challenges well and was dogged enough to press home against all odds; events proved that my assessment was correct. The least I wanted from his attack was a strong engagement of the enemy from the rear; anything more was a bonus.

Mentally, I had decided that if both these Phase 1 attacks were to get a strong grip on their objectives by the early part of the night, then I would release Bravo Company (Bajaj) to capture **Helmet** and relocate myself to **Green Patch** with Charlie Company (Kale) and Ghataks ready to exploit the success of three points of contact, **Helmet** being top priority. This I did not share with my company commanders. But they could sense it, and one of the company commanders asked, "*Sir, between me and you, how hard should we try to engage the enemy?*" I replied, "*Between you and me, if I ask you to capture any objective, I expect you to try with all your might to capture it.*"

We have attacks classified as Primary, Secondary, Diversionary, Holding, Feint, etc. These are all battle designs that affect where you will locate your resources for maintaining the momentum. For the success of operations, the enemy should not be able to distinguish one from the other until it is too late. That is only possible if the impact at the point of contact has the same vigour and intensity. Without this, these attacks will not achieve what they were designed for. Hence, it is a good practice for a commander to keep the battle design to himself and reveal to his subordinates their task and not its effect. For instance, if you want to feint an attack on some objective, you will task some subordinate unit to launch an attack. Once the process of attack is underway, you will halt and/or call back this attack at a moment when you assess that the purpose for which you had launched this attack has been met or you assess that the enemy has seen through the game and is not reacting the way you thought he would. You should not task the subordinate commander to launch a feint; he should be tasked to capture the objective. It is for the commander to come up with a believable narrative and to select the right man to execute it. This is combat psychology at work; it implies knowing your troops as much as knowing the enemy and how they will react.

What if you are told your task is only a feint? If you are extraordinarily capable, you will plan and execute it without letting your subordinates know the purpose while conveying to the enemy a sense of real threat. If you are ordinary, you will inform everyone that it is a feint and not the real thing, ensuring everyone has pulled back that wee bit. A combined result is that the enemy is not convinced that this is a real attack and does not react as expected, and the superior commanders' design is not executed.

Hot Food before Battle

The body tends to become sluggish without balanced food; it was even more pronounced at those altitudes. After two days of continuous activity without proper food and water, I observed that the actions became laborious and physical output reduced drastically. Any serious mountaineer will vouch for this; they stock up the camps enroute to a summit before finally assaulting it. What we were attempting was no less, the difference being that we had an enemy waiting for us at the top!!

Some of the troops, especially those in the firebase and commanders at various levels, had been in the firebase continuously for three to four days, surviving on packed dry food items like 'Churma', 'Puri – Sabji' they had brought with them, or that was later supplied. I thought a good supper of 'Watery Dal and Rotis' would go a long way in re-energising the troops just before the assault. Major Rathore, in response to my direction that troops would be provided with a hot meal before the assault, had pushed up the 'Pre-Cooked Meals' packets that had become lately available. This was more than I had expected. It was a novelty for the troops as the packet came with its stove stand and fire briquettes; they soon cooked their meals in the small utensils they invariably carry in preference to the government issued 'Mess Tin'. The meal brightened the general mood as any satisfactory meal would. Major Rathore had also ensured adequate water; all assaulting troops drank as much as possible and filled their water bottles. The administrative battle had been reasonably won. It was now time for the tactical battle.

The combined effort of Major Rathore, Subedar Major Madan Singh and Subedar Adjutant Kuldeep Singh, under the unrelenting stewardship of Major Sandeep Kala, had ensured all men and materials required for the battle were pushed up, and all arrangements had been made to receive and evacuate the inevitable casualties.

The Legend of Karni Mata

I decided to talk to Alpha Company (Acharya) as they were the first ones out; their smooth launch would set the ball rolling for the battalion. There was another peculiarity of Alpha Company: they were having an 'Aarti' (prayer meeting and hymn singing) to invoke the blessings of **'Karni Mata'**, the presiding deity of the Company, which they would carry into battle, a tradition in existence since 1912. Normally, every battalion has one centralised religious institute; ours was a 'mandir' located at the rear location at Moghulpura. We had a 'Mandir' function on 26 June to invoke God's blessings for the success of the hazardous task we were about to undertake. This 'Karni Mata Mandir' of Alpha Company is different; it has a legend.

After the 'Aarti,' I spoke to the men of Alpha Company (Acharya). I told them that the name of the battalion was in their hands. I told them that others, especially Charlie Company, had proven themselves in Tololing; it was their turn now. Given the healthy rivalry between the Jats and the Rajputs of the battalion, I dropped a hint that should you fail; Jats will never allow you to forget it, however, justified your case may be. "*Just as Charlie Company was always barbed for their poor show in Sonapindi Gali, you too will be heckled at most competitions in future*", I gently reminded them. I spoke to them of the blessings of **Karni Mata**, which this Company always enjoyed, and their obligation to their presiding deity. "*You are carrying your God into battle; you owe it to her to be victorious whatever the price, or else don't carry her and disgrace her with your cowardice.*" This got them fully agitated, and troops vied with each other to assure me that **Knoll** would be taken at all costs. Satisfied that Alpha Coy was ready to be launched, I asked them to be ready to attack in about two hours. As

I was departing, I told the company I would come to see them at **Knoll** the next day. I bit my tongue even as I uttered these words; I was challenging fate, I felt. The thought that I was not sure which of us would see the daylight of morrow ran across my mind; I silently prayed for everyone's safekeeping and asked for pardon to have had the audacity to have thought all of us to be immortal.

As commanders, we can only plan, provide and enthuse; the execution is in the hands of the junior commanders and the troops. They, with their sweat and blood, grit and determination, courage and conviction, implement on the ground what we commanders have in our minds. In victory, we tend to underplay this most important aspect while cornering the accolades.

Preparing the Target

With the Fire Base Commanders, Battery Commander and Sandeep Kala giving me the thumbs-up sign, we were ready to go. At 1930 hours, the preparatory bombardment started and lasted for 30 minutes. **Knoll**, **Three Pimples Complex** and **Lone Hill** were effectively engaged with artillery; **Knoll** and **Three Pimples** were also engaged by direct firing of Bofors gun. The enemy weapons had fallen silent. We reserved the fire of the Fire Base for later use. As this was happening, Alpha Company (Acharya) had moved up to be launched into attack. The passage from the security of Fire Base 2 into the forward slopes was through a natural tunnel about five metres long, allowing a single person at a time. So, we moved up, a platoon at a time that permitted crossing in an orderly manner. Lieutenant Vijayant Thapar's platoon moved to the Fire Base 1 location, followed by Shivnayak's and Bhupinder's platoons. By the time the preparatory bombardment ended, Alpha Company (Acharya) was poised to launch the assault. At 2030 hours, we staged Delta Company (Mohit) forward to the Fire Base area to prepare them to follow in the wake of the Alpha Company attack.

Then all hell broke loose!

Surprise is Lost!

The whole firebase area came under heavy artillery fire. Shells were landing all over the firebase. I instantly knew I had blundered. The enemy had been engaging us intermittently at the firebase. He was well aware of the feverish activity that had been taking place in the Fire Base area; he would have easily guessed that an attack was in the offing. The enemy had faced many attacks along the just captured Tololing ridge and must have been able to read that an attack follows preparatory bombardment and opening of infantry fire support weapons fire. He would have known that the assault troops were in the area of

Kajal, whatever name he called it. To add to our woes, it was a full moon, and the forward slopes of **Kajal** on which Lieutenant Vijayant Thapar was descending would have been visible even in failing light as the enemy was no more than about 500 metres. In a nutshell, we had failed to achieve any surprise and were at the receiving end of some intense and accurate artillery shelling.

Each blast shook us to the core like strong physical blows, like the one experienced while firing a 106 mm Recoilless Gun. Miraculously, no shell landed on Fire Base 1, probably because it was perched on a ridge no more than 10 to 15 metres wide. Shells were landing at its front and rear. Despite all the shelling, these men at Fire Base 1, under the leadership of Subedar Ram Kumar Lamba, continuously engaged **Knoll** and **Three Pimples**, thus preventing the enemy from engaging troops of Alpha Company (Acharya) that were moving under covering fire. **Sangwan Location** was also engaging the enemy at **Ledge** and moved towards it with some troops.

Delta Company (Mohit)

The crisis, however, was with Delta Company (Mohit). I had them concentrated at the firebase to give them a pep talk before they were launched into the attack. I had reckoned that with Alpha Company closing in with the enemy and about to engage them, I could talk to the men about their operation's importance and degree of difficulty. I had planned to tell them that this attack would require all their famed Rajput valour and tenacity to come into play. While their fellow Rajput Alpha Company were to bite hard at the head, they were to slip in and take a hard bite at the rear; I intended to tell them and get them fired up. Intense enemy shelling put paid to my efforts.

I was mortally scared of Delta Company suffering massive casualties in the firebase should a stray shell land where they were huddled up. I knew if anything like that happened, it would become almost impossible to launch them into attack soon. I had read and heard of many instances where the assaulting troops had lost the appetite for an attack when they suffered casualties early on. I had to get them somehow out of Fire Base and quickly. Pushing them back was not an option as shells fell as far back as the gorge area where the Regimental Aid Post (RAP) was located. The success of my whole plan depended upon Delta Company attacking Lone Hill in the enemy's depth; my strong belief was that such an attack would unnerve him and force him to create errors. Now, I could not push them ahead where Alpha Company was under severe artillery shelling, nor could I push them back nor stay put. I had to make a quick decision, and I made it.

Lieutenant Kenguruse led the Ghatak team to act as a protective patrol to Delta Company's infiltrating column. He was originally tasked to shadow Lieutenant Thapar's platoon. Once Thapar launched an attack on **Knoll** from the North, he was to skirt around Thapar's rear, keeping a safe distance from getting embroiled and sneaking in the rest of the Delta Company. Major Mohit, the Company Commander, having led a recce patrol himself, was well aware of the route and would guide his troops in conjunction with Lieutenant Kenguruse. Lieutenant Kenguruse had led a patrol to **Green Patch** on a route that started on the **Tololing Nala** about 300 metres to the East of **Kajal**.

I decided to switch the approach of Delta Company (Mohit) to follow the route **Fire Base - Tololing Nala - Green Patch - Lone Hill**. I told Lieutenant Kenguruse to take them to **Green Patch** and told Major Mohit to get to **Lone Hill** from **Green Patch**. With this, I literally chased Delta Company out of the Fire Base, wishing them good luck. I kept repeating '*Badhia Karna, Bhago*' as the only words of encouragement. That the slope to Tololing Nala was downhill helped a lot; within minutes, they were in the safety of the nala, not a launch I had envisaged for them. They had been safely launched, and I would take it any day as against the crisis I was facing just a few minutes back. The enemy artillery shelling had done its damage; there was a crisis on the edge of the Fire Base.

A section of Lieutenant Vijayant Thapar's was hit by shelling, and so was the Medium Machine Gun (MMG) and Automatic Grenade Launcher (AGL) position on Fire Base 2. Fire Base 2 was a compromise; it needed adequate cover, but it was the only location from which we could support Delta Company's attack on **Lone Hill**. While we had built protection against flat-trajectory weapons, there was hardly any protection against high-trajectory weapons. Like at Tololing, we hoped the enemy would not engage us effectively, but he did. To add to the difficulty was the fact that the area was more flattish near the weapon emplacements, making the effect of shelling even more devastating. Delta Company was still some time away from attacking or asking for fire support; hence, I ordered Subedar Ranbir to move his troops into the safety of a few rocky outcrops near the Fire Base and wait out the enemy fire. In taking this decision, I was banking on the Forward Observation Officer (FOO) Lieutenant Ajay Saxena, who was with Delta Company, to provide any fire support that should be required.

Around 2200 hours on 28 June, Lieutenant Kenguruse came on the set to report he was in the **Area Green Patch** and on their way to **Lone Hill**. He surprised me by saying he had found a WD Telephone Cable and asked me what he should be doing with it. I asked them to cut it. But the presence of a telephone cable in the middle of nowhere perplexed me. What was its purpose? I kept wondering. Could it be for communication between the defences of **Three Pimples** and **Point 4700** Ridge? If so, why in the open, unprotected area? It was not falling into any pattern of enemy deployment I had in my mind. Having cut it, I was satisfied that it would help isolate the enemy troops further; that is all that mattered to me.

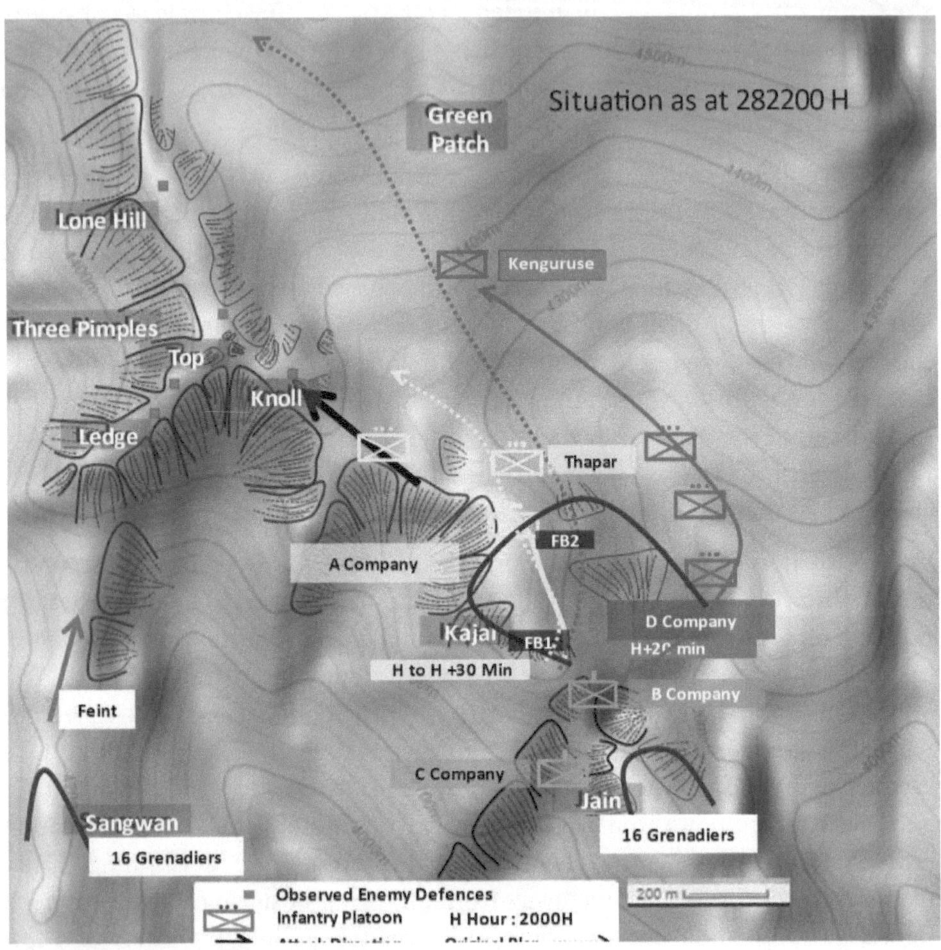

Actions of Alpha Company (Acharya)

Captain Thapar was, in the meantime, attending to his casualties and regrouping and was held up. All I could do was wait for the situation to develop. Around this time, Fire Base 1 started receiving enemy machine gun fire. Nothing effective, but we knew the enemy bullets were flying our way, the shock of preparatory bombardment was wearing out, and the enemy was regaining his composure; our attacking troops had not yet made contact with the enemy.

I then took stock of what was happening in Alpha Company. Captain Vijayant Thapar was still reorganising his sections after being hit by shelling. They had taken a few injuries, and the sections had scattered and mingled with Fire Base 2 troops in a scramble for cover. On enquiry of what his plans were, Major Acharya said that he had moved Subedar Shivnayak's platoon to the base of **Knoll**. He had moved with this platoon and said he would launch the attack from SE with Subedar Bhupinder's platoon as a reserve. I asked him about Thapar's platoon. He said he had tasked him to stand down from attack, gather his men, and come to **Knoll**.

Major Acharya attacked **Knoll** from SE with close fire support from Fire Base 1. Around 2300 hours, Major Acharya came on the radio net and reported that they had cleared a major portion of **Knoll** and were left with probably one bunker. He asked us to stop the fire on **Knoll**, which was now endangering his troops. On enquiring, he said that he was level with the enemy, not more than 15 to 20 metres away, and was trying to figure out how to assault it.

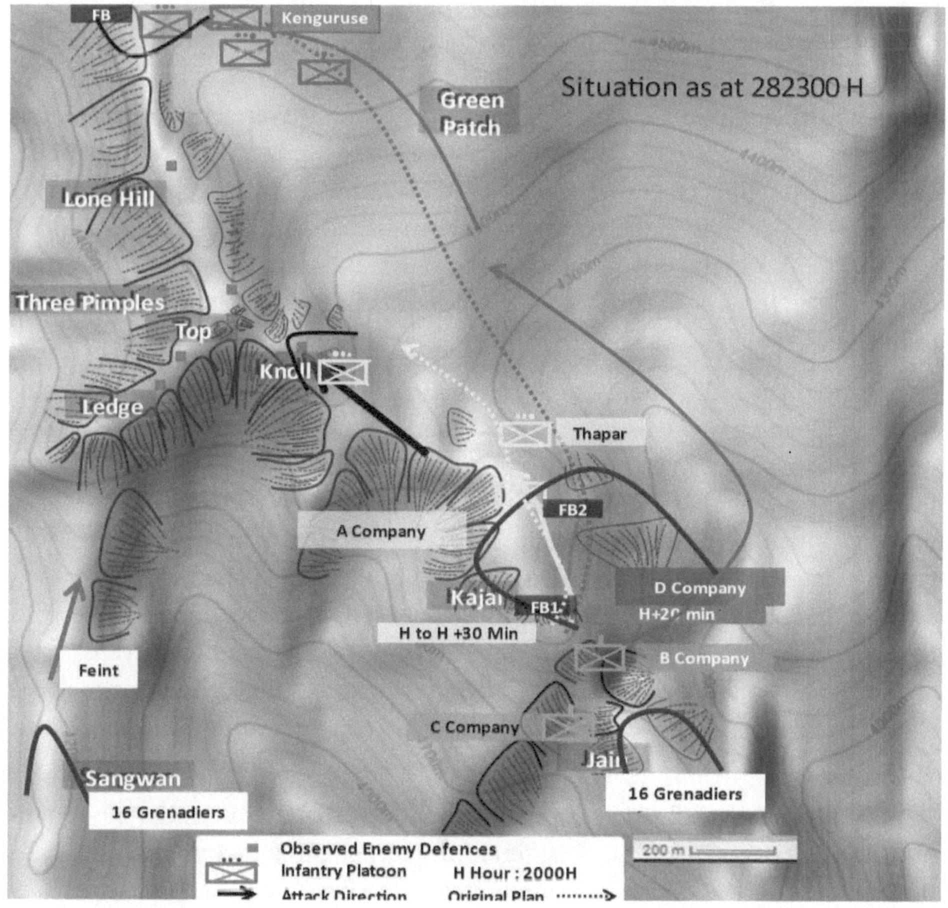

From my side, the objective of the attack of Alpha Company had been met; we had established a foothold in enemy defences and engaged him closely from SE; he could not move without yielding **Knoll**. I ordered Major Acharya to firm in his current location, build sangars and start engaging the enemy. I told him that we would plan the final clearance of **Knoll** during the daytime when terrain information would become clear.

Actions of Bravo Company (Bajaj)

Elated that one part of the plan had gone well, I released Bravo Coy under Major Bajaj, which had been moved up to the Fire Base area, to move to **Area Green Patch**. Lieutenant Rautela's platoon was the first one to move around 2330 hours.

Around this time, we started having interference in our battalion radio net. I could recognise CO 18 GARHRIF, Colonel Chakravarthy's voice. It was a case of two battalions' nets working on the same frequency. My radio operator informed me that this was the frequency allotted to us. I got on to the net and contacted Colonel Chakravarthy, revealing my identity; I asked how they also have the same frequency. He informed me that they, too, had been allotted the same working frequency. We decided that we should switch to a different frequency. In the middle of the operation, this could be tricky. However, our Signal platoon had retained the previously used frequency on different channels. We all shifted to this reserve frequency and encountered no interference. But we had another peculiar challenge. We had been issued new STAR V sets in place of ANPRC 25, which we had been used to thus far, even as recently as the attack on Tololing. STAR V sets came with programmable channels with pre-loaded frequencies, which was a challenge in itself.

Earlier the radio operators would manually change frequency through the whole range; here we had some prefixed channels. While a runner could be sent with frequency information, now one required a device, making it less flexible. Luckily for us, our Signal platoon had decided to keep the regular frequency used in counter-insurgency operations as a reserve; thanks to them, we switched quickly. There was another peculiarity of this radio set. One had to speak slowly and softly. If one spoke quickly or loudly, as often happens with men in the thick of the action, the receivers could not determine what was being transmitted as the signal would get disturbed. The only way to be intelligible was to speak slowly and softly. It was really a great effort to keep it so, failing this, one could always hear 'Say again over!'

This probably helped us appear in total control of the situation, though the ground reality was many times different. Enemy shelling had moved away, and the Fire Base parties breathed a sigh of relief. Fire Base 2 was back in its position to support the Delta Company (Mohit) attack. The shelling had moved to cover the approaches to **Three Pimples**. We had adopted a movement pattern where a platoon was spread over about 200 metres, and a gap of 500 metres was kept between the platoons. The platoon was located according to their place of likely use and sequence. As a result, we did not suffer much from this defensive fire of enemy artillery, but what we suffered was to have a telling effect.

By midnight, Major Mohit informed me that they had established a Company Fire Base for an attack on **Lone Hill.** This meant, to me, an absolute cut-off route of withdrawal for the complete **Three Pimples** defence complex of the enemy. I was highly elated that despite initial hiccups and setbacks, the troops had achieved the design that I had in mind.

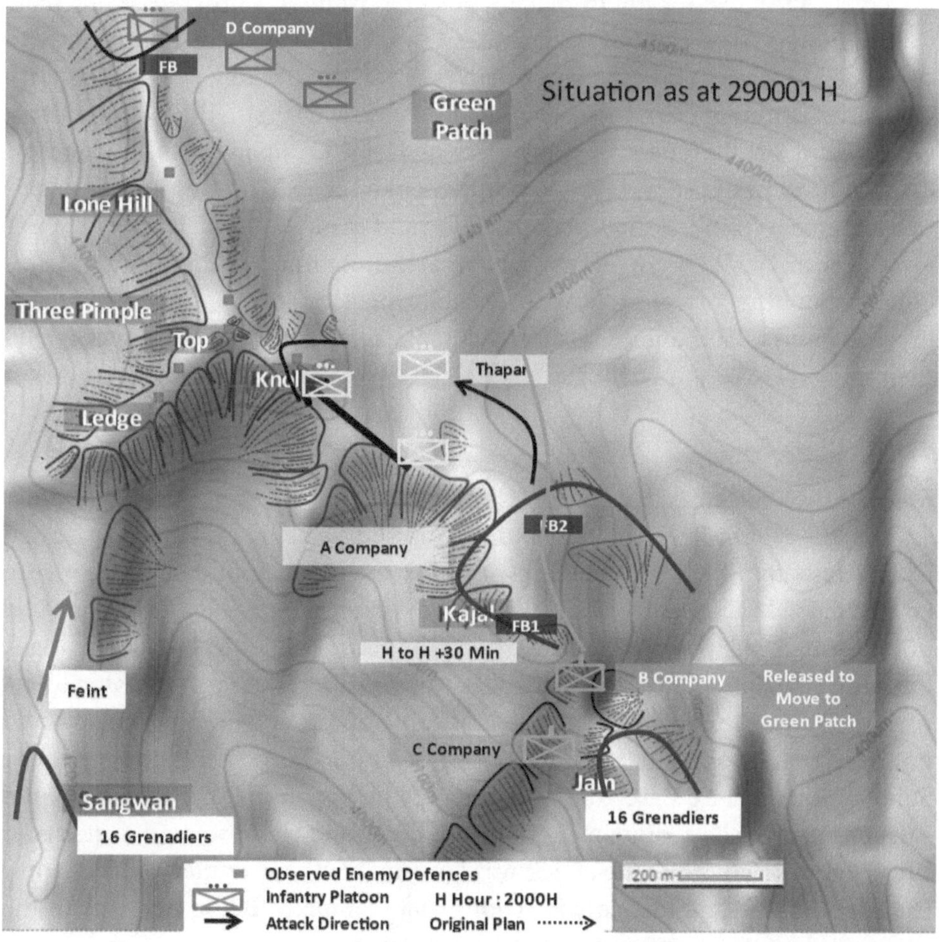

Alpha Company fully engaged the front at **Knoll** and Delta Company, sitting astride the ridgeline running to **Helmet**; we had fully invested and cut off **Three Pimples Complex**. If we could prevent the only enemy troops capable of linking up to relieve the enemy at **Three Pimples**, then this feature with the complete enemy would be ripe to capture without a fight once their water was finished. The objective that had that capability, in my view, was **Helmet** and **Junction Area**. Lieutenant Rautela was already on his way to **Green Patch**; Major Bajaj, Bravo Company Commander, and Subedar Ram Kumar Lamba's platoon were with me.

As Alpha Company (Acharya) was firmly in possession of a major portion of **Knoll** and suppressive fire on **Three Pimples** could be ensured with the help of detachment commanders, Subedar Lamba reverted to the command of his platoon. In the meantime, 18 GARHRIF attacks on **Point 4700 ridge** had been launched, and the fight was fully joined. With the enemy so fully engaged, it was extremely attractive for me to make a push for **Helmet**. I ordered Major Bajaj to capture the **Area Helmet** with Bravo Company. Lieutenant Rautela was to continue to **Helmet** and establish a firm base for an attack by Bravo Company. The earliest time of attack we calculated would be at first light. I was waiting for a report on the operations progress of Delta Company (Mohit) before I decided to commit the troops. Everything looked so exhilarating and tied up; I was extremely confident that Major Bajaj would easily capture **Helmet** by sheer force of surprise. We were on the brink of achieving much with minimal losses. One was looking forward to it with certain expectations; it was just a matter of time. Around 0030 hours, I wished Major Bajaj good luck, and he set off. But then things started unravelling.

Things Go Awry!

Major Ashok Sharma, the Battery Commander, informed me that Captain A Saxena, the FOO with Delta Company (Mohit), was being evacuated as he had been a casualty of enemy shelling; with him, the FOO team had also gone. In effect, Major Mohit had continued to bravely press on despite this loss; he had not informed me when he had reported that he was about to launch an attack on **Lone Hill** half an hour earlier. I was worried and asked my operator to get Major Mohit on the radio set; he tried for some time and reported that he could not raise Delta Company on the net. I asked him to keep trying and called for Subedar Ranbir, Fire Base 2 commander. He informed me that they had fired in support of Delta Company some time back, and there was no request for fire. That worried me as the attack was launched without artillery and infantry fire support. We had lost contact with Delta Company. Being unaware of the situation, I postponed my decision to commit to the capture of **Helmet**. But with every passing moment, the situation was becoming critical. Lieutenant Rautela was approaching **Helmet**. It was a matter of an hour or so before he would contact **Helmet**. Even by 0100 hours, we had been unable to contact Delta Company, and I was becoming slightly apprehensive. Then, the situation worsened.

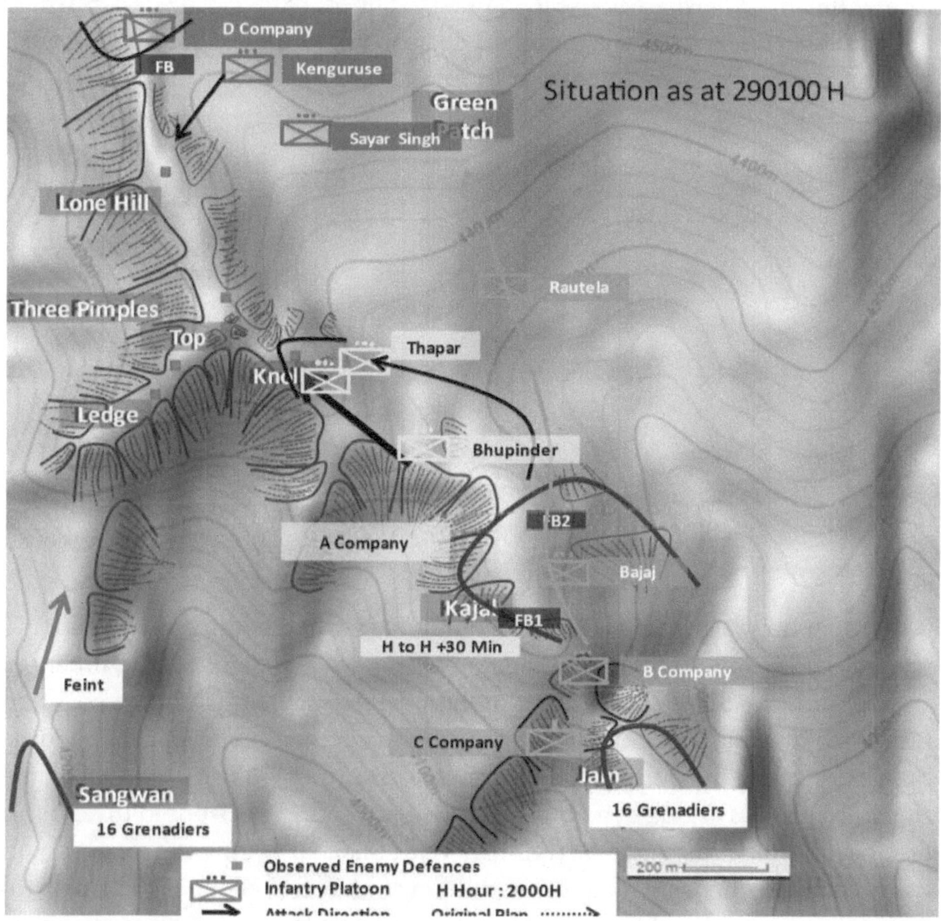

Tragedy Strikes in Alpha Company

Subedar Shivnayak of Alpha Company came on the radio and informed that in an exchange of hand grenades with the remaining bunker on **Knoll**, Major Acharya had been killed. This grenade had also incapacitated the Alpha Company radio operator Chandrabhan and senior JCO Sub Man Singh.[34] That

[34] *Kargil Victory The Battle from Peak to Peak,* Colonel SC Tyagi, Speaking Tiger Publishing Pvt. Ltd., 2019, Page 100. Major Acharya now led the assaulting troops. Knoll had two enemy sangars. The first was soon captured. However, the next one was still firing and holding on. Acharya called one of his JCOs aside and started working out a plan to tackle this position. It was around midnight when the enemy saw them closing in. A hand grenade landed between Major Acharya and the JCO. Major P. Acharya lost his life in the explosion, while the JCO was severely wounded in the thigh. Major Acharya had been very close to his men and was loved by them as he could speak to them in their own language, despite not being from the area.

hit me like a punch on the solar plexus. I was clueless about what I needed to do now. Do I roll back, or do I press onto **Helmet**? Bravo Company (Bajaj) was the only reserve with an effective commander available to me; the question tormenting me was where to use it. I talked to Subedar Shivnayak; he confirmed he could hold on. With that assurance, I decided not to change Bravo Company's mission. I was confident success at **Helmet** would ensure the success of our complete operation.

Then hope blossomed again. Captain Thapar had got his platoon up and had reached **Knoll**. I spoke to him and told him to take charge of the situation. I spoke to him at length, appreciating how he had rallied his men, and I told him to hold on till morning and to ensure the safety of the troops by building sangars. I asked him to prevent the troops from bunching up and exposing themselves. I was asking of a youngster, who was more predisposed to action, a task beyond his experience or training. With Subedar Bhupinder's platoon on its way up, they had adequate strength to beat back any effort of the enemy to recapture the position. I then explicitly ordered him to hold on till morning for further orders.

By around 0130 hours, Lieutenant Rautela reported reaching Area **Green Patch**. With Bravo Company (Bajaj) well on the way, our plans to surprise and shake up the enemy were about an hour from manifesting. Our efforts to raise Delta Company (Mohit) on the radio were, however, turning out to be futile. I was getting anxious by the minute. Knowing the criticality, everyone tried to contact Delta Company somehow, but to no avail.

We saw some firing in the **Lone Hill** area. There was sporadic fire from the **Three Pimples** area, and we tried to suppress it from our Fire Base 1.

He was always the Master of Ceremonies at the functions held in the battalion. He had been married just a few months ago. He was awarded posthumous Maha Vir Chakra.

Since Subedar Ram Kumar Lamba had left, I had become 'de-facto' Fire Base Commander and was in constant touch with Alpha Company (now led by Thapar) from my command post. The whole battle hung in balance; we had gained some initial footholds despite the heavy and accurate enemy shelling that nearly ruined our launch from the firebase and despite the attrition and disorder it caused to the assaulting troops. Yet, we did not have the capture of any substantive feature to report. We were unaware of the situation of Delta Company (Mohit). Based on initial successes, I had gambled and released Bravo Company (Bajaj) to capture **Helmet**. Should I order Lieutenant Rautela to halt at **Area Green Patch**, concentrate Bravo Company there and revert to my original plan? That was the question that was racing in my mind. Even though Delta Company (Mohit) was out of communication, I was confident that they too, like Alpha Company (now under Thapar), had the enemy engaged closely despite the loss of their company commander.

Even now, my best chance for capturing **Three Pimples** without the costly fighting through the objective was by isolating it by capture / contact of **Helmet**, so I decided to continue with the plan. The plan's success depended entirely on Alpha Company (now under Thapar) consolidating its substantial foothold on **Knoll** and bringing **Three Pimples** under fire from close ranges. While Major Bajaj (Bravo Company) was onto his task, and I was confident that Major Mohit (Delta Company) was causing the required fear in the enemy's rear, I decided to personally guide Alpha Company (now under Thapar) to consolidate.

Second Tragedy in Alpha Company

Another disaster struck us immediately. Subedar Shivnayak reported that Captain Thapar had been killed in an attempt to clear the enemy bunker.[35] Shock is a very mild word to describe my feeling. There was a strong taste of bile in my mouth; there was this heart-wrenching at having lost such a young life; there was this sense of helplessness, and there was the loss of ability to think. I went numb; I had this unrealistic feeling of floating over the battlefield in

[35] *Kargil Victory The Battle from Peak to Peak,* Colonel SC Tyagi, Speaking Tiger Publishing Pvt. Ltd., 2019, Page 100. Lt Vijayant Thapar had by now regained his command and control. He was ordered to take control of the situation at the Knoll. On reaching the scene of battle, Lt Thapar quickly assessed that while this sangar was holding onto the Knoll, the enemy could not be defeated. He ordered his men to follow him while he personally assaulted the enemy sangar. He wanted to avenge the killing of Major Acharya. Lt Vijayant Thapar was barely a few feet away from the enemy sangar when a burst of fire tore through him, killing him instantly. Vijayant was a fourth-generation military officer; his father is a retired Colonel. He was fond of cricket and music. He had shared an audio cassette full of peppy songs with me while under training at the Corps Battle School just before this war. He left behind an emotional note to his parents. One of his obituaries read, 'A soldier at 19, an officer at 20 and a martyr at 22.' He was awarded posthumous Vir Chakra.

slow motion. All I could see was blooming failures everywhere. Without Alpha Company holding out, both Delta Company (Mohit) and to an extent, Bravo Company (Bajaj) would be endangered. If that were to happen, the Ghataks and a depleted Charlie Company were insufficient reserves to be decisive anywhere. The time was around 0200 hours, and first light was two hours away, which would blow away all our surprise and expose us to the observed fire of the enemy, both direct and indirect. Something deep within me was screaming **'Act' 'Act' 'Act'**. Then, I decided to recoil Bravo Company (Bajaj).

My first task was to establish contact with Delta Company (Mohit). Lieutenant Rautela had crossed **Area Green Patch** and was the closest to it. Lieutenant Rautela was tasked to move to **Lone Hill**, contact Major Mohit and report back.

My second task was to get a strong commander to **Knoll** to rally Alpha Company, which had lost both its officers and some key junior leaders were wounded. I tasked Major Bajaj to reach **Knoll** with a platoon of Bravo Company immediately. The third platoon that was in the process of leaving the Fire Base 2 area was ordered to stay put and await further orders.

With recovery action in motion, I got on to keeping Alpha Company (now under Subedar Shivnayak) on the **Knoll** until Major Bajaj arrived. Having established direct communication with Subedar Shivnayak, I assessed he was shaken but composed. The platoon was running low on ammunition, having expended it during capture and firefight during the night. The nearest troops capable of relieving them were Subedar Bhupinder's platoon. They had been moving from Firm Base around 2330 hours; it was strange that they had yet to reach **Knoll**, about 600 to 700 metres. I contacted Subedar Bhupinder on the radio set and asked him where he was; he was not sure. He said they had been among high rocks for the last hour, but they had not been able to find a way up. I asked him if he could hear the firing. He reported that it was somewhere about 100 to 200 metres ahead of him. I asked him to reach Subedar Shivnayak's platoon quickly.

I ordered Subedar Shivnayak to hold on until reinforcements arrived, and I told him to conserve the ammunition. We would provide fire support from Fire Base 1, and he would have to direct it. We earmarked one MMG, one RL and one AGL for close support of Subedar Shivnayak; with the rest, we concentrated on **Three Pimples**. Without knowing the exact location of our troops on **Knoll**, it was quite some task to engage enemy defences barely 10 to 20 metres away from our own troops. I was aware that more than our ability to pin down the enemy, the sure knowledge that we were with them was more important. I had to keep their morale up till reinforcements arrived. We decided to start with machine gun firing tracers. We chose a line well to the left of **Knoll** and asked Subedar Shivnayak to watch for the fire and correct it towards the enemy bunker on **Knoll**. He kept correcting it, and at one point, he asked us to stop it, saying they were in the line of fire and it was impossible to continue. With relative positions unclear, engaging the enemy with rocket launchers was impossible.

It was around 0230 hours on 29 June 1999, when Major Bajaj (Bravo Company) reached the base of **Knoll**; he still had about 30 to 45 minutes before he could reach the top of **Knoll**. Lieutenant Rautela had moved towards **Lone Hill** after returning to **Area Green Patch**; he had not been able to raise Delta Company (Mohit) on the radio set.

Bofors Saves the Day

We were sitting on sandbags in the makeshift command post, I was occupying a slightly higher position for a better view of the battlefield. At this juncture, Major Ashok Sharma, the Battery Commander supporting us, said, pointing to something on his board, "**Why don't we try fire of Bofors in direct firing?**" I bent down to have a closer look, and no sooner a burst of machine gun fire swept through the command post, hitting the rock face behind us. Looking up, I saw that it was in the line my head was just a second earlier; I turned to Major Ashok and said, "**You just saved my life**". Such are the chances in battle. I was not sure if we could lay the gun onto the target at night; I was not even sure if the gun was available for our use.

Nevertheless, I asked him to check if we could engage with Bofors. To our good luck, not only was the Bofors gun available, but it was laid on the Knoll, the last target to be engaged. Major Kala was available at the gun position to direct the fire. I decided to try the direct fire of Bofors.

Using a Bofors gun was easy, but managing its repercussions was challenging. We could not leave our troops exposed to the fire of Bofors shell; hence, we had to withdraw them. I asked Subedar Shivnayak to retreat about 200 metres to get a clear shot at the target. He refused flatly, stating that if we retreated, it would be very difficult to regain the objective again. I was in a quandary; the commander on the ground was recommending me not to withdraw him, and at the same time, it was impossible to ensure their safety from the fire of Bofors gun without such a withdrawal. Firing might destroy our own troops who were holding on tenuously. I instinctively knew that Subedar Shivanayak's recommendation was militarily sound, so I was looking for a solution in which the troops continued to hold on, and we still used the Bofors.

From my experience of seeing the locals milling around our field firing ranges in Infantry School, Mhow and other field firing ranges, I was sure they would be reasonably safe if they could take some solid cover on the leeward side of the line of fire. I enquired from Subedar Shivnayak whether he could find some solid rocks where the troops could take cover, and he replied in affirmative. I asked him to protect himself and his troops and report back. We asked the Bofors gun to stand by for firing on Knoll on orders.

Within a few minutes, Subedar Shivnayak was on the radio, confirming they were ready to receive the fire. Bofors gun opened up and a solitary shot impacted Knoll; one could see the flash. Subedar Shivnayak was on the radio set in a jiffy, asking us to stop the fire. My heart sank again, fearing the worst. The luck this time had rolled on our side; the single shot had hit the very same bunker on Knoll that was holding up Alpha Company. That shot had caused shock, confusion and disorder in enemy defences. Subedar Shivnayak reported that the enemy was in disarray, and he wanted to attack immediately.

Ordering the Bofors to stop the fire, I asked Subedar Shivnayak to go ahead with his assault. Within minutes, he reported that the enemy had withdrawn from **Knoll** in confusion and that we were in full control of **Knoll**. I asked him to firm in to await the reinforcements. Subedar Bhupinder's platoon had by now managed to reach the top.

The time now was around 0300 hours. An RL Illumination Round was fired, followed by a barrage of small arms fire in the bowl near **Lone Hill**; we did not know what it was.

Delta Company Resurfaces!

Major Mohit (Delta Company) suddenly burst on the radio net. There was so much I had to find out from him. From his voice, I could make out he was shaken. I asked him for the status. He reported that Lieutenant Kenguruse's platoon had attacked **Lone Hill**, and when they were near the top, the enemy had rolled stones, which had taken this platoon down. This platoon had fallen down a steep slope of 100 to 150 feet, and Lieutenant Kenguruse and Havildar Sarman had died, and all others were injured.

Major Mohit had done great work by pressing forward his attack despite a lack of artillery support, despite a lack of fire support from the unit Fire Base and despite having his radio set shot up. With the CO's intent as his sole guide, he had launched a series of assaults on the ridgeline, some of which were false crests until they contacted **Lone Hill**. They had decided to climb to it from a flank with a vertical face protecting it. Lieutenant Kenguruse, with few men,

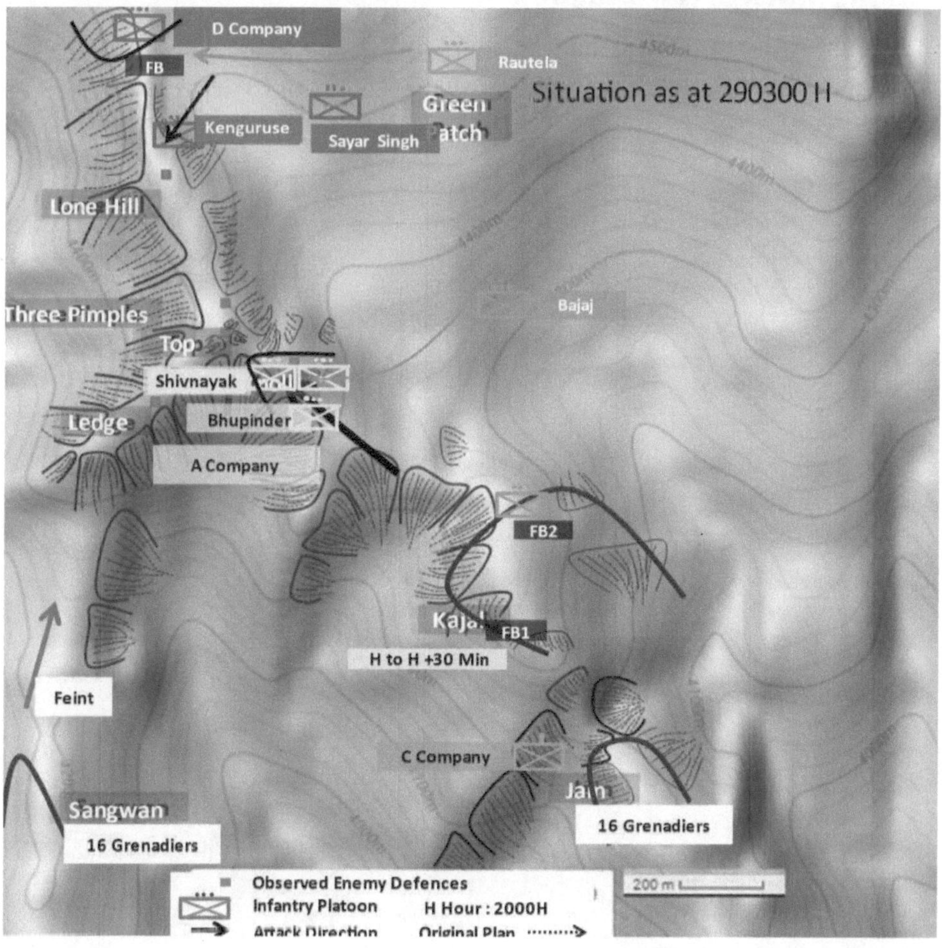

had fought his way to the top and surprised the enemy. Enemy panicked and pushed the sangar stones, rolling them up on the platoon assaulting along the near vertical cliff face. The stoned Lieutenant Kenguruse and his section fell down the precipice, a sheer fall of over 200 feet. Delta Company's reserve platoon (Subedar Sayar Singh) was about 500 metres behind. Overall, in my assessment, Delta Company had expended itself, and despite the heroic efforts, we had yet to capture **Lone Hill** or succeed in establishing a tactical foothold. With first light barely an hour away, I had to decide on the future disposition of Delta Company quickly.

Tactically, they were in a disadvantageous position, being dominated by **Lone Hill, Three Pimples** and the ridgeline leading in from **Helmet**. They had suffered substantial casualties and needed to be taken out of battle; hence, I decided to withdraw them to the safety of the firm base.

Taking Stock of the Situation

Brigadier Amar Aul, who had been following the battle on the radio set, intervened to suggest we hold on to what we have in the area of **Lone Hill.**

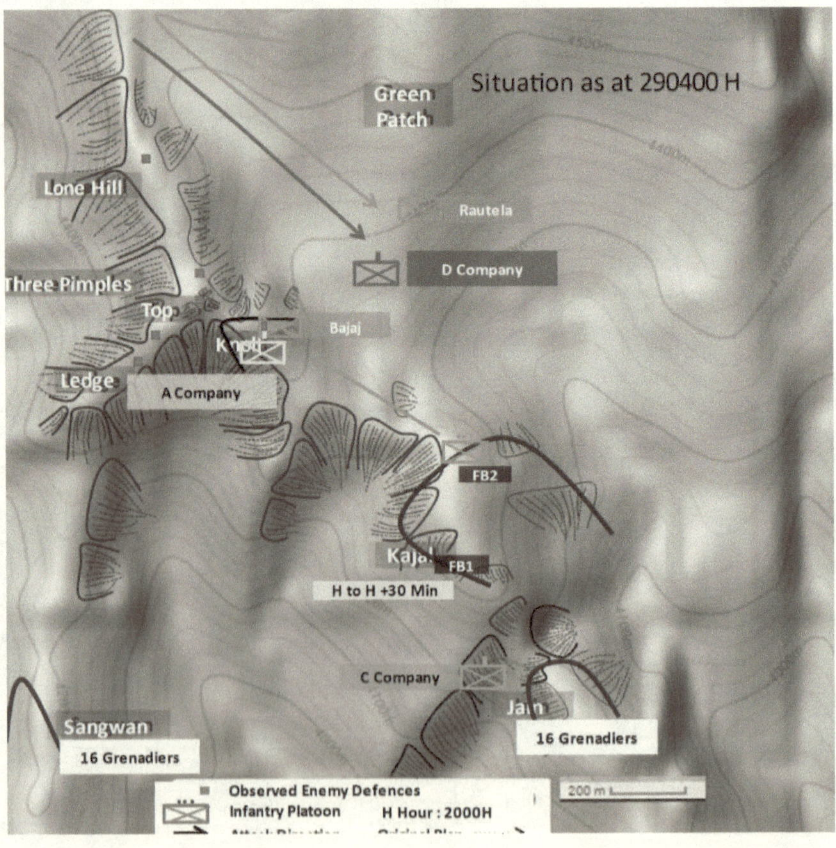

I apprised him that the ground around was more a bowl dominated by imposing heights not more than 300 to 400 metres, and there was no point in holding on to it. Further, with **Knoll** firmly in our hand, I added that we could progress the operations to **Three Pimples** through it and that I needed time to regroup my forces in the safety of the firm base, to which he conceded. I ordered Major Mohit Saxena to fall back on the firm base carrying his dead and wounded. I informed him that Lieutenant Rautela was already nearby to assist him.

Around 0330 hours, Maj Bajaj (Bravo Company) reported that he had reached the **Knoll**. I asked him to take charge of the situation and report back on the situation in **Three Pimples**. I decided to progress the operations from **Knoll**; accordingly, we despatched the third platoon of Bravo Company that had been held back at the firebase to join their Company Commander at **Knoll**.

The battle was chaotic until now, and I needed to reorganise myself. I asked for a head count, which started to come in by 0400 hours. While all others were on the expected lines; I was shocked by the Delta Company report, which had 30 soldiers unaccounted for. The news hit me hard, and I felt utter remorse at such a great loss. Major Mohit had reported the misfortune that had struck his company, and I had mentally prepared myself for a shock, but this was beyond comprehension. It felt like sitting on the ruins of a disaster, helpless, and all I could do was wait for the reports to come in from Major Bajaj and Major Mohit Saxena. Field Marshal Slim wrote in his book Defeat into Victory that the initial reports are as good or bad as the final reports. I was to experience it soon.

29 June 1999

At daybreak, there was no fire from **Three Pimples**. Was it unoccupied, or was the enemy just holding fire? It was hard to tell. By 0530 hours, Delta Company was getting back into the safety of the Firm Base. Lieutenant Rautela and his platoon were enroute to join Major Bajaj (Bravo Company) at **Knoll.**

Actions of Delta Company (Mohit)

I had a long chat with Major Mohit Saxena to understand clearly what had transpired with him through the night. Delta Company had made a clean getaway from the artillery fire of the Fire Base and reached the Saddle on the **Lone Hill – Helmet ridge** unmolested, commencing its advance towards **Lone Hill**. They had met many false crests, and the enemy had been alerted. Finally, they had established a firebase with Naik Gaid Singh's LMG Detachment. (Incidentally, Naik Gaid Singh's claim to fame had been as an accomplished hedge trimmer at Gwalior, much in demand; here he was to anchor the effort of his company's effort in a more professional manner!). The enemy targeted his detachment with machine gun fire, and Rifleman Jai Hind Prakash received a burst on his face. Despite this, Naik Gaid Singh inspired others by manning the LMG himself. In the meantime, one of the enemy MMG bursts shot up Major Mohit's radio set, putting him out of communication.

Kenguruse's Daredevil Assault

Failing to find a way to **Lone Hill,** Lieutenant Kenguruse was tasked with finding a route. He had led his troops through a rock face, climbing it with bare feet and hands, and had gained a route to the top, and together, they had fought their way to the top. It was then that the enemy, in desperation, had pushed the stones down on this team. These rolling stones had swept this team down the precipice at the edge of which Lieutenant Kenguruse's team had gathered to launch a final push to the top. It was a merciless tumble for the team, resulting in the death of Kenguruse and Havildar Sarman, whose hands still held the grenade he had intended to throw.

Naik Gaid Singh had re-established communication after fetching the reserve radio set from Subedar Sayar's platoon located in the bowl area where the ground was rising from the nala towards **Three Pimples**. Subedar Sayar's platoon had reported a skirmish with enemy troops in the area where he was located. That was strange; I had expected interference from **Three Pimples**, but there seemed to be none. This skirmish in the nala was not falling into any of the patterns for enemy movement I had envisioned. Did he try to block our troops? I had no answer. This company had been through a very tough operation; victory had been snatched from their hands by cruel luck and the enemy's desperation.

We soon received reports that a group of our unit had landed at the base of 18 GARHRIF. On enquiry, it was revealed to be the platoon of Subedar Sayar, some casualties and some other troops of Delta Company. The count was 30; it was a great relief that casualties were not as bad as I had imagined.

Delta Company, in their retreat, had brought in all their wounded. Now, with the wounded safe and under medical care, Mohit Saxena said he wanted to go back and fetch the bodies of Lieutenant Kenguruse and Havildar Sarman. Tactically, I considered it unwise. For me, it does not make sense to expose troops to the possibility of casualties and further death for recovering fallen comrades; however unsentimental it may appear, I would not have permitted it under different circumstances.

Three Pimples is Captured!

Major Bajaj (Bravo Company) reported that he could not spot enemy movement at **Three Pimples.** "*Is the enemy still holding Three Pimples*?" was a question for which I had to find an answer. Given the terrain conditions, it was too risky for

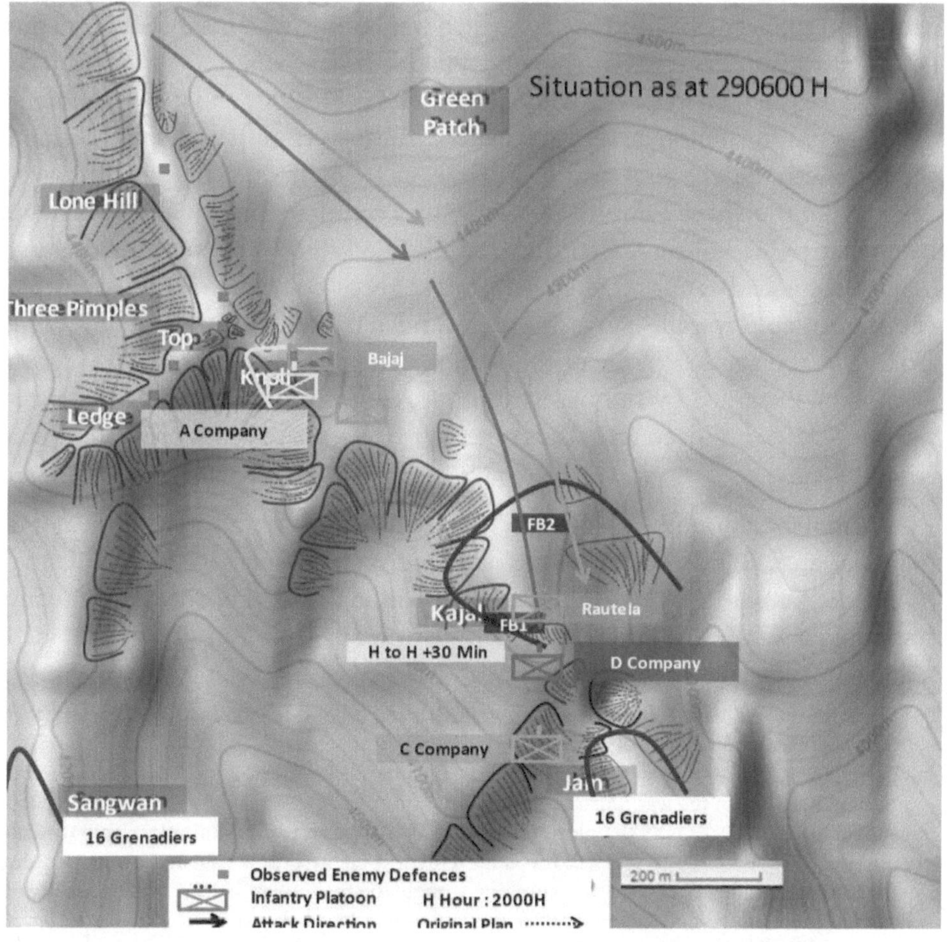

Major Bajaj to probe forward. So, I readily agreed when Major Mohit expressed his desire to retrace his steps to **Lone Hill**. A flanking move in broad daylight would surely force the enemy to react and reveal his position.

Major Mohit left **Kajal** around 0700 hours with about a platoon, supported by Fire Base 2. Around this time, we received news that the attack of 18 GARHRIF had succeeded in capturing **Point 4700** and **Tommy.** That was great news; with **Knoll, Point 4700** and **Tommy** in our hands, the area secured from enemy interference had expanded. **Lone Hill** was only 500 metres ahead.

We waited for the return of Major Mohit. They recovered the bodies without any interference and returned to the safety of the Firm Base by around 0900 hours. He also brought in some enemy weapons, equipment, maps and rucksacks. My hopes soared, imagining that he had got these from **Lone Hill.**

When asked, he reported these were recovered in the Nala area, and they had found some enemy dead bodies, which was confusing. This information did not fit into any of the enemy deployment patterns. The captured items included a map; it was an inch map with contours marked every 200 feet, unlike our maps that had contours marked every 200 metres. These were like the maps I had seen when we were taught map reading at NDA in 1976. The map had markings of defences for the **Three Pimples** area showing a company and roughly coincided with what we had observed on the ground. Interestingly, the new feature that Major Mohit had reported after his ground recce could be identified on the Pakistani map. Overall, it had more ground details than our maps.[36] While looking at the rucksack, one of the jawans quipped, "*This rucksack belongs to an officer*." Intrigued by the observation, I asked him to elaborate. He said it was very clean; it indeed was. The contents further proved his observation was accurate.

Amongst the clothes, we found rank epaulettes, a tracksuit with the name "Saifulla" and "**Sikkis**". "**Sikkis**" probably indicated 6 Northern Light Infantry (NLI), the battalion raged against us and "Saifulla" was probably its company commander.[37] Another interesting thing was a souvenir issue of the 'Golden Jubilee of Pakistan Army'.[38]

36 Brig MPS Bajwa, Commander 192 Mountain Brigade, later told Colonel Ravindranath that they had used photocopies of the map for planning attack on Tiger Hill.

37 Later, during the remainder of my battalion command, I wore this occasionally as a war trophy! It is now in the war museum of the battalion.

38 All such journals recount the glorious history of the respective organisation; this was no different. What surprised me was the achievement it claimed as a golden moment for the Pakistan Army. It stated that the combined might of the Indian armed forces could not subdue the courage and valour of 90,000 of its troops in Dhaka in 1971. The surrender, it

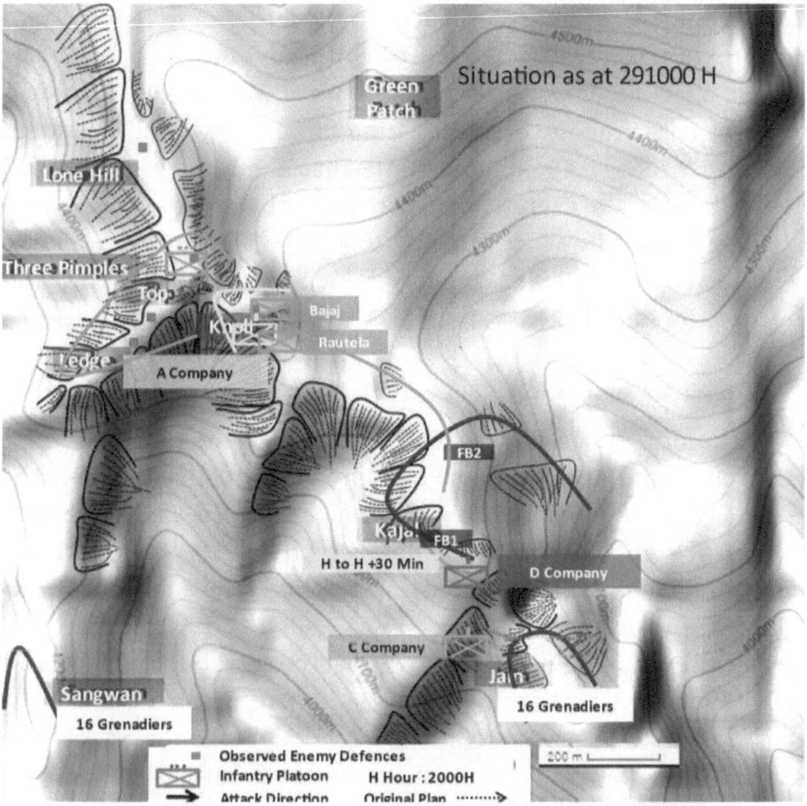

By now, I was reasonably assured that **Three Pimples** had been abandoned. Major Bajaj was immediately ordered to secure **Three Pimples.** The operations started around 0930 hours, and securing the initial area went off without

claimed, was a letdown by the political class. How delusional? It is a recurrent theme for the Pakistan military leadership, a story well sold that the political class has always nullified the great achievements of the Pakistan Army. It was repeated at the end of the Kargil War, too.

incident. Around 1000 hours, a platoon moved to secure it, and as we were watching, there was a blast when a two-man team entered a bunker; we froze and waited. Was the enemy still holding? Were we too exposed now? These were the types of thoughts that were racing through my mind. We waited, and nothing happened; I was gaining in confidence and assessed it to be a '**Booby Trap**' left behind by the enemy. I could see Major Bajaj move in with additional forces. **Three Pimples** was captured by 1000 hours. Major Bajaj reported that two of his men had been killed, and it was due to a Rocket Launcher fired from the direction of **Lone Hill.**

The Enemy Put to Flight

From what information was available, it was becoming clear that the enemy, attacked from both in the front and rear and with an attack on **Point 4700** by 18 GARHRIF now in full flow, had panicked and vacated **Three Pimples, Knoll** and **Lone Hill** complex around the time we brought Bofors direct fire on to the enemy holding up Subedar Shivnayak at **Knoll**. The enemy had withdrawn from **Three Pimples** towards the nala as we had not contacted them from that direction. Once near the nala, their path had crossed close to where Subedar Sayar's platoon was. An instance was reported where, near a big boulder, soldiers from both sides had come face to face. Each realised who the others were when they opened their mouth to communicate, and both turned back and scooted - our men towards the nala and the enemy towards **Lone Hill.**

Sensing some danger, the platoon fired an RL illuminating round in the direction. They could see the enemy about 100 metres away, silhouetted on higher ground, on whom they immediately opened fire. This was the firing I had heard earlier during the night. The enemy ran helter-skelter shouting, '*Hame wapis jaane do Pakistan, dobara nahin ayenge Hindustan*' (Let us go back to Pakistan, we will not return to India). "Saifulla" was one of those killed.

We were ahead of time in the capture of **Three Pimples**, and only **Lone Hill** stood between us and the completion of our mission "**Capture Three Pimples Complex By 1800 on 29 June**". I had intended to press on with the remainder of Bravo Company (Bajaj) to **Lone Hill.** The fire from the

direction of **Lone Hill** was not a good sign, so we thought it prudent to attack with proper fire support.

Major Ashok, the Battery Commander, got going to organise artillery fire support, and I ordered Lieutenant Tomar to move with his company to act as a reserve. Given the deployment and state of enemy defences, I did not envisage any counterattack. I decided to de-congest the objective area of troops. I moved Alpha Company and Delta Company to revert to the safety of the Administrative Area, near the improvised cook house we had created, now safe from enemy observation. This also reduced the load on the troops ferrying food and water to **Kajal**.

By about 1500 hours**, Lone Hill** was registered for artillery fire. H Hour was fixed at 1600 hours. At 1600 hours, with artillery providing continuous fire support, Lieutenant Rautela led his platoon towards **Lone Hill** along the narrow, flat, open ridge. I held my breath helplessly as the artillery fire lifted,

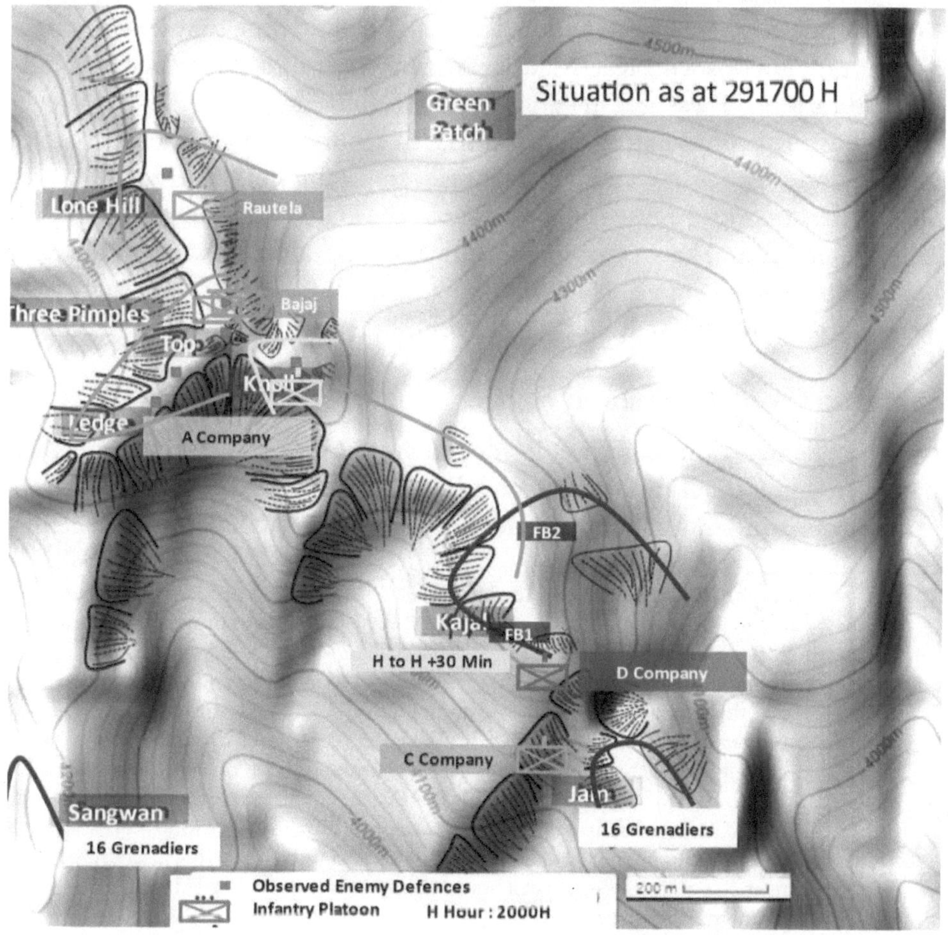

and Lieutenant Rautela started moving his sections forward using fire and movement. There was no opposition, and tense moments passed, so we secured **Lone Hill**. By 1700 hours, Major Bajaj had reached Lone Hill and reported that Lone Hill was captured and secured.

Mission Accomplished!

I reported the mission accomplishment to Brigadier Amar Aul, and a sense of relief came over me, as though someone had just lifted a heavy weight off my shoulders. With it came all the suppressed turmoil in my heart. The see-saw battle soaring to great hope, falling to great depths of hopelessness, and finally ending in success in the last 48 hours had stressed me to the limits. Though my heart ached for each death as they occurred, my mind kept reminding me of the task at hand and the imperative to pursue it relentlessly; a machine-like zeal possessed me.

We had lost three Officers and 10 Other Ranks. I had seen or heard each of them fall, all to execute an order I had passed. I had no time to spare a moment in their thought or shed a tear. All this came rushing out from the bottom of my heart in torrents. I was not in control of my feelings anymore. Try as I would to suppress it, I could not; it came out first in whimpers, with ever-increasing intensity, and my sorrow and helplessness were in full flow. There was no way I was able to control myself. Major Ashok, the Battery Commander, put his arm around me and kept consoling me; my radio operator passed me the water bottle and kept saying all this is not your fault. But the volcanic eruption of suppressed emotions would not subside for quite some time.[39]

Walking Over the Field of Battle

Once I regained composure, we decided to go to **Lone Hill**. Many of my men had been going up and down the nala by now. We moved down to the nala, skirted **Knoll** and moved up along the steep slope. We landed near the enemy's

[39] Vijayant at Kargil, Thapar & Dwivedi, Penguin e bury Press, 2020, Page 164. This had been the toughest battle fought by the Indian Army. It cost 2 Raj Rif the life of three officers and eight ORs, while fifty - two others were wounded. The victory was not savoured that day. In fact, no fire was lit in the cookhouse. With so many killed and so many wounded, there was a grim realization that the cost of war was beyond computation. Early that morning, Maj Bhanwar Rathore, the quartermaster of the unit, heard sounds of sobbing from the commanding officer's snow tent. He ventured in to see Lt Col Ravindranath crying with his head in his hands for the men he had lost, for the young fighter Vijayant, for Archie the sutradhar, for the beloved Kengruze. He was a strict commander, but deep within, he was a kind man who loved his men like his kids. Rathore, who was elderly, put his arms around the commanding officer, consoled him and requested him to get a hold of himself as the unit needed him to be strong, to take care of them. He explained.

cook house. Frozen snow was still available, and it was their source of water. The cookhouse had Corrugated Galvanised Iron (CGI) sheet roofing on an angle iron frame; the walls were loose stones. There were jerry cans with kerosene and some CGI sheets on the ground. It gave an impression that the enemy had been around for some time.

I was looking at **Lone Hill** and **Area Junction**; the ridge line was scraggy. I wondered how they could have humped up the provisions and materials for construction. The Sando Valley was clearly visible, and so was the Sando Post. It got me wondering how this was not detected.

We then moved to **Lone Hill,** where most of the defences faced Sando Valley; this was strange since the slopes leading up from the road to Sando Post were extremely steep, making it almost fortress-like.[40] There was a small hollow in the rock face, in which there was a small igloo tent. This appeared to be the company commander's location. It had a steep face to its North on the ridge towards **Helmet – Junction** and the enemy had ropes established to get down. It was really creditable that Delta Company (Mohit) had assaulted from this direction despite all its difficulty, and one could only imagine the surprise and shock of the troops here to be suddenly assaulted from the rear. All the actions till then were concentrated at **Knoll** and the feint on **Ledge**. For me, it was unbelievable that a platoon led by Lieutenant Kenguruse had actually performed the impossible cliff assault, that too without any equipment. Few people of Delta Company had tenaciously pressed on and doggedly held on to the rear of the

---

40 *Kargil Victory The Battle from Peak to Peak,* Colonel SC Tyagi, Speaking Tiger Publishing Pvt. Ltd., 2019, Page 100. The battle had taken a very heavy toll on our men. In the entire operation, three officers and ten men from other ranks* had sacrificed their lives. Fifty-one men from other ranks were injured, out of which thirty-six were critical. However, plenty of arms and ammunition were recovered, including five machine guns. The Company Commander's documents, including maps marked with Pakistani artillery positions were also captured, alongside his personal clothing and equipment. The sangars of the enemy were very strong and had not been affected by our artillery firing; only one of them was found to be slightly damaged. This suggested that the enemy had had a lot of time at hand to prepare these sangars, and strengthen them. It appeared that the Three Pimple area had been strongly held by a single company, with their route of maintenance along the nalas—as opposed to along the ridgelines, as commonly believed earlier. This reality emerged during the day. Major Mohit Saxena recounted cutting telephone cables along the nala during the night, but at that time, it did not strike anybody that it could well be their route of maintenance.

enemy. They had not been able to capture it, the prize slipping from their hand in a deluge of rocks the enemy pushed against Lieutenant Kenguruse and his platoon, sending them tumbling down the precipice.[41]

We returned to **Three Pimples** and were helped up by someone at the top. This feature had gaps and crevices in the rock faces on all sides. No wonder, despite heavy artillery bombardment and continuous battering with MMG, RL and AGL fire, the enemy continued to retaliate with fire as soon as he got a respite. He would withdraw to the safety of these crevices and bounce back as soon as we stopped firing. There was no identifiable route to the top; one had to zig-zag through steep openings easily covered by fire from higher rock faces. Looking all around, one realised the solid defence potential this feature offered to a determined enemy. I could not figure out a way to take this citadel-like feature other than by besieging or at a high cost in fighting through the objective. I realised how lucky we had been that we did not have to do either.

We next went to **Knoll**; the gap between them was less than I had imagined. Alpha Company had, in fact, faced much interference from **Three Pimples**. We found two bodies of enemy soldiers; one was in the bunker at the top, and another was down the slope towards the nala. The bunker holding out was the one at the very top and was the last defensive position on **Knoll**. It was about 10 feet higher and about 20 metres from the bunker Major Acharya had captured. He had been trying to get his 84 mm Rocket Launcher up while an enemy hand grenade did him in. The ledge that Captain Vijayant Thapar and Anand used to assault was narrow, not

41 *Kargil Victory The Battle from Peak to Peak*, Colonel SC Tyagi, Speaking Tiger Publishing Pvt. Ltd., 2019, Page 100. The Ghatak platoon was under the command of Captain Neikezhakuo Kengruze. He was extremely fit and could outrun the other commandos with a heavy rocket launcher on his back. Hailing from Kohima in Nagaland, he was engaged to a doctor back home. Captain Kengruze was very popular with his troops and was affectionately known as Naga Saheb or Nimbu Saheb amongst them. A good guitarist, singer and drummer, he was deeply religious as well. I had known him while his battalion was undergoing pre-induction training at Kashmir. I had to tick him off one day, because while playing basketball, he wouldn't pass the ball to anyone. But he scored every time he took the ball back thereafter! He was to score big yet again, when he was specially chosen and sent ahead to prevent any enemy movement to and from the Three Pimple area. He was awarded posthumous Maha Vir Chakra.

more than three feet. It would have taken indomitable courage for the young officer to charge across.

I had carried the nagging doubt about Subedar Bhupinder's inability to join up and reinforce Subedar Shivnayak's exhausted forces. I ascertained from him about his operation, and he showed me the route they had taken and where they were stuck up. While climbing **Knoll**, they had moved, hugging the Fire Base and taking a route to the left of a jutting rock. That had led them to hardly 100 metres from where Subedar Shivnayak was, but separated by a rock face through which they could not find a break.

Such are the chances that dictate the course of battle, which is why we require a very high numerical superiority for attack in the mountains. Given that troops need to move in small subunits and can easily lose the way, one needs a larger strength to create the required numerical superiority while fighting through the objective. Reviewing the area 2 RAJRIF had captured, it dawned on me how incredibly lucky we were to capture a company location in the mountains with only one battalion, that too with depleted strength.

We assessed that we did not face any real threat of a counterattack as the enemy was under attack on **Point 4700 Ridge** by 18 GARHRIF. Ordering Bravo Company to firm in at the **Three Pimples**, **Lone Hill** and **Knoll** areas, I started back for **Kajal Fire Base**. I had walked just ten steps sliding down the sharp, small, loose stones, and the sole of my DMS boots broke. It was in reasonable shape just ten days earlier; the wear and tear had occurred during this operation. If this was the condition of my boots, I could only imagine the state of the boots of those continuously moving up and down from the cookhouse. While I was wondering what to do, my radio operator climbed back to fetch a pair of shoes. When he returned, I was surprised; they were not of the pattern issued to us. On enquiry, he said they were Pakistani shoes; when asked where he found them, he shocked me with his answer. "*He does not require it anymore. You require it.*" I understood and had no argument against this earthy logic. I squeamishly wore them and returned to **Kajal.**

Though action was on barely 1500 metres to our North on **Point 4700** ridge where 18 GARHRIF was progressing its attack, most of the troops of 2 RAJRIF had collapsed into a heap, exhausted from the tensions and exertions of the last 48 to 72 hours. Many of the troops had not slept for more than five to six hours during this period, and commanders and key elements even less. Charlie Company and Ghatak Platoon were in the Fire Base.

Post Battle Musings

At **Kajal**, in my pup tent, I reviewed the intense activities of the period starting from when we were tasked to capture **Junction** on 20 June. These ten days had been one rush, each day and moment revealing something new, providing a tantalising opportunity here, delivering a knockout blow there, forcing us to adjust our thoughts and plans, taking us through a roller coaster ride of highs of exhilaration, where the future looked limitless in opportunities, and lows of desperation and despondency when one failure followed another. Against all this, the battalion had pulled through. While I had many moments of self-doubt, the battalion displayed a quiet and firm determination. While I had feared a breakdown of attack in the face of murderous enemy shelling, the troops had walked through it nonchalantly, even while their comrades were falling. Such was the determination and valour of 2 RAJRIF that even an insipid man is inspired to great acts of heroism.

How else can one explain the phenomenon where every tradesman, 'Dhobi', 'Nai', 'Sweeper' et al., carried ammunition, food and water for days on end so that the fighting man who had to launch the attack did not tire themselves? How else can one explain a mess waiter picking a telephone and moving out to check a break in the line when the enemy was shelling all around? How else can one explain why soldiers, medically unfit, who took painkillers and injections, went into the attack, fully aware that if the enemy would not get them, the high-altitude rare air and cold would, probably? How else can one explain the calmness with which they went into attack through murderous enemy artillery fire, not being deterred by comrades being hit all around them? How else can one explain the grit of the MMG, RL and AGL detachments in the firebase which continued to rain fire on the enemy while they were being smothered by enemy fire so that their comrades in attack would not be stopped? How else can one explain companies continuing to press home the attack even after they have been deprived of supporting fire, even when their communications have snapped and even when commander after commander has fallen? How else can one explain when a soldier encourages and comforts the distraught CO by saying, '*In attack and war, soldiers will die. Why blame yourself*"? I was blessed to command such troops; with these thoughts swirling in my mind, I sank into a deep sleep.

30 June 1999

On 30 June, I woke to the good news that 18 GARHRIF had captured **Sangar** and **Rocky**. Newspapers were full of the success of operations by 2 RAJRIF and 18 GARHRIF. Unprecedently, General Ved Malik, Chief of Army Staff, had '*suo* *moto*' awarded the '**Chief's Citation**'. The Chief awards this in recognition of outstanding operational achievements of units after a lengthy vetting process with recommendations of intermediate formation headquarters. 2 RAJRIF was the first unit in the history of the Indian Army to receive it '*suo moto*'.

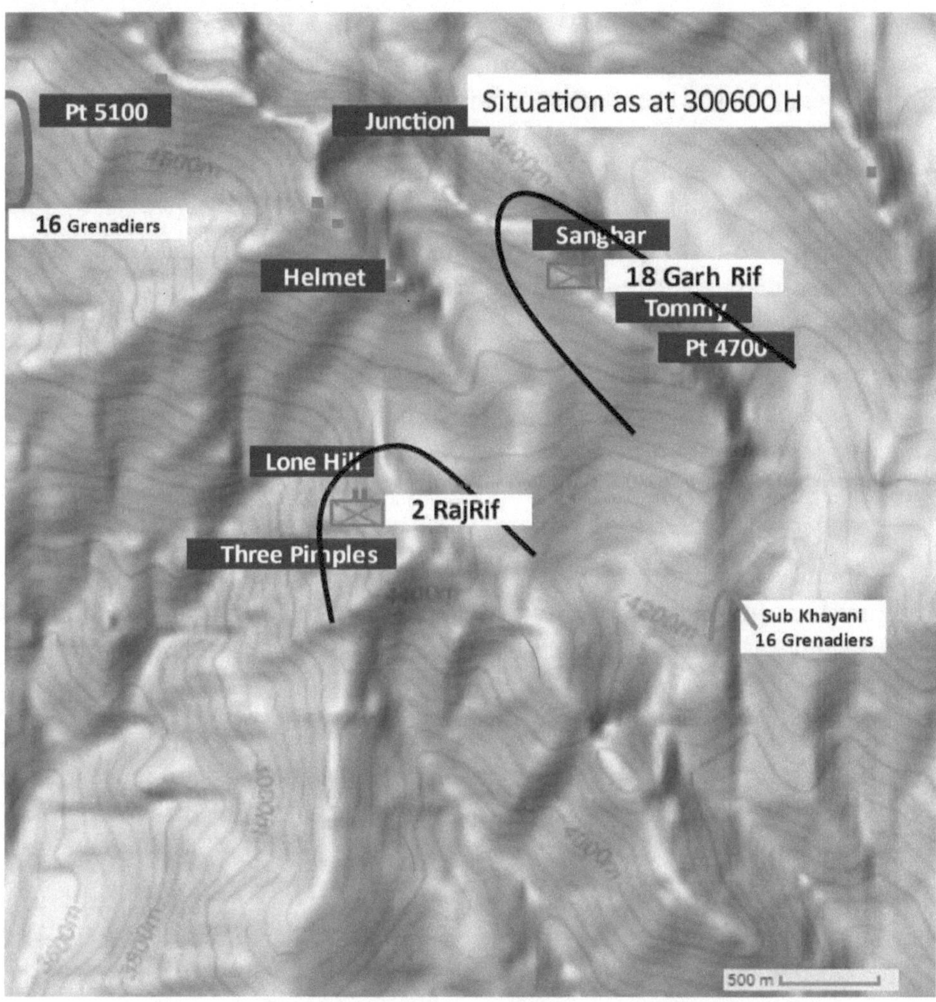

While I was asleep, Bravo Company was relieved by 16 GRENADIERS; Major Jain took over **Lone Hill** and **Three Pimples** and Major Sangwan **Knoll**. Bravo Company moved back to the Administration Area. In the night, Major Sangwan became a casualty when he stepped on a stray mine in **Kajal** area. Given the quantum of troops milling around **Knoll**, we had been incredibly lucky not to have had any mine casualties.

Mindless Application of Theory

The reason for being relieved became clear when around 1000 hours, the Brigade Major 56 Mountain Brigade informed me that 2 RAJRIF was to capture **Area Junction** by first light 01 July. I was flabbergasted and asked him if he knew the state of my unit. He just replied it was the Commander's orders. That left me wondering why the Brigade Commander had not given me the order directly. It was a mindless application of what was taught in the Staff Course. In all the war games and field exercises, the holding formations relieve the offensive formations who continue with assault. In theory, it may sound okay, but in practice, it takes a greater understanding of the troops' morale. In peacetime, both troops and commanders accept such orders. With no live bullets or casualties, such manoeuvres are easy to execute. But the Commander should have known better.

I got in touch with Major General Mohinder Puri, the Divisional Commander. He was not aware of any such tasking, and he said "*Ravi, as far as current operations are concerned your battalion's role is over. You will be pulled back and not employed till you are brought to fighting fit standards.*" Here was a commander who understood war and knew how to employ his troops.

Soon, we received amended orders. 16 GRENADIERS were tasked to capture **Area Junction**, and 2 RAJRIF was tasked to capture **Area Helmet**. I accepted the task since we had Charlie Company and Ghatak Platoon available.

The 16 GRENADIERS attack was to be by troops currently occupying **Knoll** and **Three Pimples**; they had to be relieved and moved to attack **Area Junction** from the SW direction from Sando Valley. The operation was postponed to the night of 01 July. I ordered the Ghataks and Charlie Company to move to **Lone Hill** in preparation for an attack.

While we were regrouping, 18 GARHRIF was pressing on boldly in a daylight operation towards **Area Junction**, and their further progress was halted by impassable terrain along the ridge. We got on to organising the firebase in support of this attack. We decided to attack **Helmet** with **Area Green Patch** as the Forming Up Place with fire support from artillery and close support from the firebase in the **Lone Hill** area.

01 July 1999

By 1200 hours on 01 July, along with Major Ashok Sharma, the Battery Commander, I moved **to Lone Hill**. Major Ashok started registering the target, which was completed by 1400 hours, and after that, he started degrading it with the direct fire of Bofors.

While he was at it, I connected with Colonel Chakravarthy, CO 18 GARHRIF, to listen to his witty remarks. 'Chaks', as he was known, had this witty streak in him that could surmise in few words a complex situation. During our exchange, I learnt that he too was to attack that night. I was guessing his objective would be some feature to the North and not visible to us. He surprised me by saying that he was attacking from the South-Eastern direction. On further exchange of notes, we realised we were attacking the same feature. We were lucky; one can only imagine what could have happened if troops had come face to face, unaware of the presence of the other; so much for coordination by staff.

The staff is charged with the duty of supporting the commander in the execution of his task. To this end, their prime functionalities include continuous monitoring of situations, collecting, collating and interpreting information, besides others that ensure the logistic and operational role of the commander's plan. Estimating enemy capabilities and, based on this estimation, divining enemy intention and forecasting enemy possible plans are the most important functions of the Intelligence Staff. This ought to be the starting point of any worthwhile operation. Even more important is to continuously monitor the ebb and flow of battle and raise red flags if '*blue on blue*' clashes are possible due to blurred boundaries, especially in the mountains.

We reverted with our observations to Brigade HQ. The whole issue was resolved by tasking 18 GARHRIF to capture **Helmet**, 16 GRENADIERS to capture **Area Junction**, Charlie Company and Ghataks of 2 RAJRIF to act as reserves. This whole operation was put under my command for close coordination. There was nothing much I could do except to bring both the Company Commanders Major Jain (16 GRENADIERS) and Major Bisht (18 GARHRIF) on the same radio net and went along with the plans they had made.

The Attack on Area Junction

The attack started at 2100 hours after preparatory bombardment. By 2300 hours, the company of 18 GARHRIF had captured **Helmet**. The attack of 16 GRENADIERS, led by Lieutenant Vishal, was progressing. They had a formidable rock wall facing them, through which they were trying to break through. Lieutenant Vishal started closing in with the wall by fire and movement. By around 0200 hours, he had closed in with the wall and found a breach. Covered by this officer, the remaining troops under Major Jain fetched up and secured the feature. Surprisingly, there was no opposition, and by 0300 hours on 02 July, we received confirmation that **Area Junction** was captured.

02 July 1999

With Major Ashok, I reached **Helmet** around 0900 hours on 02 July and congratulated the troops for their successful conduct. We reached **Area Junction** by about 1100 hours. **Point 5100**, barely 600 metres away, was still held by the enemy, who could be seen moving around freely behind neatly made stone walls.

Junction was a highly jagged rocky feature to the North of the feature captured by 16 GRENADIERS. It dominated **Point 5100** from the East, but climbing and creating a defensive position was difficult. This was probably the reason why it was not occupied. Moving around, one saw that the position was well stocked for rations, and the tell-tale marks showed it had been occupied longer than **Lone Hill** or **Tololing**. The sangar walls were about two to three feet thick, with perfect plumb lines and adequate loopholes. If the enemy had decided to fight from here, we would have had a big challenge on our hands, so why had he chosen to quit so strong a position without a contest? The enemy had tried to sabotage all the assets by pouring kerosene on the flour, other ration items, and broken or punctured oil tins. It was becoming obvious that the enemy had withdrawn without a fight, but there was no visible route to **Point 5100** along which he could have withdrawn. I was sounding out Major Ashok as to where and how the enemy could have withdrawn.

Lieutenant Praveen Tomar, now commanding Charlie Company, who had accompanied us, let the cat out of the bag. He said they had withdrawn the previous afternoon when 18 GARHRIF had started closing in on it along the ridge line. Given his service and experience of barely six months, he had yet to realise the importance of what he had observed and, hence, did not bother to share it. He narrated how they had observed enemy troops running into the re-entrant to the East and crossing the **Point 4700** ridgeline at its lowest point in the re-entrant. We checked and soon found ropes to get down into the re-entrant. The Ghatak team with me was immediately tasked to go and occupy the crossing point and recce for a route to **Point 5100** from the North of **Junction**. We started engaging **Point 5100** with artillery fire and tasked Major Jain to find a route to the top of **Junction**.

Major Sandeep Kala was asked to move to **Kajal** and prepare to lead an attack on **Point 5100** with Charlie Company and the Ghataks. Around 1400 hours, having briefed Major Jain of 16 GRENADIERS to establish a firebase for an attack on **Point 5100** and also to keep the enemy under constant harassment with fire, we started towards the **Saddle** area, now occupied by the Ghatak team led by Havildar Rajbir.

Major Ashok Gets Injured

Just as we were starting, Major Ashok slipped on the ice, fell on his back and let out a cry. Considering it a normal ice skid, I jokingly chided him and asked him to get up. He was in much pain and was unable to get up. He was not able to stand or take any weight on his legs. Worried, we tried to massage his legs and back. He stated that he had received a sharp blow on his back. I examined the area where he had fallen and was shocked to see the sharp edge of a buried ice axe jutting out about an inch in length. It had so transpired that while he had slipped and fallen on his back, the sharp edge had come under his lower backbone. No wonder he was in considerable pain. We quickly rigged up a stretcher, and with great difficulty, we lowered him into the re-entrant. We started his evacuation with the BC party's and my team's help. I saw them off and moved with my radio operator to join the Ghatak team of Havildar Rajbir at the **Saddle**.

Pieces of the Puzzle Fall in Place

The view on the other side of the **Saddle** was very revealing. Just to the North of the **Saddle,** at about 50 metres, was a well-constructed stone hut. A couple of WD cables for line communication were passing through the **Saddle**, and so was a well-beaten track. This track led further to the NE, where we could see a lake at about 500 to 600 metres around which it disappeared behind the **Point 5060** feature. One could see stone walls and sangars on the Western slopes of the **Point 5060** feature. The hut had rations dumped in it. Now, the whole scheme of enemy intrusions started falling into place.

The intrusions had not taken place along the ridgelines emanating from **Marpola** to occupy the **Marpola ridge, Point 5100, Area Junction** and then

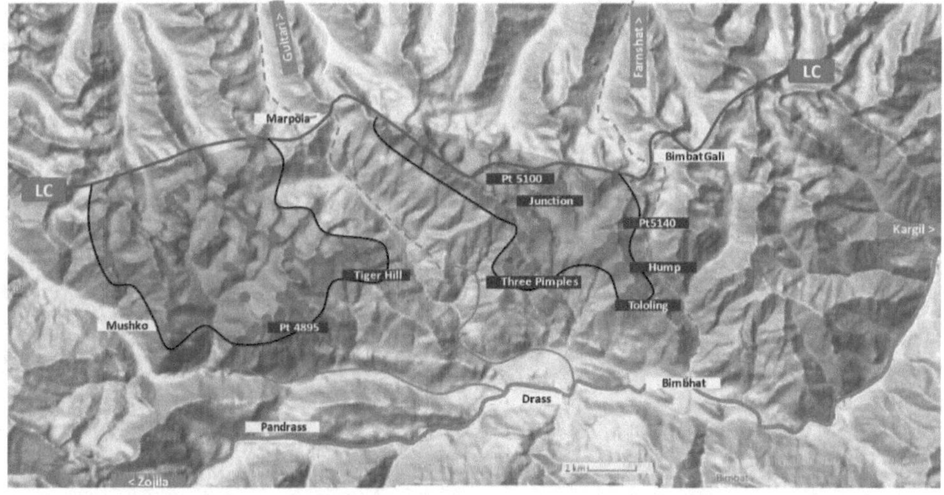

further branching out to **Lone Hill**, **Three Pimples Complex** on one side and **Rocky**, **Tommy** and **Point 4700** on the other side. Nor had the occupation of **Tololing Ridge** started from the ridge on the West of Bimbat Gali, occupying **Point 5140**, **Hump** and **Tololing** progressively.

I guess the intrusion started with Pakistan crossing the LC North of **Point 5060** and occupying **Point 5060 Ridge** to start with and progressively its Southern slope by about a company. This would have been followed by the occupation of **Point 5100**, **Area Junction** and **Point 4700** ridgeline on one side with a company / company plus and **Point 5140** with a platoon on the **Tololing Ridge** on the other side. The last stage of intrusion would have been to push troops to occupy, with one company, the **Lone Hill** and **Three Pimples Complex** from **Area Junction** and **Hump** and **Tololing** from **Point 5140** on the **Tololing Ridge** with a platoon each making it a company. All these intrusions would have been supported by an administrative base and Battalion HQ established North of **Point 5060** on the other side of the LC. This, in turn, would have been serviced on tracks along the Nala leading up from Farnshat in POK. In my opinion, this would have been the layout of 6 NLI in the Drass intrusion. The complete intrusion and its maintenance would have been hidden from troops located in the winter posts of 16 GRENADIERS, the unit holding the LC. Only aerial platforms could have detected this intrusion.

This explained the telephone cable D Coy found while infiltrating, why the enemy had slithered down to the re-entrant from **Area Junction**, by which route the enemy had escaped from **Three Pimples Complex**, and the confusing clash with enemy troops in the bowl North of **Three Pimples** and South of **Area Green Patch**.

It appears that the enemy commander, attacked vigorously at the two extremities of his defences, with his route of withdrawal now blocked was on the horns of a dilemma. As Sun Tzu succinctly states in his Art of War, troops under such circumstances have '*One eye on the enemy attack, another on the escape route*'; he advises the attacker to deliberately leave an obvious escape route while pursuing the attack with vigour. In our case, it was out of ignorance and not by design.

The sudden collapse of enemy defences was by no small measure influenced by the attack of 18 GARHRIF around midnight on **Point 4700** ridgeline, which had the threatening possibility of isolating him. Thus, two under-strength battalions had routed two companies, albeit holding not so well entrenched defences nor compact defences, in about 24 hours. These had been recce-pull operations; manoeuvre warfare at its best, albeit in the highest of high mountains!

Comparing this with the Tololing operation is interesting. The attack on Tololing had been a classic two-direction attack preceded by proper recce and preparation. The opposition was about a platoon / platoon plus. Before yielding, this feature consumed two infantry battalions, 18 GRENADIERS and 2 RAJRIF. If one considers the whole of Tololing Ridge, possibly held by a company, it took five battalions and nearly ten days to capture.

We evacuated Major Ashok, who was literally in tears, feeling extremely guilty for getting himself to such a position and not being able to support the battalion. I assured him that he had done enough, and what had happened was neither intentional nor out of neglect; it was a pure and simple accident. Major Sandeep Kala, my 2iC, fetched up after handling the casualty evacuation and all the administrative work involved. I felt bad that I could not render a final salute to the brave officers and soldiers before they were flown to their kin.

I discussed with him all that had emerged from the day recce and that the best direction attack on **Point 5100** would be from the rear while we held him in the front by fire from **Area Junction**. He was to get Charlie Company and the Ghataks ready for it. We reported this to Brigade HQ and requested artillery support and the OP/ BC party for the planned attack on 03 July; we were tasked to go ahead with preparations and await final orders. Charlie Company was pulled back to the Administrative Area for preparation, and the Ghataks concentrated at **Kajal.**

03 July 1999

The attack on **Tiger Hill** was launched on 03 July night, and we had a gallery view of the plastering it was receiving from laser-guided bombs of the Air Force, rockets of the MBRL and shells of direct-firing Bofors. Having been at the receiving end of enemy artillery fire, one could imagine the impact of all this destructive fire; it was awe-inspiring.

Dealing with the Shirker

On 03 July around 0900 hours, Major Kala informed me that Major Madan had spoken to him, expressed his guilt and wanted to come up and be part of the operation. My first reaction was total anger at the officer's sheer opportunism; hence I responded, '*What is there to do? I don't require him now*.' On second thought, this was an opportunity to call the bluff of Major Madan's invalidity claim.

I instructed Major Kala to call him up. Major Madan reached us around 1300 hours and brought air photos of **Three Pimples**. The air photos had taken nearly ten days, far from the 48-hour- 'Wet Print' and 72-hour- 'Annotated Print' taught to us at the Staff Course. The arrival of Major Madan in good time confirmed to me what I had all along suspected: that he was malingering. To confirm this further, I tasked him to recce for an attack on **Point 5100**. He set off and returned by evening, having completed his recce. By then, we had been tasked to be prepared to clear area **Point 5060**. Hence, Major Madan was tasked to recce for its clearance from **Point 4700** ridge. He took off for recce on 04 July morning. I was asked to report to HQ 56 Mountain Brigade at Drass.

Later, Major Kala reported the successful completion of the recce. Whatever small doubt I had about Major Madan's malingering was cleared. I reported the matter to the higher ups, resulting in disciplinary action. Major Madan later regretted his behaviour and requested I withdraw the case. Since he was expressing regret, I offered him a way out. I asked him to plead guilty and accept to be summarily tried by the GOC, whom I could request for leniency of sentence. Major Madan refused this offer and opted to be tried by a General Court Martial, claiming that the medical state of his knee prevented him from discharging his duties in the attack. He was later found guilty of malingering and dismissed from service. The clinching evidence was his act of coming to **Kajal** and subsequent recce.

The unit was asked to fall back to Drass on 05 July, and by 06 July, we had established ourselves near **Bimbat** at the base of Tololing, where we stayed till the end of the war.

CHAPTER TWELVE

THE ROLE OF ARTILLERY IN KARGIL

Every arm, especially the combat arms, tends to staunchly believe in their overbearing importance for success in military operations. To an extent, this type of one-upmanship is healthy and required; it enhances self-worth and builds up legends that can be passed on from generation to generation. After all, in these modern times combat units get a rare opportunity to script history in combat, and hence icons and legends must be idolised to join the pantheon of heroes in regimental histories.

We should take a leaf from the Greeks on this account, who created and idolised a hero after every war. The Kargil War saw something akin, which neutral observers may call a 'tussle for glory' between the Infantry and the 'Gunners.'

Though we were at the wrong end of enemy rifles and machine guns and 'very close' to the 'business end' of our Big Guns, our views including that of my men, are unambiguous - Indian Artillery performed commendably both in the tactical battlefield and as an institution. The first relates to the role envisaged for it in warfighting, and the second relates to the professional management of the arm by the elders of the larger Artillery family.

As an infantryman, I believe that victory resulted from my grit and determination. I grudgingly acknowledge that others too were seen on the battlefield with their guns and ammunition! Ask an artilleryman - he will tell you that he blasted the "damn enemy" with his Big Guns, and the infantryman merely walked to the objective and planted the Tricolour; the truth lies somewhere in between.

Artillery as an Arm

Artillery is a specialised arm for fire support; it entails bringing down artillery fire to produce the effect the supported arm requires. In military parlance, this is the application of fire, which is distinct from allotment, never to be mistaken one for the other. The organisational structure of artillery is designed to achieve this: Observation, Gun Position, Survey and Communication. The main role of artillery is to pulverise the targets so that the commander can achieve his objective. In the Kargil War, this mainly boiled down to supporting the infantry in evicting the enemy from dominating features and preventing the enemy artillery from interfering with our attacks and preparations.

Kargil was a Peculiar Situation

Given the limited arena of the war, there was a preponderance of Indian Artillery in Kargil, more than what normally can be expected in a general war situation with a wider geographical spread. This helped establish a level of artillery domination that the infantry must not take for granted as the norm.

The terrain had forced the artillery to deploy along the main road artery; there was neither the time nor the resources to create elaborate gun positions away from the main artery and tucked into the numerous folds the ground offered. If the artillery could operate with relative impunity, it was due to the absence of an enemy air threat and the ability of our equipment to out-range his guns. While we could concentrate our artillery, the enemy could never match our numbers. Given the peculiar layout of the road network, he could not denude artillery from another sector to reinforce the Drass battle, while we could.

I will explain this. The Zojila - Kargil Road runs along the LC at distances varying from five to 10 km. Our main artery for movement was parallel to the line of contact, while his was perpendicular. At that time, long stretches of this road were under enemy observation, who could easily engage any movement on these roads. On the other hand, the roads leading from Pakistan's Northern Areas were, for most stretches, never under Indian observation, roads leading to the Drass- Mushko sector more so.

Even the vagaries of nature turned against Pakistan. Unusual for the region, in 1999 the Zojila pass opened in April itself which was at least a month before its usual opening time. This facilitated the early return of the Indian Army and redeployment of its artillery from across the Pir Panjal ranges. The early buildup and quick launch of attacks caught the Pakistani Army planners by surprise as they had estimated that serious engagements if any, would not commence before mid-June and the replenishment of ammunition was planned accordingly. But due to the operation having started much earlier, and as the Burzil Pass had still not opened until mid-June, movement of Pakistani artillery into the sector and supply lines replenishment became very difficult.[42]

---

42 Zehra Nasim, From Kargil to the Coup, Events that Shook Pakistan

In war, like in life, potential does not naturally transform into ability; one must plan and work at it. The enemy could not use his advantage and effectively block the Zojila - Kargil Road. One can dominate roads by fire but never block them. To block, you must occupy - or a determined opponent will continue to use it as we did. What was otherwise a great tactical disadvantage turned into a great tactical advantage for us, given the range of Bofors guns.[43] We could cover wide frontages by side-stepping a few kms while the enemy had to cover long distances. And before the Pakistani commander ordered such redeployments, he had to first be convinced that these would not be needed for switching back, paralysing his mental flexibility, an attribute that operational-level commanders bring to the table for battlefield success.

It is interesting to hypothecate what would have happened if the enemy had physically cut off the road. This would lead us to the flaw in the enemy's plan, which I will come to later.

Drawing out Some Lessons

I must also point out a flaw in the infantryman's thinking. The most glaring flaw was the incessant demand for direct fire support, in which the Gunners were expected to literally blast the enemy off the objective area through pinpoint direct shots, and any amount of covering fire was always less when assaulting enemy positions, especially in daylight. We need to realise both the capability and limitation of artillery fire and use it to the best effect; I will touch upon the limitations first and the capabilities later.

Artillery fire is not precision fire; it is an area fire. It is not designed to pick and eliminate enemies like a sniper does; even most infantry support weapons, including the much-vaunted machine gun, are not designed for it. Yes, 'smart projectiles' have been introduced in artillery, which can be directed to the target in many armies, including ours. Still, due to their exorbitant cost, these are few and meant for use against armoured vehicles. The infantrymen must, therefore, never expect the artillery to eliminate the opposition from the objective and never judge them on the inability of artillery fire to do so. In some cases, they did so in Kargil as an exception due to the peculiar circumstances and not as a norm.

The second impact of this imprecision is on the unmatched geometry of the beaten zone and the target layout. Due to weapon-ammunition design

---

[43] 400 x 155 mm FH77 Bofors guns were procured from the Swedish arms manufacturer AB Bofors in a controversial March 1986 deal. However, it proved to be a battle-winning factor in Kargil. Since then, these guns have been upgraded with extended ranges and continue to form the backbone of the Indian Artillery arm.

limitations, the artillery beaten zone is oval with a statistically determined distribution pattern of shells / bombs. On the other hand, the geometry of objective areas is determined by the lay of the land, enemy weapon systems and his tactical doctrines. In the mountains, there will often be pockets of fire-free zones where artillery fire will not be able to reach due to the selected line of fire. In a nutshell, it will never be possible to cover the objective with uniform fire; there will always be gaps in the fire. The assaulting infantry must cater for this and plan the attack accordingly, taking steps to mitigate the lessening of fire effect on the objective by catering for more robust intimate fire support from the integral fire support weapons of the battalion like machine guns, automatic grenade launchers, rocket launchers and mortars. **The task of "shooting in the infantry onto the objective" cannot be outsourced to artillery.**

Artillery support can never be enough for an infantryman; the more, the better! But remember, like the Indian Air Force, it is a flexible arm. It concurrently performs a host of battlefield tasks ranging from preparatory bombardment through covering fire and responding to enemy fire assaults with counter bombardments. Depending upon the ebb and flow of battle, artillery fire will switch from one target to another, and the infantry soldier is never aware of the larger operational picture. Pressuring the attached Battery Commander (BC)/Observation Post Officer (OP) to ask for counter bombardment and the attached BC/OP repeatedly asking for CB fire over D5 net due to a misplaced zeal for the supported troops is counterproductive on two accounts. To ascertain the effectiveness of his fire, all that the enemy has to do is to monitor our D5 Net, and he will get very authentic confirmation. Secondly, artillery ammunition is a precious commodity that is more useful in supporting an attack and enhancing the chances of its success rather than warding off irritable enemy artillery fire for which getting into foxholes / slit trenches and keeping mum would be a better option.

The third impact of this inherent lack of precision is on fire control. Infantrymen must understand that correcting artillery fire is not precise; it is always gross. The problem gets even more accentuated in the high altitudes due to unpredictable meteorological conditions. To expect fine adjustment of fire in terms of metres shows a lack of understanding of the procedure of ranging as well as the subsequent artillery bombardment pattern. Such a lack of basic understanding leads to assuming a capability that does not exist and basing one's plans on such wrong assumptions.

Much is made of peacetime affiliation between artillery units and the supported arm, but we saw that it did not matter. Forget about the unit getting the BC and OP party from the affiliated unit; there were no affiliated units at the infantry battalion level. More often than not, the BC and OP parties belonged to different units and to their credit, they were passed from one assaulting unit to another, just like infantry support weapons. This ad hoc arrangement did not really affect the quality of fire support the units enjoyed; the pressure of the situation brought about innovative solutions for which the Indian Artillery must be justifiably proud.

Giving a snapshot of the tremendous effort put in by the Indian Artillery, Major General Jagjit Singh wrote in the Indian Defence Review (22 January 2019) an article "**Battle Winning Role of the Gunners in the Kargil War**," quoting from his book of the same name. He writes, "*In the capture of Tololing heights, a significant part of the fire plan, was the employment of Bofors guns, and the MBRLs in direct firing role. Direct firing was conducted from a distance of nearly 10,000 metres, with the Bofors deployed in three tiers, employing "Shoot and Scoot" tactics, to avoid damage by the enemy's counter-bombardment. [...] The Indian artillery fired over 2,50,000 shells, bombs and rockets during the Kargil conflict. Approximately 5,000 artillery shells, mortar bombs and rockets were fired daily from 300 guns, mortars and MBRLs while 9,000 shells were fired the day Tiger Hill was regained. During the peak period of assaults, on an average, each artillery battery fired over one round per minute for 17 days continuously. Such high rates of fire over long periods had not been witnessed anywhere in the world since the World War II. Even during the World War II, such sustained artillery firing was not common at all. The men at the guns had blisters on their hands from carrying and loading shells and cartridges. Very few of them got more than a couple of hours of sleep in every 24 hours cycle. They had no time for proper meals and were often themselves under enemy artillery fire. Yet, they carried on relentlessly.*"[44]

---

44 http://www.indiandefencereview.com/spotlights/battle-winning-role-of-the-gunners-in-kargil war/

EPILOGUE

"WHY DID THE DOG NOT BARK?"

Of the two battles 2 RAJRIF fought, Battle of Three Pimples was far more challenging professionally. The challenges in the Tololing Battle, in hindsight, were more psychological. There, we had the luxury of detailed recce, thorough preparations and overwhelming superiority against an enemy position that had been hemmed in and continuously engaged by 18 GRENADIERS since 25 May.

Inducted into the Drass Sector on 01 June 1999, we were tasked on 03 June 1999 to capture Tololing. What little information we could gather was patchy and often contradictory. The first task was to get all the required information for executing our task, which we accomplished by conducting close recce, talking to troops in contact with the enemy, and firming up our plan. The plan's success hinged on our ability to move 15 tons of ammunition close to the enemy. Then, we surreptitiously built up the assaulting troops and launched a ferocious and determined attack on an enemy holding strategic high ground. In doing this, I witnessed the awe-inspiring capability to suffer great privation, face adverse physical and professional challenges and willingness to take risks of men, junior leaders, and officers of 2 RAJRIF. A night-blind carpenter, Uttam Singh, lugged ammunition, trekking every night for eight hours, catching the coat tail of the soldier in front of him. Such was the level of motivation and professionalism of this battalion.

The attack commenced at 2100 hours on 12 June, to the booming of 100-gun artillery gun support. After a night-long operation, 2 RAJRIF was able to wrest Tololing Top from the enemy with 10 dead besides 92 injured. This was a great morale booster for the Indian Army, which never looked back. General VP Malik, Chief of Army Staff, personally congratulated the battalion. He said, **"You (the Battalion) have done the Army Proud, the Nation Proud"**, he later termed this **the ' Turning Point' of Kargil War.**

2 RAJRIF launched another ferocious and successful attack on 28 June 99 on **Three Pimples** with heavy losses. Three officers and eight soldiers died. The **Battle of Three Pimples** stretched me and my unit to extreme limits physically and professionally. Such was the doggedness of the troops and their

वीर भोग्या वसुन्धरा

2ND BATTALION

OP VIJAY : 1999

MAJ VIVEK GUPTA	- MVC (POSTHUMOUS)
MAJ P ACHARYA	- MVC (POSTHUMOUS)
CAPT N KENGURUSE	- MVC (POSTHUMOUS)
NK DIGENDRA KUMAR	- MVC
COL M B RAVINDRANATH	- VrC
CAPT MOHIT SAXENA	- VrC
CAPT VIJAYANT THAPAR	- VrC (POSTHUMOUS)
SUB BHANWAR LAL	- VrC (POSTHUMOUS)
CHM YASHVIR SINGH	- VrC (POSTHUMOUS)
HAV SULTAN SINGH NARWARIA	- VrC (POSTHUMOUS)
RFN JAI RAM SINGH	- VrC
CAPT PRAVEEN TOMAR	- SM
CAPT MRIDUL KUMAR (ARTY OP)	- SM
CAPT SOMNATH BASU (RMO)	- SM
SUB SUMER SINGH	- SM (POSTHUMOUS)
SUB SUNAYAK SINGH	- SM
HAV SHRI BHAGWAN SINGH	- SM
HAV SHARMAN SINGH SENGAR	- SM (POSTHUMOUS)
HAV RANBIR SINGH	- SM
NK KARANBIR	- SM
L/NK NARAYAN SINGH	- SM

MENTION-IN-DESPATCHES

CAPT S S RAUTELA

COAS COMMENDATION CARD

SUB MAN SINGH CHAUHAN
HAV NAWAL SINGH
NK JAI SINGH RAJPOOT
RFN MAHESH SINGH

GOC-IN-C-COMMENDATION CARD

MAJ S S BAJAJ
NK/CPTR UTTAM SINGH BHAKUNI

commanders in pursuing their objectives set forth by me that when we were done, the Chief of the Army Staff took personal cognisance of the valour and fortitude of the troops of 2 RAJRIF. Setting aside all the existing protocol, he bestowed, for the first time in the annals of the history of the Indian Army, `suo moto` '**Chief's Citation**', an award given to units in recognition of sustained and collective outstanding performance in operations.

The reader can gauge for himself the impact this battle made. The nation bestowed four Maha Vir Chakras (MVC), seven Vir Chakras (VrC), nine Sena Medals (SM) and two Mention-in-Despatches for the display of individual valour to our unit (list of winners on previous page). **Two Battle Honours: 'Tololing'** and **'Drass'** and a **Theatre Honour 'Kargil'** were accorded for our collective achievement. In the battalion, we felt we deserved at least one '**Param Vir Chakra**,' the highest gallantry award, an oversight that I did not hesitate to convey to the highest level of command in our Army.

An aspect of the battle that I shall never be able to erase from my consciousness is the loss of so many young officers who led from the front. Nothing would explain the spirit of our young officers than the letter dated 19 June 1999 by Major Acharya, reproduced hereafter.

Dear Papa

Hope this letter finds you in the best of health and spirits. Thanks for your letter and card dt.14 June 1999...We are already getting ready for our next task. Our unit now has to live up to the higher expectations of the Army, Regt, as well as the media. You know what, even the Chief sent a letter of congratulations to the unit. It was indeed an honour for our unit to have been given such a task. Hard work and a sound ethos does have its merits, don't you think? We now have to work harder to preserve the hopes and aspirations of our well-wishers.

Please don't worry about casualties. It's a professional hazard which is beyond our control, so why worry; at least it's for a good cause. In the Bhagwad Gita Lord Krishna briefs Arjun on the following lines: Hato va prapyasi swargam, Jitva va bhokshijasey mahim, taduthisht kaunteya, yudhaya kritnishchayaha. *("Die and you will go to heaven; conquer and you enjoy sovereignty of the earth; therefore, stand up, Arjuna, and fight with determination.")*

No we are not air maint(ained), but food is good and we have a Bengali doctor if not Chinese. Yes, the PM's Kargil visit was a good motivation. Good chap. I am quite a sight now with an unkempt beard and vaseline cream all over my ugly face to counter the icy winds.

Please tell manam (his mother) that combat is an honour of a lifetime and I would not think of anything less. What better way to serve the nation? I am proud to be in the Infantry and esp(ecially) in our illustrious Bn (battalion).

Take care of your health as well as manam's. Don't worry and lose sleep. Tell a story a day of the Mahabharata to Charu (his wife), so that your grandchild imbibes good values. Jai Mataji ki.

Yours affly

19 June 1999 Babloo

(He died fighting on 28 June 1999, awarded Maha Vir Chakra)

We were brought up on a diet of leading from the front. It has been glorified and glamourised to an extent where every officer who is commissioned thinks it a dereliction of duty if he is not within the first few to face the bullets. My analysis of the incidents of the actions which had taken place of 4 JAT, 18 GRENADIERS, and 8 SIKH all indicated that patrols led by young officers had established contact with the enemy and the death of officers had normally led to the withdrawal of his leaderless platoon. This, I surmised, was the reason why so many bodies of our dead could not be brought back. My analysis of the situation convinced me that the young officers were in a Catch-22 situation. The troops, brave as they are, cannot be expected to perform tasks for which they are not trained. The mere fact that it is their bread-and-butter task does not mean they can do it. Tasks to be performed under hostile fire require far more practice than we train for.

When expected to suddenly perform tasks they know how to do but are not trained for, they look at the officers around them. The officers themselves have now to do the job that ought to be done by their subordinates. So, the officer is in a dilemma; if he orders the jawans to perform the tasks they should rightfully be doing, he fears they will consider him a coward. If he takes the lead and does the job a subordinate should rightfully do, he reduces his effectiveness as an officer. Most young officers tend to choose the latter course of action. The high rate of attrition among junior officers is due to this.

I personally feel that this should be treated as a symptom of the failure of our training system in ensuring the soldiers are trained for tasks expected of them, rather than gloating over the needless deaths of so many young officers, however brave and romantic it is. War is ruthless, you must pay in blood for what you do not possess in talent or skill.

In this war, we and several other battalions essentially restored an adverse situation in our favour at an enormous cost to human life. The question that begs - why did we get into such a situation in the first place? In my opinion, this was a monumental intelligence failure. Border security has many layers of protection. The troops physically guarding it are the penultimate layer; the force that restored the status quo ante, like our battalion, is the ultimate layer. There are many more layers before them, starting from RAW assets, the Air Force, the air surveillance assets of the Army, ground intelligence assets of the Army, the troops deployed there and the Intelligence Bureau.

Have we learnt our lessons? *Had the dog barked, the story would have been different.*

Dear Colonel Ravindranath,

I write to wholeheartedly commend and to say how filled I am with pride at the performance of 2 Rajputana Rifles.

It is not the taking of any one single feature that is the real mark of the great excellence of your Battalion; it is the totality of the courage and spirit that all ranks of the 2 Rajputana Rifles have displayed in this challenge to our nation.

With salutations of one soldier to another. And with the request that my letter and its contents may please be made known to all ranks the 2 Raj Rif. More strength to your arms.

Yours sincerely,

Jaswant Singh.

(Jaswant Singh)

Letter of Appreciation to CO 2 RAJRIF from Shri Jaswant Singh, the then External Affairs Minister of India

Before I conclude, I must pay my respects to all my men who were killed in action in the Drass Sector in June 1999 (names listed below). They laid down their lives for the nation, the Indian Army and for the *izzat* of the unit. I salute them!!

A Company

Major Padmapani Acharya, MVC, 28 June 1999

Captain Vijayant Thapar, VrC, 28 June 1999

Subedar Sumer Singh Rathore, SM, 13 June 1999

Rifleman Kanwar Pal Singh, 26 June 1999

Rifleman Jagmal Singh Shekhawat, 28 June 1999

Naik Anand Singh, 28 June 1999

Lance Naik Satyaveer Singh, 28 June 1999

B Company

Lance Naik Om Prakash, 28 June 1999

Lance Naik Jasvir Singh, 13 June 1999

C Company

Major Vivek Gupta, MVC, 13 June 1999

Subedar Bhanwar Lal, VrC, 13 June 1999

Company Havildar Major Yashvir Singh, VrC, 13 June 1999

Naik Chaman Singh, 13 June 1999

Naik Surender Singh, 13 June 1999

Lance Naik Satpal Singh, 28 June 1999

Lance Naik Bachan Singh, 13 June 1999

Rifleman Ashish Kumar, 28 June 1999

Rifleman Jasvir, 13 June 1999

D Company

Captain Neikezhakuo Kenguruse, MVC, 29 June 1999

Havildar Sultan Singh Narwaria, VrC, 13 June 1999

Havildar Sarman Singh Senger, SM, 28 June 1999

Rifleman Vikram Singh, 28 June 1999

Lance Havildar Satyabir Singh, 28 June 1999

FEW REMINISCENCES FROM HIS OFFICERS

Major Sandeep Bajaj (later Major General) remembers

25 years have passed since the war, my mind often goes back to the iconic battles of Tololing and Three Pimples which my unit fought in and in which I was privileged to participate in. One enduring question has always come to my mind "*What motivated the unit to perform like it did?*" *What set it apart? Was it individual valour or leadership or sound planning or synergy with other Arms?*

As time passed and I was fortunate to command a Division, I kept seeing flashes of the same energy in certain units. It boiled down to two factors which when meshed, unleashed an unstoppable force like no other.

The **first** being the unit history - 2 RAJRIF had an incredible record of never failing in an attack in its history of almost two centuries. This was drilled into the minds of all ranks of the unit relentlessly and such was the regimentation that no one could accept the fact that his attack may not succeed. This was worth dying for! And many made that supreme sacrifice but kept the unit honour intact and always succeeded in taking the objective. Nobody wanted to be known as the first person to fail - be it an officer, JCO, or other rank.

The **second** factor was that our section level drills were traditionally very strong and with great credit to Late Col MB Ravindranath, VrC. He focused on this aspect like a possessed man during the peace tenure preceding the war. The terrain as it obtained in Kargil was tailored for section level attacks on enemy positions (bunkers) and here the section commander was king. We had planned that each section had a designated objective and once the battle was joined it was the junior leaders who led us to victory.

Artillery was a critical battle winner but the Pakistani Army knew that we would be able to concentrate enormous fires prior to the infantry assault. To obviate the same they made full use of the reverse slopes to take shelter from the artillery barrage and once they were certain that the artillery fire had lifted, they then occupied the bunkers on the forward slope and were thus able to conserve their forces for the main battle.

Realising this, we decided on a deception plan and proposed to the brigade HQ that once the artillery fire lifted and the enemy assumed that the main infantry assault was coming in, there would be a second artillery assault after 30 minutes. This led to quite a few Pakistani soldiers being caught in the open prior to our assault on Tololing on 13 June.

The true extent of the enemy deployment across the Drass sector was known once we captured Three Pimples on 28 June and while going through the rucksacks of the enemy we came across a meticulously marked Artillery OP map with clear depiction of the Pakistani positions and our disposition. A tiny dot in red indicated Tololing as being captured. We rushed this map down to the Brigade HQ.

As I walked through the Pakistani platoon positions on Tololing, I was struck by the well planned and executed defensive positions with well constructed bunkers linked with crawl trenches; mutually supportive positions and well maintained and cleaned section weapons (with spare barrels properly cleaned and ammunition belts completely fired indicating a very high level of weapons maintenance). The Pakistani Army was very professional but lacked motivation under a sustained attack with Indian junior commanders using the craggy terrain to close up and fight.

Once we had captured Tololing Top, a local counter attack was launched by the enemy with ferocity. What stood out was that the enemy was in some cases in a salwar kameez with bullet proof jackets and surprisingly gas masks. A very eerie sight in a battle with gunfire and smoke all round. An image permanently etched in my mind.

As we sat exhausted next to Point 4590 (the first capture of the war) on the West shoulder of Tololing on 13 June, Rifleman Pushpender from my company came up to me holding a live Indian Artillery shell cradled in his arms like a baby and asked me to explain to him why the shell did not explode on impact (blaming the Ordnance Factory). I gently told him to keep walking on towards the reverse slope and toss the shell down the gorge. He went on arguing and after five minutes of convincing went on and tossed the shell into the gorge where it exploded on impact with the ground. Pushpender accompanied me on the second attack at Three Pimples and retired a Havildar.

Lieutenant Praveen Tomar (now Colonel) recalls:

The South Eastern approach to Tololing had a gradual slope with no cover, the nearest cover was at Tololing Top over 800 metres away. The entire approach was under enemy observation and covered by mortar and automatic fire. By any tactical appreciation, it was an unviable approach, but the desperate situation made us attack along this axis. In case our company attack along this approach failed, it would mean the annihilation of the entire company. The enemy would surely not allow us to withdraw back along the open spur. A few shell holes near the Tololing defences were the only shelter available to us.

Both Major Gupta and I were well aware of the near suicidal nature of our mission. We went to great lengths to plan and prepare to the minutest detail. For us, victory or death seemed to be the only options. Some officers wrote their Last Letters, to be given to the families in case of their death. Maj Gupta and I did not want to tempt our fate. As if to defy destiny itself, we decided to not write any Last Letter.

We selected a feature near our camp for our rehearsals. The hill feature was also located West of the highway, had a similar gradient and a gentle slope dipping from North to South similar to Tololing. The almost impossible odds made us fanatical in our preparations. Charlie Company climbed higher, trained harder and stayed out training longer than other companies. We would stay out at night trying to see the moonlight and visibility conditions. We would judge the maximum distance that a buddy pair could venture apart without losing contact. All actions and contingencies were rehearsed repeatedly. We even practiced throwing of live grenades. Each person down to the last rifleman knew his task and what to do in case of a contingency.

The old timers had spent several tenures in CI and LC posts. They had been under small arms fire and were aware of the terrible havoc that can be wrought by artillery fire. As they saw the heavy preparatory bombardment on the enemy locations, they were sure that the enemy positions would be blown to bits. We would just need to walk-in to occupy the objective. Greenhorns like me were not so sure. Sensing an opportunity to take advantage of the raw lieutenant, my CHM bet that if we reach the objective to find it empty and the enemy destroyed, I would offer him a case of whisky. I was not too keen to take the bet, after all he had seen much more of Army life than me. Not taking up the challenge would only mean that I was not too sure of my views. I took up the bet, with a fervent prayer that God may prove the CHM right. How I wish, I had lost the bet!!

As I moved for the attack with the leading section, Major Vivek Gupta patted me on the shoulder and whispered **"Tomar, remember it is victory or death"**. The ominous words would soon ring true. It was the highest honour for me to lead my men into battle with barely six months of service. It had another personal connection too. My CHM was from my own village and several other boys of the company were from the nearby villages. In the tight knit village communities, they knew me, my father and my grandfather, just as I knew their families. With the honour of the entire clan at stake, fear or failure was not an option for any of us. Death would be the honourable choice.

The enemy was so confident that he allowed us to close in before opening fire, perhaps hoping to inflict maximum casualties in the opening volley. During the first few seconds of the contact, my entire section had been hit. Bullets tore through my clothing and my packs. A few minutes into the contact, a bullet ricocheted off my helmet and threw me to the ground. Only providence saved me. Within the first half an hour of the contact, the company had lost the Company Commander, the Senior JCO as well as the CHM. The situation hung in balance. With every passing minute the possibility increased that the enemy would reinforce his bunkers and that would spell the end of Charlie Company's attack. Luckily, I was able to find a small gap to out flank the enemy. The MMG detachment followed up behind me. The fate of the entire attack now depended on the four of us. The MMG fire pinned the enemy down while I crawled back and forth to feed them ammunition. The precarious toe hold gave me the chance to bring in more men and clear the enemy one by one. The capture of Top was the decisive point of the entire attack.

War lays bare the most noble as well as the darkest traits of human nature. Each man of Charlie Company proved his mettle and lived up to the soldierly traditions of the paltan and his clan. After the war, I have often looked back to see if I could have done it any differently. If I could have done it any better, with a lesser loss of lives. But however hard I try, I realise that our effort was almost superhuman. Even then we succeeded due to the reckless bravery of each and every man and a whole load of luck. The words of my Divisional Officer to me just before my Novices boxing bout in NDA still ring in my ears, "*In boxing, in battle and even in life, you will throw your punches and get some in return. Whatever it may be, keep your chin up and take it like a man*".

Lieutenant S S Rautela (now Colonel) writes:

I was the baby of the battalion (junior most officer) and took charge of the Ghatak Platoon. The battalion was lucky to have a CO like Colonel MB Ravindranath who had the calmness and the composure of an ocean. He kept us busy and away from rumour mongering by engaging us in acclimatisation by climbing all the mountain heights and practising field craft.

After a few days, when I gave a ring to my mother at Delhi, she asked me my whereabouts. I told her I was at our old location, but my mother told me that I was hiding something from her and I was where the battle is going on i.e., either Drass/Kargil. She confronted me and said that she had seen a video clip of mine with the boys which was very frequently flashed on the DD National

Channel during that time. I remembered that while we were training, a Door Darshan TV crew took a shot of me and my B Company boys moving on the road in double file formation with our battle loads, which we didn't even realise.

We often came under artillery fire. The flight of the projectile made a whistling sound. I told the boys, we have to take cover if you hear a whistling sound coming from the enemy side. A boy asked me "*Saab, jab seeti ki awaaz na aaye tab kya karna hai?*" I told him, "*Bhai, aise main toh joh karna hai woh bomb hi karega aur awaazein/seetin hamari hongi*".

On 28th June, we had our early meal (before the assault on Three Pimples) and promised that we will meet after the victory. By about 3 a.m. the exchange of fire had minimized/stopped and it seemed as if we have once again achieved victory in the second attack also. I was tasked to evacuate the casualties of "D" and 'A' Company. We had lost three officers and eight OR and almost 40-50 were seriously injured, but we had secured the features/complex.

At such a young age I saw enemy action, comrades falling and what it actually means to serve the nation.

ABOUT THE AUTHOR

COLONEL MB RAVINDRANATH (RAVI), VrC

Nothing would describe late Colonel MB Ravindranath (Ravi), VrC, better than this small newspaper clip describing his role in the capture of Tololing as the CO of 2 RAJ RIF.

Born in 1959 to Shri Magod Basappa and Shrimati Sarojamma in Kunduru, Honnali Taluk, Davangere District, Karnataka, Ravi went to Sainik School Vijayapura early on in his life. Selected for the National Defence Academy in 1976, he passed out from the Indian Military Academy, Dehradun in June 1980, getting commissioned into 17 MADRAS. In 1985, he was amongst the founding team of 21 RAJRIF, one of the experimental mixed-class units created in Infantry Regiments.

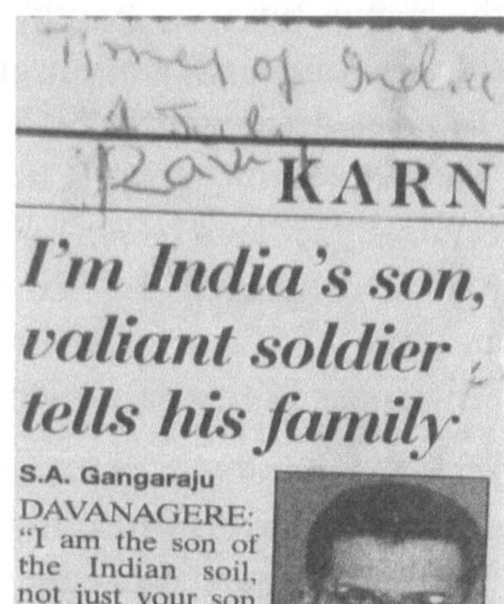

KARN

I'm India's son, valiant soldier tells his family

S.A. Gangaraju

M.B. Ravindranath

DAVANAGERE: "I am the son of the Indian soil, not just your son and I am ready to sacrifice my life for my mother-land". His son's remarks keep echoing in the mind of retired school teacher Hole-sirigere Magodu Basappa, and he finds comfort in it. Lt Colonel M.B. Ravindranath is the leader of a battalion upfront, and played a key role in capturing Tololing Hill from the enemies in Kargil recently.

Taking over command of 2 RAJRIF in 1998, he led the battalion in the capture of Tololing and later Three Pimples. He was awarded the Vir Chakra (VrC) for his gallantry and outstanding leadership on 15 August 1999.

Ravindranath voluntarily sought premature retirement in 2001, leaving behind an illustrious military career to answer the call of his larger family as the eldest son and to take hold of a family business enterprise that needed his deft touch to flourish. He proved his mettle in the industrial sector, and by 2018, he was on the Board of Directors of a number of self-owned ventures that included Magod Laser Machining, Magod Fusion Technologies, Preusse India and Tycoon Software Technologies, spread over several sites in India.

Colonel MB Ravindranath, VrC, died of a massive heart attack on 8th April 2018, with his boots on, as the soldier in him would have desired. He had just returned from his customary early morning jog in the neighbourhood park of Jayanagar, Bengaluru, when he collapsed. He and his wife, Anitha, have two daughters, Prerna and Prarthana.

As a soldier-scholar, deeply respected amongst his peers in the Army, Ravi maintained meticulous notes of his military experiences. In fact, he was at an advanced stage of completing the manuscript of this book when destiny called him to Valhalla. The manuscripts/handwritten notes remained in the loving custody of Anitha and daughters Prerna and Prarthana, who were determined that the book would one day see the light of day.

Through the efforts of his admiring coursemates of the 56th NDA Course, the manuscript was revived with the objective of releasing it on the occasion of the 25th Anniversary of Kargil's victory. The team that compiled the book from the notes/drafts written by Ravi himself included Colonel David Devasahayam (Retired), Founder and Chairman of the Radiant Group of companies (56th Course), Lieutenant General JS Sandhu (Retired) (56th Course), Major General Ajay Sah (Retired) (56th Course) and Brigadier Mohit Saxena, VrC (2 RAJRIF and one of Ravi's company commanders during the battle and a leading protagonist in this narrative).

Ravindranath, or Ravi, to his admirers and friends, wanted to change how our young officers think and lead their men in battle. His lecture to the Junior Command Course was a mandatory part of the course syllabus. It was the most highly rated training event by successive student courses and Directing Staff.

We hope that his book finds a place on the bookshelves of our budding junior leaders in the Indian Army as it has a host of valuable tactical-level lessons to be imbibed.

www.ingramcontent.com/pod-product-compliance
Lightning Source LLC
LaVergne TN
LVHW041156150826
845673LV00001B/181

* 9 7 9 8 8 9 3 2 2 9 3 5 6 *